Variation in Central Modals

Linguistic Insights

Studies in Language and Communication

Edited by Maurizio Gotti,
University of Bergamo

Volume 4

PETER LANG
Bern · Berlin · Bruxelles · Frankfurt am Main · New York · Oxford · Wien

Maurizio Gotti, Marina Dossena, Richard Dury,
Roberta Facchinetti & Maria Lima

Variation in Central Modals

A Repertoire of Forms and Types of Usage in Middle English and Early Modern English

PETER LANG
Bern · Berlin · Bruxelles · Frankfurt am Main · New York · Oxford · Wien

Die Deutsche Bibliothek – CIP-Einheitsaufnahme

Variation in central modals : a repertoire of forms and types of usage in middle English and early modern English / Maurizio Gotti ... . – Bern ; Berlin ; Bruxelles ; Frankfurt am Main ; New York ; Oxford ; Wien : Lang, 2002
(Linguistic insights ; Vol. 4)
ISBN 3-906769-84-4

British Library and Library of Congress Cataloguing-in-Publication Data:
A catalogue record for this book is available from *The British Library,* Great Britain, and from *The Library of Congress,* USA

Published with a grant from Università degli Studi di Bergamo (Italy), Dipartimento di Linguistica e Letterature Comparate.

ISSN 1424-8689
ISBN 3-906769-84-4
US-ISBN 0-8204-5898-8

Contents

Preface

He that wyl nat whan he may,
He shal nat, when he wyl.

(Mannyng, *Robert of Brunne's 'Handlyng Synne'*, 1303/1901: 159)

This volume presents the first results of work carried out by a research team based at the University of Bergamo, whose aim was the analysis of verbal modality in a corpus of Late Middle English and Early Modern English texts. Owing to the vast quantity of data available, the project was structured in two periods. The present volume represents the work of the first period, an intermediate stage when it was thought appropriate to offer preliminary findings (essentially relating to quantitative investigations concerning the distribution of modal forms in individual text types) to the scientific community in an independent volume. This is expected to be supplemented by another set of papers by the same research group (to appear at a later stage), in which data will be discussed from the point of view of their incidence on theoretical and methodological issues.

As far as this first volume is concerned, the line of research is based on an interest in the pragmatic and sociological aspects of the history of the English language, thus implying an involvement with the diatopic and diastratic variables investigated by sociolinguistics, and the codes, registers, and situational context of pragmatics. The aim of the research project was to register and comment on the formal variety of central modal verb manifestations and their relative frequency in a range of texts covering approximately four centuries, from about 1350 to 1710. The results of this analysis would then be compared with those of previous studies in order to ascertain any similarities and discrepancies, both in quantitative and qualitative terms. In particular, the analysis would take into consideration the main uses of the modal forms found in the corpus so as to provide a detailed mapping from a pragmatic point of view, as this aspect was deemed to have often been neglected in previous studies, or to have been covered only in a partial and unsystematic way.

Consistent with the methodological approach chosen, the research group decided to identify the various forms of central modal verbs occurring in the texts contained in the Helsinki Corpus of English Texts.[1] In its general framework the research work consisted of two stages: the first aimed at identifying a repertoire of the forms of English central modals occurring in the text types under scrutiny; in the second stage this repertoire was examined in order to identify what forms were most frequent in the various text types. Subsequently, the results were employed to outline significant traits of modality variation between the Late Middle English and the Early Modern English periods.

The decision of the research team to make use of the Helsinki Corpus was influenced by the latest approaches to linguistic research (from both the synchronic and the diachronic points of view), which take into account the use of computerized corpora. These present at least a twofold advantage: on the one hand, they allow quick and accurate selection of the lexical, morphological, syntactic and textual elements that occur in the various texts under examination, according to definite criteria; on the other, this approach allows researchers to compare different text types in a homogeneous and consistent way. Indeed, large-corpus linguistics has enabled researchers to analyse language 'in use', meeting the three criteria for a valid science of language (cf. de Beaugrande 1996): coverage of language data, convergence among the data being described, and consensus among linguists about how to proceed. It is important, however, that, in order to offer adequate data, a corpus should consist of a collection of representative samples (each of a standard length) taken from a number of texts, appropriately selected with the aim of presenting a reliable picture of one or more varieties of a language from one or more chronological periods.[2] The team also hoped that the use of a

---

1 The structure and rationale of the Helsinki Corpus is discussed by Rissanen / Kytö / Palander-Collin (1993) and Kytö (1996).

2 For a detailed presentation of the advantages of the use of computerised corpora in the diachronic analysis of the English language, cf. Rissanen (2000a); this article also provides a very useful review of the main English

corpus would allow them to analyze modal verb usage from pragmatic and sociolinguistic points of view.

The outcome of this analysis is reported here, and is the result of the joint efforts of the whole group coordinated by Maurizio Gotti. Although planned and discussed by all members of the research unit, the various steps of the corpus analysis have been carried out on an individual basis and the results are presented as follows: Maurizio Gotti is responsible for chapters 1, 7, 9, 11; Marina Dossena for 1, 8, 10, 11; Richard Dury for 1, 4, 5, 11; Roberta Facchinetti for 1, 2, 3, 11; Maria Lima for 6, 11. The final editing of the volume was carried out by Maurizio Gotti, Richard Dury and Marina Dossena.

Acknowledgements

Thanks are due to Olga Fischer (University of Amsterdam), Charles Jones (University of Edinburgh), Bernd Kortmann (University of Freiburg), Merja Kytö (Uppsala University), Matti Rissanen (University of Helsinki), Elizabeth Closs Traugott (Stanford University), Ans van Kemenade (University of Nijmegen) and Anthony Warner (University of York) for their careful reading of the manuscript and for their invaluable comments and suggestions; of course, they bear no responsibility for the views expressed in the final version of the book.

---

historical corpora; more information on these research tools can be obtained in Kytö / Rissanen / Wright (1994), Hickey *et al.* (1997) and from the annual reports by Kytö and Rissanen in the *ICAME Journal*.

Abbreviations

EME	Early Middle English
EModE	Early Modern English
LME	Late Middle English
ME	Middle English
ModE	Modern English
OE	Old English
PDE	Present-day English

Abbreviated titles of the works included in the corpus analysed

AELR3: Aelred of Rievaulx's *De Institutione Inclusarum*
ALHATTON: Hatton, Alice, *Letters*
ANHATTON: Hatton, Anne, *Letters*
ASTR: Chaucer, *A Treatise on the Astrolabe*
AUNGIER: Aungier, *Letters*
BEHN: Behn, *Oroonoko*
BENEDME: *The Benedictine Rule*
BOETHCH: Chaucer, *Boethius*
BOETHPR: Preston, *Boethius*
BOYLE: Boyle, *Electricity & Magnetism*
BRUT: *The Brut of the Chronicles of England*
BURNETCHA: Burnet, *History of My Own Time*
BURNETROC: Burnet, *Some Passages of the Life and Death of [...] Earl of Rochester*
CAPEL: Capel, *Letters*
CHARLES: Charles II, *Letters*
CHATTON: Hatton, Charles, *Letters*
CLOUD: *The Cloud of Unknowing*
COMMISS: Letter from the Commissioners of Customs 1672/3
COUNC: Letter from the Privy Council 1688
CTBATH: Chaucer, *The Wife of Bath's Prologue*
CTMEL: Chaucer, *The Tale of Melibee*

CTMERCH: Chaucer, *The Merchant's Tale*
CTPARS: Chaucer, *The Parson's Tale*
CTPROL: Chaucer, *The General Prologue to The Canterbury Tales*
CTSUMM: Chaucer, *The Summoner's Tale*
CURSOR: *Cursor Mundi*
EHATTON: Hatton, Elizabeth, *Letters*
EOXINDEN: Oxinden, Elizabeth, *Letters*
EPLANETS: *The Equatorie of the Planetis*
EVELYN: Evelyn, *The Diary of John Evelyn*
FARQUHAR: Farquhar, *The Beaux Stratagem*
FHATTON: Hatton, Frances, *Letters*
FIENNES: Fiennes, *The Journeys of Celia Fiennes*
FOX: *The Journal of George Fox*
FRYER: Fryer, *A New Account of East India*
GOWER: Gower, *Confessio Amantis*
HENRY5C/L: Henry V and others, *Letters*
HOOKE: Hooke, *Micrographia*
HOOLE: Hoole, *A New Discovery of the Old Art of Teaching Schoole*
HORSES: *A Late Middle English Treatise on Horses*
HOXINDEN: Oxinden, Henry, *Letters*
HS: Mannyng, *Robert of Brunne's "Handlyng Synne"*
JETAYLOR: Taylor, *The Marriage Ring*
JOPINNEY: Pinney, John, *Letters*
JPINNEY: Pinney, Jane, *Letters*
JUDG: Judgements
LANGF: Langford, *Plain and Full Instructions to Raise All Sorts of Fruit-Trees*
LISLE: The trial of Lady Alice Lisle
LLETT: Letters to the King 1417-19
LOCKE: Locke, *Directions Concerning Education*
LPROCL: Proclamations
MAND: *Mandeville's Travels*
MILTON: Milton, *The History of Britain*
NHADD: Haddock, Nicholas, *Letters*
NHOM: *The Northern Homily Cycle*
OATES: The trial of Titus Oates
OSBORNE: Osborne, Thomas, *Letters*
PENNY: *Samuel Pepys' Penny Merriments*

PEPYS: Pepys, *The Diary of Samuel Pepys*
PET3: Petitions
PHENRY: Henry, Philip, *Letters*
PHLEB: *A Latin Technical Phlebotomy and its Middle English Translation*
PRICK: *The Pricke of Conscience*
RET: Guild Returns 1389
RHADDJR: Haddock, Richard, Jr, *Letters*
RHADDSR: Haddock, Richard, Sr, *Letters*
SOMERS: Somers, John, *Letters*
SPENCER: Spencer, Robert, *Letters*
STAT7: Statutes
STRYPE: Strype, John, *Letters*
TEST: Testaments and wills
TILLOTS: Tillotson, *Sermons*
TREVISA: Trevisa, *Polychronicon*
USK: Appeal of Thomas Usk
VANBR: Vanbrugh, *The Relapse*
WALTON: Walton, *The Compleat Angler*
WSERM: *English Wycliffite Sermons*
WYCNEW: Wycliffe, *The New Testament*
WYCOLD: Wycliffe, *The Old Testament*
WYCPROL: Purvey, *The Prologue to the Bible*

Part 1:
Theoretical background and methodological framework

I. Introduction

Before presenting the results of our investigation, it seems appropriate to outline the framework within which such analysis was carried out, and – in particular – point out the view of modality shared by the research group, the ways in which modality is commonly expressed in the English language, a brief overview of the evolution of central modal verbs in English, the main features of the corpus analyzed and the principal points taken into consideration as well as a definition of the main categories adopted in the analysis of the data.

1. The concept of modality

The concepts of 'necessity', 'possibility', 'probability', and 'impossibility' are at the core of all modal logic, having been a topic of central interest and intense study since classical times. Within the scope of their analyses, logicians have further categorised such notions into a variety of different modalities,[1] each corresponding to a particular set of laws or principles to which the truth/actuality of an event is relativised.

But what exactly is 'modality' from a linguistic point of view? Indeed, although this term is easy to define in broad terms, it is notoriously difficult to define and categorize precisely. Voicing a widely shared view, Halliday / Hasan have defined modality as "the speaker's assessment of the probabilities inherent in the situation, or, in a derived sense, of the rights and duties" (1987: 135). As it is the

1 Rescher (1968: 24-26) provides a thorough review of the main types of modalities studied in logic, the most widely acknowledged being: 'alethic' (relating to the notion of truth itself), 'epistemic' (relating to knowledge and belief), 'temporal' (relating to time), 'boulomaic' (relating to desire), 'deontic' (relating to duties), 'evaluative', 'causal' and 'likelihood'.

expression of some evaluation by the speaker, modality adds an overlay of meaning to an otherwise neutral semantic value of the proposition.

Being "a strand running prosodically through the clause" (Halliday 1976: 194), modality is expressed not only by modal verbs but also by a considerable range of grammatical and syntactic items, the most common being verbal, adverbial, adjectival, and nominal expressions, together with particles, clitics and prosodic features (like intonation and stress) in speech.[2] All these linguistic items contribute to shaping the overall semantic-pragmatic value of the utterance, which we will qualify according to a three-fold categorization.

1. *Epistemic modality* concerns matters of knowledge and belief and is related to the speaker / writer making judgements about the possibility that something is or is not the case. It is concerned with his / her belief or opinion about the validity of the proposition; as such, an epistemic statement "modifies the truth of a semantic proposition" (Lew 1997: 146). Consequently, epistemic modality is the modality of propositions, or, in von Wright's words, it is modality *de dicto*, since it is "about the mode or way in which a proposition is or is not true" (von Wright 1951: 8). Depending on the linguistic items which convey epistemic modality, this may be further distinguished into: 'epistemic necessity', 'epistemic possibility' and 'epistemic prediction' (the latter expressing deduction, speculation or inference and involving human judgement on the likelihood of past or future events). This modality is linked to the moment of speech (present or reported past) and the proposition that it qualifies may refer to present, past or future states of affairs.[3]

---

2 Palmer (1986) provides an interesting overview of the many linguistic items which embody modality in a variety of classical and modern languages.

3 Palmer (2001) distinguishes propositional modality into two categories: epistemic modality (by means of which speakers express their judgements about the factual status of the proposition) and evidential modality (with which they indicate the evidence they have for its actual status). However, this distinction appears to be more suitable for the description of languages other than English and, as a result, it has not been adopted in this study.

While epistemic modality refers to propositions, non-epistemic modalities refer to acts or events and consequently they are modalities *de re*, in so much as "they are about the way in which an individual thing has or has not a certain property" (von Wright 1951: 25). These modalities, often subsumed under the label 'root',[4] can be divided into two main types: deontic and dynamic. Their main difference is that with deontic modality the conditioning factors are external to the relevant entity, while with dynamic modality they are internal.

2. *Deontic modality* involves "the issuing of directives and is associated with such notions as permission or obligation" (Lew 1997: 146), in so much as it "is concerned with the necessity or possibility of acts performed by morally responsible agents" (Lyons 1977: 823). Consequently, the issue is not whether a proposition is true, but whether something is to be done. The speaker gives permission, makes a promise or a threat, expresses a wish, or places someone under an obligation.[5] Unlike epistemic modality, therefore, this modality is intrinsically connected with 'futurity', since it qualifies the speaker's attitude towards the realization of the events to which reference is made in the utterance, thus conveying the value of 'intention', 'volition', 'permission', or 'obligation'.

---

4 The term 'root' was first introduced by Hofmann (1966) and was subsequently employed by Ross (1969), Huddleston (1976), and particularly by Coates (1983) and Sweetser (1990). Although many linguists make use of this term to refer to all non-epistemic modality, some prefer not to use it on the grounds that the term 'root' suggests that it is the more basic of the two (Hoye 1997: 46). Although it is undoubtedly true that non-epistemic modality developed first from a purely diachronic point of view, the implication of 'basicness' that 'root' implies is not so useful in synchronic studies (van der Auwera / Plungian 1998: 84) nor in the type of studies such as the present one, in which the coexistence of different semantic and pragmatic values as expressed by the same modal form is investigated.

5 Because of this strict link between the subject and the rest of the predicate, deontic modality has commonly been considered to have a narrow scope, although this view has recently been called into question by Nordlinger / Traugott (1997), who – referring to the meaning of *ought to* – have argued that deontic modals can also be used to make an assertion about the proposition as a whole (i.e. with a wide scope).

3. *Dynamic modality* is a third type of modality suggested by von Wright (1951: 1-2), the first logician to deal with modality exhaustively. He used the word 'dynamic' in order to classify those uses of modal verbs which express ability and disposition, such as *can* in English. Such cases cannot be categorized as deontic modality (expressing an order, permission or promise) or epistemic modality (expressing a judgement on the proposition). Instead, they indicate "the relationship which exists between circumstances and unactualised events in accordance with natural laws – e.g. those of physics, chemistry, biology, etc." (Perkins 1983: 11). Starting from this premise, the concept of dynamic modality has been further developed by Palmer (1979a, 1986, 1990) and is now generally applied to modal expressions of 'ability', 'power', 'habit', 'prediction', and 'circumstance'.[6]

Semantically, epistemic, deontic and dynamic modalities might seem to have little in common; yet in many cases it is difficult to establish a clear-cut distinction between one type and another. This is due to three main reasons: first of all, modality is a fuzzy system,[7] subject to cases of indeterminacy and strongly affected by the context; secondly, in English and in other languages the same linguistic forms may be used to express any of the three kinds of modality; finally, one type of modality may be conveyed by a great variety of linguistic forms, as shall be presently discussed.

---

6 'Dynamic circumstantial' modality occurs when what is possible is dictated by the circumstances, as in 'Bill can only relax in his summer house' (= the circumstances are such that...).

7 The notion of modality as a fuzzy system has been applied by Coates (1983) on the basis of Zadeh's theory of linguistic fuzzy sets (1965, 1970, 1971), qualified as systems where the movement from 'belonging' to 'non-belonging' is gradual and unabrupt.

2. The expression of modality in English

English modality is realized by linguistic items from a wide range of grammatical classes, including modal auxiliary verbs, lexical verbs, adjectives, nouns, adverbs, particles, as well as mood and prosody in speech. Nevertheless, discussion on modality in linguistics has been concerned almost exclusively with the modal auxiliary verbs, which formally are the most coherent class of modal expressions in English.

Modal auxiliary verbs – All linguists feel the need to subdivide the class of modal auxiliaries into various sub-classes according to shared syntactic and morphological features. The most common distinction divides the principal modals from those more marginal modal forms like *ought to, need*, and *dare*, which have more complex morphological characteristics. For example, Quirk *et al.* (1985) distinguish between:

(i) central modals (*can/could, may/might, will/would, shall/should,* and *must*);
(ii) marginal modals (*dare, need, ought to, used to*);
(iii) modal idioms: *had better, would rather, be to,* and *have got to*;
(iv) semi-auxiliaries: verbal idioms introduced by one of the primary verbs *have* and *be* (*have to, be about to, be able to, be bound to, be going to, be obliged / supposed / willing to*).

Perkins (1983) distinguishes the following categories:

(i) primary modals (*can, may, will, shall*, and *must*);
(ii) secondary modals (*could, might, ought to, would*, and *should*);
(iii) quasi-auxiliary modal expressions (among which *have got to, need,* and *had better*);

Finally, Palmer (1990) makes the following distinctions:

(i) modals (*will/would, shall/should, can/could, may/might, must,* and *ought to*);

(ii) modals to a lesser extent (*used to, dare, need,* and *be to*);
(iii) more marginal modals (*had better* and *would rather*).

It is interesting to note that, despite the different terminology applied, the list of all the verbs considered is always more or less the same. We consider the following categorization the most suitable for our purposes:

1. *Central modals*: *can, may, shall, will, must*, and their past / tentative forms *could, might, should,* and *would*; all share a set of important syntactic features, which might be summarized as follows:

a) they have only finite forms and do not occur in any syntactic environment where a non-finite form is required:
ex: *They wouldn't be able to go* (**They wouldn't could go*);

b) they do not co-occur (in Standard English):[8]
ex: **He might could come*;

c) they do not enter into person-number agreement with the subject, as they have a single present tense form:
ex: *She can sing very well* (**She cans sing very well*);

d) they present an abnormal mapping of form onto time reference; both their present and past forms can be used to refer to present and future time, often with hypothetical or tentative meaning:
ex: *I might help you now / tomorrow*;

e) they admit verb-subject inversion. This occurs not only in interrogatives, where the modals exhibit no *do*-support, but also in sentences with introductory negatives or semi-negatives:
ex: *Will he come?*
Only then could I finally understand;

---

8 For an overview and recent bibliography of modal combinations in non-standard English varieties see, among others, Nagle (1994) Fennell / Butters (1996), and Facchinetti (1997).

f) negation: in forming negative clauses *not* is added after the modal verb:
ex: *You must not leave.*

2. *Marginal modals*: *dare, need, ought to, used to*; all of these have some of the properties typical of the central modals mentioned above, but are anomalous in various ways. For example, *need* and *dare* have both a modal and a main verb form, *ought* is always followed by the particle *to*, and *used to* occurs with reference to past events or states no longer corresponding to the encoder's reality.

3. *Modal idioms*: two multi-word verbs (*had better, would rather*) and verbs introduced by one of the primary verbs *have* and *be* (*be to, have (got) to, be about to, be able to, be going to, be supposed to,* and *be willing to*).

The central modals, marginal modals, and modal idioms quoted above express modality verbally, while non-verbal modality is realized by one or more of the following:

(i) *Superordinate clauses incorporating non-verbally-derived adjectives*; they can all be used impersonally with an *it*-subject, can be employed either predicatively or attributively, and convey either an epistemic (*be sure / certain / likely / possible / necessary / probable / apparent / clear / evident / obvious ... that*) or a deontic value (*be imperative / compulsory / mandatory / obligatory / lawful / legal / legitimate / permissible ... that*).

(ii) *Superordinate clauses incorporating verbally-derived adjectives and participles*; these include:
1. epistemic past participles referring to an act (*be advertised / affirmed / declared / implied / observed / reported ... that*);
2. deontic past participles referring to an act (*be advised / advocated / forbidden / invited / ordered / supplicated / warned ... that*);

3. past participles referring to an epistemic state (*be assumed / doubted / fancied / imagined / surmised / thought ... that*);
4. past participles referring to a deontic state (*be allowed / compelled / obliged / forced / bound / required ... to*);
5. epistemic verbally-derived adjectives (*be conceivable / arguable / debatable / doubtful / questionable ... that*).

(iii) *Modal adverbs*: these sentence adverbs convey epistemic modality, as they express the speaker's judgement in relation to the content of the whole proposition (*allegedly, arguably, evidently, necessarily, obviously, seemingly* ...).

(iv) *Modal nouns*:
1. referring to an epistemic act: *affirmation, argument, deduction, inference* ...;
2. referring to a deontic act: *call, demand, order, request*...;
3. referring to an epistemic state: *thought, feeling, presupposition, conviction*, ...;
4. referring to a deontic state: *compulsion, exemption, obligation, prohibition* ...;
5. referring to a dynamic state: *ability, capacity, potential* ....

(v) *Modal lexical verbs*: these are mostly epistemic or deontic performatives (*attest, estimate, infer*...; *allow, order, command, forbid, prohibit* ...) or lexical verbs referring to an epistemic state: *assume, feel, guess, presume, think* ...).

(vi) *Mood*: as remarked by Palmer (1986: 21), "the distinction between mood and modality is [...] similar to that between tense and time", in so far as mood is a morphosyntactic category of verb forms, expressing the degree or kind of reality assigned to a sentence. Several moods are to be distinguished, the three basic types being indicative, imperative and subjunctive.[9] In the expression of modality, the subjunctive is frequently employed (ex. *I suggest that he leave immediately*).

9 For a thorough discussion of the different moods and for a detailed bibliography on this topic, see von Wright (1951) and Palmer (1986).

(vii) *Prosody*: in speech, intonation and stress are of great importance in the communication of the speaker's attitude.

3. The evolution of central modal verbs in English

3.1. Old English[10]

PDE modal verbs derive from the OE proto-modals or pre-modals *cunnan*, *magan*, *motan*, *sculan*, and *willan*. In OE these verbs were part of the larger inflectional category of preterite-present verbs, including also *agan, durran,* and *þurfan*. They shared most of the properties of main verbs:

a) they behaved like ordinary full verbs with respect to negative placement and inversion;
b) they were ordinary complement-taking verbs;
c) they could be followed by finite or non-finite clauses.

While from a grammatical and syntactic point of view very little distinguished this group of verbs from the other main verbs, they were semantically distinctive; indeed, right from the OE period, they have been the most frequent conveyors of the concepts of permission, obligation, wish, will, and mental capability, which can be subsumed under the general labels of deontic and dynamic modality. In contrast, it is only in ME that the concepts of 'probability', 'possibility' and 'certainty' – currently subsumed under the term 'epistemic modality' – are fully conveyed by *can*, *may* and *must* and it is not until EModE that such values are acquired by *will* and *shall*.

Let us now consider each OE proto-modal in detail, starting with *cunnan*. The Indo-European root of *cunnan*, which can be traced in *kin-n-*, *ken-n* or maybe even *gen-u-*, probably meant 'perceive', 'understand', 'know'. In OE, the proto-modal translated Latin *scire*,

10 Although no analysis of OE data was carried out in this research, an outline of the modal history in OE is given here as a necessary background to an understanding of the ME situation.

meaning 'have the intellectual capability, know how to'. Therefore, right from the beginning the modal verb *can* has always expressed some kind of dynamic modality, as testified in (1):

(1) Ne con iċ noht singan
'I can't sing' (Bede's account of Caedmon)

In OE, however, as in (1), the proto-modal *cunnan* basically conveyed the value of intellectual rather than physical capability. Consequently, it occurred only in contexts with animate subjects possessing mental faculties. The PDE dynamic value of *can* expressing physical ability, independent of the mind, would only develop in ME and would become prevalent in EModE.

Such a value was already present in OE, expressed by the proto-modal *magan*, semantically very close to *cunnan*. Indeed, utterances equivalent to PDE 'I can think'pertained to the domain of OE *magan*:

(2) iċ mæg ġeðenċean (*Anglo-Saxon Chronicle* in *OED2* on CD-ROM)

This proto-modal translated Latin *posse*, with the value of 'having the physical capability / the strength of, being able to'. Only in very limited contexts did it also express permission,[11] which became dominant in the following centuries. Indeed, among the proto-modals, **motan* (PDE *must*) was the only one to express this deontic concept of permission prototypically:

(3) þonne rideþ ælc hys weges mid ðan feo, hyt motan habban eall.
'and then rides each his way with the money and it may/are permitted to-have all = and then each goes his own way with the money and can keep all of it' (Traugott 1972: 71-2)

However, if it is true that in a number of examples *motan* can be interpreted as an equivalent of the modern 'be allowed' or 'be permitted', in other instances – especially when found in non-complex sentences – its meaning is often considerably less self-evident, the

11 Traugott (1972) claims that at times *magan* expressed the deontic value of permission, but she also acknowledges that this was very limited, while physical ability was the predominant interpretation.

idea of permissibility being tinged with an idea of objective possibility, as underlined by Standop (1957: 67-93).

As for deontic obligation imposed by the speaker, it was conveyed by OE **sculan*, with the value corresponding to that of PDE *must*. *Sculan* is peculiar among the proto-modals, since it was the only one which started its grammatical and semantic re-categorization already in OE; this led to it losing its main-verb features and taking on those typical of PDE modal verbs much earlier than the other pre-modals. At the same time, from the semantic point of view, it evolved from the narrow scope of pecuniary obligation or indebtedness to wider moral obligation and command laid down by an external superior authority, including the operations of nature, gods and fate.

From this it was only a small step to reach the fully-fledged meaning of futurity, since commands necessarily have a future time reference. When it simply indicated futurity, *shall* frequently occurred either with the infinitive form of the following verb or with some other words in the sentence like *weorþan*, clarifying the futurity of the event. Consequently, the idea of futurity was established as an integral part of the semantic value of this auxiliary, although the verb also maintained its meaning of obligation and of the speaker's certainty about the necessity or the actualization of the event. Similar meanings, but less defined, were expressed by *willan*,[12] which mainly conveyed the deontic value of wish or intention,[13] corresponding to the current verbs 'to want', 'to wish', as in (4):

(4) he æt sumum cirre wolde fandian hu...
'he at one time wanted to discover how...' (Traugott 1972: 69)

In the rare non-deontic cases, *willan* was mainly employed to express the predictability value that we still find in 'Oil will float on water'

---

12 In OE there were three different lexical verbs expressing 'will' or 'desire': *wilnian*, *willian*, and *willan*; the first two were regular weak verbs and are represented by the modern *to will*; the verb *willan* is the origin of the ModE modal auxiliary. Although in OE the three verbs could not be confused due to their different endings, their forms coalesced in the following centuries, on account of the loss of inflections which occurred in late OE and ME.

13 Mitchell (1985) also points out a second general use of *willan*, which the OED classes as "natural disposition to do something, and hence habitual action".

and which is identified by Jespersen (1949) in terms of 'power', as (5) testifies:

(5) elpendes hyd wile drincan wætan.
'elephant's hide will drink wet = elephant's hide will absorb water.'
(Traugott 1972: 69).

Such cases occurred at first only when *willan* was employed with inanimate subjects, consequently with no hint at volition. Later, used with animate subjects, it is hard to determine "how far *willan* had gone along the road to simple futurity" (Mitchell 1985: 1/115), yet a number of occurrences testify to the strong undertones of dynamic futurity carried by OE *willan* in a variety of contexts.

(6) wen is, þæt hi us lifigende lungre wyllen sniome forsweolgan
'expectation is that they us living quickly intend at-once swallow-up = it is likely that they will swallow us up at once' (Denison 1993: 299)

As shown in this brief review, right from the OE period dynamic and deontic modality found ample expression through the proto-modals, epistemic values developing only in ME on the basis of further semantic changes of these verbs. As a group, the distinctive morphology and syntax of proto-modals was clearly established towards the end of ME, but their full semantic re-categorization was much slower and took place mostly in EModE.

3.2. Middle English and Early Modern English

In ME, the proto-modals could no longer be followed by a direct object; this change affected all proto-modals, although *cunne* (the ME form of *cunnan*) was the slowest to evolve and instances can still be found in late ME where this modal retains its OE syntactic properties. The past forms were increasingly used in non-past contexts with hypothetical and tentative meanings (Molencki 1999: 135-136) and decreasingly in narrative past contexts, to the point that we can no longer distinguish clearly two tenses for this class of verb.

The particle *to* marking the infinitive form started to be used more and more frequently in ME, but never followed the modal verb;

moreover, all the non-pre-modal verbs in the preterite-present category disappeared. These and other minor changes led to the isolation of the proto-modals from all other main verbs and towards the end of the 15th century they became an autonomous verbal class, which was morphologically and syntactically even more defined in the following century:

1) the old pre-modals no longer occurred in non-finite forms;
2) they rarely co-occurred in standard dialects;
3) the negative particle remained after the modal verb (i.e no DO-periphrasis);
4) verb-subject inversion remained in interrogative contexts.

As previously mentioned, unlike morphology, the semantics of modals did not change greatly before late ME. Indeed, it was only towards the end of ME that *cunne* lost the value of intellectual capability, as it was more and more frequently used not only with animate but also inanimate subjects, which cannot 'know'. Consequently, *cunne* came to express the dynamic value linked to physical capability corresponding to the current *to be able to*. At first, this occurred with inanimate subjects, but the meaning of physical capability was gradually extended also to animate subjects. Currently, however, *can* also expresses the deontic value of permission, a meaning which only became widespread in the 19th century, following a pattern of development similar to that which had been previously followed by *may*.

In late OE texts there are already cases of *magan* used deontically in the granting of permission and then in EME we find the first uses of *mow* with the meaning of epistemic possibility. The two new meanings remain undeveloped until the EModE period.

As for ME *shall*, this remained definitely more frequent than *will*, especially in predictive contexts. Wycliffe, in his translation of the *Vulgate*, used *shall* regularly to translate the Latin future tense, while *will* was employed to gloss the Latin *volo*. In LME the idea of futurity inherent in *shall* strongly increased at the expense of the sense of obligation which was steadily weakened, up to Shakespeare's time, when the two auxiliary verbs had almost reached the present pattern. By the end of the 15th century, the idea of futurity latent in the notion of volition became predominant in the use of *will*, with the result that this came to be used as an auxiliary expressing futurity. During the EModE period, *will* superseded *shall* in second and third person dynamic futurity contexts and by the end of the 16th century its volitional sense had been further weakened.

As can be seen from this overview, in LME and EModE, the period of time taken into consideration in our study of modal forms in the Helsinki Corpus, the central modal verbs were undergoing significant changes particularly from a semantic point of view. Indeed, this was the time when some of them were re-categorized from one type of modality to another.

4. The Helsinki Corpus of English Texts

The diachronic section of the Helsinki Corpus includes a programmatic selection of texts compiled from the Old, Middle and Early Modern English periods (850-1710) for a total of over 1,500,000 words. The text extracts (which vary in length from 2,000 to 20,000 words) have been chosen to give a representative selection of

- historical periods (diachronic coverage)
- geographical dialects (diatopic coverage)
- sociolinguistic variants (diastratic coverage)
- a range of text types, genres and registers (diatypic coverage).

- *Historical periods*

The corpus presents the following period divisions:

Old English		*Middle English*		*Early Modern English*	
OE1	-850	ME1	1150-1250	EModE1	1500-1570
OE2	850-950	ME2	1250-1350	EModE2	1570-1640
OE3	950-1050	ME3	1350-1420	EModE3	1640-1710
OE4	1050-1150	ME4	1420-1500		

- *Geographical dialects*

The geographical place of origin is given for OE and ME texts only; EModE texts are all in southern standard. However, dialectal coverage was not a priority in the choice of samples, and the Scots corpora already available or in preparation allow more useful regional comparisons.[14]

- *Sociolinguistic variants*

Sociolinguistic parameters are given from ME onwards: age, sex, social status of authors, relationship between correspondents.

- *Text types*

Twenty-two text type categories have been used in the classification of extracts, eight of which occur in all three main diachronic sections. Both literary and non-literary texts are included, with preference for the non-literary; most texts are in prose. Some – such as sermons, trial records, and official correspondence – are classified as 'formal'; others – such as private correspondence, light fiction and comedy – are classified as 'informal'. Spoken English is reflected in speech-based text types such as drama, sermons and trial records, and therefore interesting comparisons can be made with the other, non-speech-based texts.[15]

---

14 Cf. Meurman-Solin (1995 and 2001). In addition to the numerous studies by Meurman-Solin (see especially 1997 and 1999), reference may be made to the studies of modality in Older Scots recently undertaken by Dossena (2001a and 2001b).

15 More detailed information about the various parts of the Helsinki Corpus can be found in its manual (cf. Kytö 1996). Several analyses have been carried out using this corpus; for the results of some of them cf. Rissanen *et al.* (1993, 1997a and 1997b).

5. The subsections taken into consideration

For the purposes of this research the LME and the EModE periods were taken into consideration, as very important processes of change in the English modality system are believed to have taken place in the period from the late 14th to the late 17th century. Due to the abundance of data available in the Helsinki Corpus, a further selection then had to be made: only two subsections were analyzed, those appearing at the beginning (M3) and the end (E3) of the three centuries to be investigated, a selection which still allowed us to make appropriate comparisons in the use and development of verbal modality. The texts included in the corpus are listed below.

5.1.The M3 subsection

The M3 subsection consists of extracts from texts written in the period 1350-1420, for a total number of 184,230 words. The various texts have been grouped into different textual categories, each representing a single genre. The specific texts and textual categories included in the subcorpus are as follows (the date, length and percentage of each text are added in brackets):[16]

- DOCUMENTS (15,390 words; 8.35%):
  - Appeals (1384-1420; 2,220 words; 1.21%)
  - Petitions (1388-1419; 5,110 words; 2.77%)
  - Guild Returns (1389; 3,710 words; 2.01%)
  - Judgements (1396-1419; 1,410 words; 0.76%)
  - Testaments and wills (1387-1408; 1,420 words; 0.77%)
  - Proclamations (1383-1419; 1,520 words; 0.83%)
- HANDBOOKS (19,150 words; 10.40%):
  - Chaucer, *A Treatise on the Astrolabe* (1391; 6,840 words; 3.71%)
  - *The Equatorie of the Planetis* (1392; 6,200 words; 3.37%)
  - *A Late Middle English Treatise on Horses* (a1450; 6,110 words; 3.32%)

16 For detailed bibliographical references see Kytö (1996: 167-230).

- SCIENCE (3,580 words; 1.94%):
  - *A Latin Technical Phlebotomy and its Middle English Translation* (1400-1420; 3,580 words; 1.94%)
- PHILOSOPHY (12,614 words; 6.85%):
  - Chaucer, *Boethius* (c1380; 10,170; 5.52%)
  - Chaucer, *The Tale of Melibee*[17] (c1390; 2,444 words; 1.33%)
- HOMILIES (7,280 words; 3.95%):
  - *The Northern Homily Cycle* (c1400; 7,280 words; 3.95%)
- SERMONS (13,460 words; 7.31%):
  - *English Wycliffite Sermons* (c1400; 13,460 words; 7.31%)
- RULES (5,390 words; 2.92%):
  - *The Benedictine Rule* (a1425; 2,380 words; 1.29%)
  - Aelred of Rievaulx's *De Institutione Inclusarum* (c1400; 3,010 words; 1.63%)
- RELIGIOUS TREATISES (37,080 words; 20.13%):
  - Purvey, *The Prologue to the Bible* (c1388; 3,020 words; 1.64%)
  - *The Cloud of Unknowing* (?a1400; 15,690 words; 8.52%)
  - Mannyng, *Robert of Brunne's "Handlyng Synne"* (a1400; 8,050 words; 4.37%)
  - *The Pricke of Conscience* (a1400; 5,910 words; 3.21%)
  - Chaucer, *The Parson's Tale* (c1390; 4,410 words; 2.39%)
- HISTORY (24,500 words; 13.30%):
  - *Cursor Mundi* (a1400; 10,390 words; 5.64%)
  - *The Brut or the Chronicles of England* (c1400; 8,160 words; 4.43%)
  - Trevisa, *Polychronicon* (a1387; 5,950 words; 3.23%)
- TRAVELOGUE (5,530 words; 3%):
  - *Mandeville's Travels* (c1400; 5,530 words; 3%)
- FICTION (14,336 words; 7.78%):
  - Chaucer, *The General Prologue to The Canterbury Tales, The Wife of Bath's Prologue, The Summoner's Tale, The Merchant's Tale* (c1387-95; 7,000 words; 3.80%)
  - Chaucer, *The Tale of Melibee* (c1390; 2,106 words; 1.14%)
  - Gower, *Confessio Amantis* (a1393; 5,230 words; 2.84%)
- LETTERS, NON-PRIVATE (5,010 words; 2.72%):
  - Henry V and others (various dates; 5,010 words; 2.72%)
- BIBLE (20,910 words; 11.35%):
  - Wycliffe, *The Old Testament* (a1382; 9,910 words; 5.38%)
  - Wycliffe, *The New Testament* (c1388; 11,000; 5.97%)

---

17 As regards this text, the figure of 4,550 words given by the handbook (cf. Kytö 1996: 182) has been divided into the two text types of Fiction and Philosophy as classified in the tags provided for each sample.

5.2. The E3 subsection

This part of the corpus consists of 171,040 words, drawn from texts published in the period 1640-1710. The specific texts and textual categories included in the corpus are as follows (the date, length and percentage of each text are added in brackets):

- LAW (13,180 words; 7.71%):
  - Statutes (1695-99; 13,180 words; 7.71%)
- HANDBOOKS (11,370 words; 6.65%):
  - Walton, *The Compleat Angler* (1676; 5,370 words; 3.14%)
  - Langford, *Plain and Full Instructions to Raise All Sorts of Fruit-Trees* (1699; 6,000 words; 3.51%)
- SCIENCE (11,280 words; 6.59%):
  - Hooke, *Micrographia* (1665; 6,060 words; 3.54%)
  - Boyle, *Electricity & Magnetism* (1675-6; 5,220 words; 3.05%)
- EDUCATIONAL TREATISES (11,320 words; 6.62%):
  - Locke, *Directions Concerning Education* (1693; 5,200 words; 3.04%)
  - Hoole, *A New Discovery of the Old Art of Teaching Schoole* (1660; 6,120 words; 3.58%)
- PHILOSOPHY (8,820 words; 5.16%):
  - Preston, *Boethius* (1695; 8,820; 5.16%)
- SERMONS (12,470 words; 7.29%):
  - Tillotson, *Sermons* (1671/1679; 6,600 words; 3.86%)
  - Taylor, *The Marriage Ring* (1673; 5,870 words; 3.43%)
- PROCEEDINGS, TRIALS (13,760 words; 8.05%):
  - The trial of Titus Oates (1685; 7,730 words; 4.52%)
  - The trial of Lady Alice Lisle (1685; 6,030 words; 3.53%)
- HISTORY (11,640 words; 6.80%):
  - Burnet, *History of My Own Time* (1703; 5,820 words; 3.40%)
  - Milton, *The History of Britain* (1670; 5,820 words; 3.40%)
- TRAVELOGUE (10,470 words; 6.13%):
  - Fiennes, *The Journeys of Celia Fiennes* (1698; 5,140 words; 3.01%)
  - Fryer, *A New Account of East India* (1698; 5,330 words; 3.12%)
- DIARIES (11,210 words; 6.56%):
  - Pepys, *The Diary of Samuel Pepys* (1666-7; 5,140 words; 3.01%)
  - Evelyn, *The Diary of John Evelyn*, (1689-90; 6,070 words; 3.55%)
- BIOGRAPHIES (11,730 words; 6.86%):
  - AUTOBIOGRAPHY: Fox, *The Journal of George Fox* (1694; 5,560 words; 3.25%)

- OTHER: Burnet, *Some Passages of the Life and Death of ... Earl of Rochester* (1680; 6,170 words; 3.61%)

- FICTION (12,040 words; 7.04%):
  - *Samuel Pepys' Penny Merriments* (1684-5; 6,560 words; 3.84%)
  - Behn, *Oroonoko* (1688; 5,480 words; 3.20%)
- DRAMA, COMEDIES (12,740 words; 7.45%):
  - Vanbrugh, *The Relapse* (1697; 7,190 words; 4.20%)
  - Farquhar, *The Beaux Stratagem* (1707; 5,550 words; 3.25%)
- LETTERS (19,010 words; 11.09%):
  - PRIVATE: Haddock (Richard, Sr; Richard, Jr; Nicholas), Strype, Oxinden (Henry; Elizabeth), Hatton (Charles; Frances; Alice; Anne; Elizabeth), Pinney (Jane; John), Henry (Philip) (various dates; 13,140 words; 7.67%)
  - NON-PRIVATE: Somers, Spencer, A letter by the Privy Council, Capel, Charles II, Osborne, Aungier, A letter by the Commissioners (various dates; 5,870 words; 3.42%)

5.3. Comparison between the two subsections

As shown by the figures above, the two subsections do not differ greatly in quantitative terms (184,230 words in M3 against 171,040 words in E3). In addition, the periods covered have the same temporal length (i.e 70 years) and constitute the beginning and end of a 300-year time span (1350-1420 / 1640-1710).

Most text types appear in both subsections; this is the case of handbooks, scientific treatises, philosophical works, sermons, history books, travelogues, fiction, and non-private letters. Others, instead, only appear in one of the subsections; documents, homilies, rules, religious treatises, and biblical texts are only present in M3, while statutes, educational treatises, trial proceedings, diaries, biographies, comedies, and private letters are only included in the E3 subsection.

As previously mentioned, most samples included in the two subsections are non-literary; fictional works in M3 are in verse, while those in E3 are in prose. Both subsections include formal text types – such as official correspondence, sermons and trial records – while informal ones (such as private correspondence, light fiction and comedy) are only found in the E3 subsection. In the two subsections there are both non-speech-based and speech-based texts; the latter includes sermons in both subsections, and comedies and trial records in E3.

6. The foci of our investigation

The two subsections were analyzed so as to trace the most important changes in the development of verbal modality in the period of time under study. For this purpose, all the quotations were analyzed in order to determine various features of the modal verbs included in them; the main characteristics taken into consideration were the following:

- spelling variants;[18]
- the structure of the verb phrase comprising the modal (e.g. Modal + bare / perfect / passive infinitive, etc.);
- the lexical context of the occurrence (to ascertain regularity in the occurrence of a specific central modal with a particular type of verb or adverb);
- the time reference (i.e. the temporal position of the state or act expressed by the verbal complement in relation to the modal verb: past, present, future or timeless);[19]
- distribution according to the text types included in the Helsinki corpus (to ascertain whether certain modal verbs and certain meanings of these verbs are associated with particular text types or with speech-based rather than non-speech-based texts or with formal rather than informal ones);
- the type of modality expressed by the modal verb analyzed.

As regards the last of these parameters, it was generally possible to identify the main semantic and pragmatic value for each occurrence by the following procedure:

i) translation of the quotation into PDE, making use of periphrastic expressions that make meaning explicit (e.g. 'it is possible that' vs 'it is possible for');

18 In the following chapters capitals will be used to denote the lexeme (eg. SHALL), while italics will be used for its graphic variants (such as *shall, shalt, shan't*, etc).

19 This categorization of time reference is drawn from Mindt (1995).

ii) where necessary, an examination of the wider context (e.g. to judge between subjective and objective possibility);

iii) where there was still ambiguity or meanings were found to co-exist, placement of such occurrences in a category of 'indeterminate' or 'ambiguous' cases in the various tables. Several of these quotations have been explicitly presented and discussed, as possible instances of uses giving clues to a change in progress.

The identification of the prevalent modal meaning was primarily made according to whether the semantic value of the modal occurrence was deontic, epistemic or dynamic; the three categories were then divided into the following subcategories:

1. DEONTIC	*2. EPISTEMIC*	*3. DYNAMIC*
1.1 VOLITION	2.1 POSSIBILITY	3.1 ABILITY
1.1.1 Intention		
1.1.2 Refusal	2.2 INFERENCE	3.2 POSSIBILITY
1.1.3 Threat		
1.1.4 Promise	2.3 NECESSITY	3.3 PREDICTION
1.1.5 Offer		3.3.1 Neutral prediction
1.2 NECESSITY		3.3.2 Prophecy
1.2.1 Order		3.3.3 Assurance
1.2.2 Prohibition		
1.2.3 Instruction		3.4 NECESSITY
1.2.4 Proposal		
1.2.5 Advice/ Request for advice		3.5 HABIT
1.3 POSSIBILITY		

The primary distinction into deontic, epistemic and dynamic was mainly derived from Palmer (1986), as illustrated above (cf. §1). Although for the other semantic categories no single source was used, the taxonomy outlined here mainly relies on those proposed by Coates (1983) and Palmer (1990). These semantic categories have further been subdivided into detailed sets of pragmatic subcategories, whose names have been drawn from the current literature; however, as these subcategories seem to be employed to express different concepts in the various studies analyzed, a specification of the semantic values attributed to them in this volume is required. This is how these subcategories were identified:

Deontic meanings:

- *Intention / Refusal*: the modal expresses the (non-)intention to carry out an action.
- *Promise / Threat*: to be interpreted as the declared intention to carry out an action which is fruitful / harmful to the interlocutor or someone not present.
- *Offer*: expresses the speaker's availability to carry out an action to the interlocutor's advantage.
- *Order / Prohibition*: expresses a command (not) to carry out a certain action.
- *Instruction*: expresses an indication of what to do in order to carry out a process or obtain a result.
- *Proposal*: the modal may be paraphrased by the verb *suggest*.
- *Advice*: expresses a subjective opinion given to someone about what they should do in a particular situation.
- *Possibility*: mainly concerns the semantic field of permission; indeed, the modal may be paraphrased with the idioms *be allowed to* or *give permission to*.

Epistemic meanings:

- *Possibility*: is commonly paraphrased by *it is possible that*.
- *Inference*: can be paraphrased by *I (etc.) deduce that*.
- *Necessity*: is commonly paraphrased by *it is necessarily the case that*.

Dynamic meanings:

- *Ability*: the modal may be paraphrased by *be able to*.
- *Possibility*: the modal may be paraphrased by *it is possible for*.
- *Prediction*: the modal expression can be paraphrased with the use of the verb *predict*.

- *Prophecy*: refers to all cases of prediction based on an appeal to authority, and which thus acquire a stronger predictive force.
- *Assurance*: is realized whenever the locutor strengthens the illocutionary force of the predictive speech act by means of some 'guarantee', which usually takes the form of an emphasizer or booster (Holmes 1984).
- *Necessity*: concerns those cases of obligation deriving from external factors (in contrast to deontic obligation, which derives from a person's decision) and which are paraphrasable by the expression *it is necessary for*.
- *Habit*: the modal form is used to express habitual actions and typical behaviour.

Throughout the text quantitative findings are offered in terms of normalized figures per 10,000 words, unless otherwise stated.

7. The aim of our investigation

Although an ultimate aim of all historical linguistics research is to understand the principles behind the modes and mechanisms of language change, we have here limited ourselves to seeing what emerges of immediate interest from an analysis of the chosen comparative data. Our aim has been, by applying a system of semantic and pragmatic uses to the many examples of modal auxiliaries in the corpus, to make a contribution to the understanding of their meanings and uses in the single historical periods, in the two compared periods and, within and between these, in the different text types. As 'number-crunchers', close relatives of lexicographers (Samuel Johnson's 'harmless drudges'), we hope that the map we have provided here, the fruit of much labour, will prove a useful guide for future explorers, both practical and theoretical.

Part 2: Central modals in Late Middle English and Early Modern English

II. Can

It is generally acknowledged that PDE modal verbs developed their auxiliary features relatively early and qualified as a separate class in all major respects by the beginning of the EModE period. However, CAN followed his cognates "as a hesitant companion" (Nagle 1986: 73), since it did not fully qualify as a modal auxiliary before the 17th century and instances of the verb with non-modal values can still be found in the 19th century (van Kemenade 1992; Rissanen 1999: 233).

The M3 and E3 sections contain 113 (M3) and 415 (E3) verb forms that, at first sight, can be seen as examples of the verb CAN. However, while all E3 occurrences have modal meaning, 32 (27%) of the M3 tokens are non-modal lexical verbs. This leaves a frequency for modal CAN of 5 per 10,000 words in M3, against 24 in E3. The great increase between the two periods and the disappearance (in our corpus at any rate) of lexical-verb use gives us an indication of the process of grammaticalization. Undoubtedly, this increase is largely due to the corresponding decrease in the use of MAY, which expressed the role of PDE CAN for centuries.

Three of the 81 M3 occurrences have been recorded in combination with either *may* or *shall*, as double modal constructions. The form *can* occurs 8 times in the Northern poem *Cursor Mundi*, as a variant form of *gan*, past tense of OE *(on)ginnan/gin* (PDE 'begin'). This form started to be used before the 13th century, was fully established early in the 14th century in Northern use (Visser 1963-73: 1379, 1571-1575; OED), and was particularly frequent in ME poetic texts (Denison 1993: 161). Originally, it was followed by an infinitive with *to*; later, it was also employed in a weakened sense as a simple auxiliary of past tense, as in (1) and (2), from *Cursor Mundi*:

(1) þai mai quen sco *can* vnderstand / þat iacob suld be hir husband, / To laban tald sco new tiþand, / And he him ledd in be þe hand. (CURSOR: 226)

(2) Wit þat stan he laid in sling, / Sua stalworthli he lete it suing / þat in his frunt þat stan he fest, / þat bath his eien vte *can* brest. (CURSOR: 438)

In 23 of the remaining 24 non-modal occurrences, CAN is a transitive lexical verb meaning 'know', retaining the lack of inflectional morphology for the 3rd person singular typical of the OE preterite-present verb from which it derives:

(3) And soudeinly, er sche was war, / As he which alle guile *can*, / His forme he torneth into man, / And cam to bedde, and sche lai stille. (GOWER: II, 223)

(4) A Frere ther was, […] / In alle the ordres foure is noon that *kan* / So muchel of daliaunce and fair langage. (CTPROL: 26.C2)

(5) and if he ascke þee what is þat God, sey þou þat it is God þat maad þee and bouȝt þee, and þat graciously haþ clepid þee to his loue. And in him sei þou *kanst* no skile. (CLOUD: 26)

(6) iugement ys a þing þat men knowen not, for þey ledon not þer wit aftyr Godes lawe, for þei presumen as þe fend to *connen* þat þei knowen not. (WSERM4: I, 238)

The object of CAN here is always inanimate, as in (5), where it is expressed by *skile* and thus forms a set phrase which was common up to the 17th century and meant 'to have discrimination or knowledge'.[1] In 3 cases CAN is used as an infinitive preceded by *to*, as in (6). The following is the last non-modal instance of CAN:

(7) For of alle oþer creatures and þeire werkes – ȝe, and of þe werkes of God self – may a man þorou grace haue fulheed o knowing, and wel to *kon* þinke on hem. (CLOUD: 26)

In (7) *kon* is dependent on *may*; although semantically close to its PDE cognate, since the last part of the quotation can be paraphrased by 'and *know how to* think clearly about them', the infinitive introduced by *to* testifies to the still incomplete development of CAN into a modal, both syntactically and semantically. Lexical-verb CAN appears to be in free variation with *know* and *wit*: Chaucer, for instance, frequently employs CAN both as an auxiliary and as a lexical verb in great proximity:

1 As was typical of this set phrase, the matter in which the subject has discrimination or knowledge is added by means of an adjunct introduced by *of* or *in*.

(8) Thus shulde ye speke and bere hem wrong on honde, / For half so boldely *kan* ther no man / Swere and lyen, as a womman *kan*. / I sey nat this by wyves that been wyse, / But if it be whan they hem mysavyse. / A wys wyf, if that she *kan* hir good, / Shal beren hym on honde that the cow is wood, / And take witnesse of hir owene mayde / Of hir assent. (CTBATH: 108.C1)

In the first two instances of *kan* in this extract of *The Wife of Bath's Tale*, the verb is used as a modal, and the clause can be paraphrased by 'no man *can* swear and lie half so boldly as a woman *can*'; in contrast, the third use has a non-modal value and can be paraphrased as 'if she *knows* what's good for her'. Similarly, in the following speech by Melibee's wife, the first occurrence of *kan* conveys ability, while the other two mean 'know':

(9) "My lord," quod she, "I yow biseche as hertely as I dar and *kan*" [...] And Senec seith that 'whoso wole have sapience shal no man dispreyse, but he shal gladly techen the science that he *kan* withouten presumpcion or pride; and swiche thynges as he noght ne *kan*, he shal nat been ashamed to lerne hem, and enquere of lasse folk than hymself' (CTMEL: 220.C2)

1. Spelling variants

In M3 the commonest variant is *kan/can* with a total of 61 occurrences. Interestingly, *cunne/kunne*, which was common in OE with present-tense values, is very rare in the ME subsection of this corpus, while the infinitive *cinnan* and *cunnan*, which were also very frequent in OE, have not even been recorded. The *c*-forms (*can, canst, cone, conne,* and *cunne*) are less frequent than *k*-forms. However, this should not lead to any hasty conclusions with regard to the graphic variants of CAN in ME, since it is generally acknowledged that even in OE the letter *k* was a mere variant of *c*. In fact, both in OE and in ME this spelling is not uniform and largely depends on the copysts of the manuscripts, to the point that in the same extract one might find two different variants, as in (10). In E3, all the *k*- and *con-/cun-*, *kon-/kun-*forms have disappeared.

(10) þe mercy of þis fadur *kan* we not telle fully, for he ys þe moste worchere þat may ben in þis world; and he *can* not worche (WSERM4: I, 236)

In M3 negation was still largely obtained by means of a separate adverbial (*nat/not/no(u)ght*); indeed, of 20 occurrences of CAN followed by a negative adverb in the M3 corpus, only 4 (3 with *cannot* and 1 with *can-not*) are found in one word or hyphenated form, while in E3 only one-word forms or contracted forms are in use, with the sole understandable exception of *canst*, employed 3 times with a separate *not*, as in (11):

(11) If Thou *canst* not send him thether, yet I pray send him to Ospring to our Brother Cater's (HOXINDEN: 292)

The OED recalls the following as the first use of one-word negative form of CAN: "?a1400 *Cursor M.* (add. to Cott.) p. 959. 105 And Þou Þat he deed fore cannot sorus be". There are not contracted negatives in M3; the 3 forms of *cannot* recorded in M3 are respectively from Wycliff's sermons and from *The Cloud of Unknowing*, all of which are strongly linked to informal, dialogic contexts, and therefore most liable to variation. Indeed, Lass (1999: 179-180) remarks that there is no clear sign of negative cliticisation of modals before the 16th or the beginning of the 17th century, although he concedes a few metrical examples in Shakespeare, with full-form spellings. Yet Denison (1993: 309) remarks that *can't* was first recorded in 1597. As for the 2nd person singular morphologic marking *-st*, this is still employed in E3; indeed, in both subperiods, it seems to have maintained the same frequency of occurrence of 1.2 in M3 and 1.7 in E3.

2. Distribution according to text type

The distribution of CAN is widely diversified within the different text types of each subperiod. In M3 it is found with some frequency in 'speech-related' texts, namely texts written to be spoken, like Sermons (frequency of 6 per 10,000 words), texts where the writer addresses his interlocutor directly, such as Letters (6) and Religious treatises (8), and, most of all, texts including dialogue, such as extracts from the *Canterbury Tales* (16); cf. Table 1:

Text type	*No.*	*o/ooo*
FICTION	23	16
RELIGIOUS TREATISES	28	8
DOCUMENTS	9	6
SERMONS	8	6
LETTERS	3	6
HOMILIES	2	3
PHILOSOPHY	3	2
RULES	1	2
TRAVELOGUES	1	2
HANDBOOKS	1	1
HISTORY	2	1
All texts	81	4

Table 1. Distribution of CAN in M3 (in order of descending frequency per text type).[2]

Both in Fictional works and in Religious treatises, where CAN occurs most frequently, the modal is widely employed in dialogic sections, as in (12):

(12) "For who *kan* teche and werchen as we *konne*? / And that is nat of litel tyme," quod he. (CTSUMM: 134.C1)

History and Handbooks have a very low frequency of occurrences of CAN (1 per 10,000 words), while Science and Bible exhibit no instance at all. However, in this subperiod the limited number of occurrences and the idiosyncrasies of the authors seem to play a great role with regard to the concentration of CAN in different text types. In contrast, the larger number of data recorded in E3 provide material for interesting considerations (cf. Table 2).

As in M3, the relatively formal History and Law samples are the ones with the lowest frequency of occurrence (2 per 10,000 words). In contrast, the 'speech-related' texts in this subcorpus (Sermons, Trials, Letters and Drama) all show a high frequency of

2 In this and the following tables and figures only the text types exhibiting occurrences of CAN have been mentioned.

occurrence of the modal under scrutiny. Unsurprisingly, the large majority of the instances in these texts are from conversational extracts, or from samples exhibiting some sort of interaction between speaker and interlocutor. Indeed, it is in dialogues that the instances of contracted *can't* have been recorded, while *cannot* is equally distributed among all text types, be they speech-related or not.

Text type	*No.*	*o/ooo*
PHILOSOPHY	69	78
SERMONS	56	44
TRIALS	57	41
LETTERS	75	39
DRAMA	49	38
EDUCATIONAL TREATISES	25	22
HANDBOOKS	22	19
FICTION	19	16
DIARIES	14	12
TRAVELOGUES	8	8
BIOGRAPHIES	8	7
SCIENCE	8	7
LAW	3	2
HISTORY	2	2
All texts	196	11

Table 2. Distribution of CAN in E3 (ranked in order of descending frequency).

Philosophical texts are the category with the highest frequency of CAN, although being generally considered to be non-speech related. This apparent incongruity is easily clarified: the E3 philosophical section covers five extracts from Preston's translation of Boethius' *De Consolatione Philosophiae*, which is in dialogic form. The study of all the samples from *De Consolatione Philosophiae* recorded in the different subperiods of the Helsinki Corpus testifies to the fact that the frequency of CAN increases gradually, with a particularly interesting increase in normalized frequency between 1556 and 1593 (from 28 to 67) throughout all the subperiods of the E3 section (cf. Table 3).

This increase of CAN in the different translations has been found to be largely at the expense of MAY, the use of which conversely decreases in the same texts, as exemplified in (13.a) and (13.b), by Chaucer and Preston:

(13a) "For sothe," quod I, "I se wel now that suffisaunce *may* nat comen by rychesse" (BOETHCH: 429.C1)

(13b) I now see plainly that Men *cannot* arrive at a full Satisfaction by Riches (BOETHCO: 124)

Author	*Period*	*No.*	*o/ooo*
Chaucer	c.1380	-	-
Colville	1556	29	28
Elizabeth	1593	47	67
Preston	1695	69	77

Table 3. Frequency of CAN in the Philosophical subsections of the Helsinki Corpus.

The gradual substitution of MAY with CAN in these philosophical texts may exemplify the changing linguistic situation with reference to the two modals CAN and MAY, which were still separate semantically at Chaucer's time but then shared roles and gradually became established as two distinct modals, diversified in terms of contexts of occurrence and use.

Further confirmation of this claim can be found in the wide increase in frequency of CAN from M3 to E3 in all the text types represented in both samples, as shown in Figure 1.

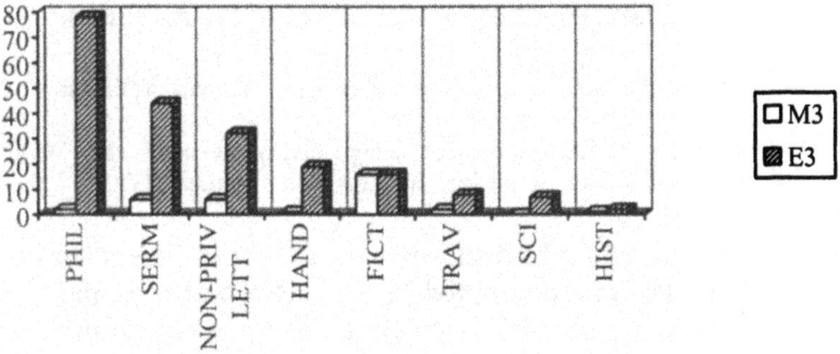

Figure 1. Frequency of CAN in M3 and E3 per text type (normalized figures).

Overall, almost all text types show a wider use of CAN in E3, the only exception being Fiction, which has an unchanged frequency of CAN between the two subperiods. In some cases such increase is minimum, as in History texts (M3 1 vs E3 2); in contrast, M3 Science texts do not use CAN, while in E3 the modal occurs 8 times. Although the small M3 Science sample does not prove that CAN was never used in Science texts in the M3 period, we can be confident that it was very rare, as the verb continues to be infrequent in this genre in E3 as well. The largest discrepancy can be seen in non-private Letters (6 in M3 vs 32 in E3), Sermons (6 in M3 vs 44 in E3), and Philosophical texts (2 in M3 vs 78 in E3). All these text types are speech-related, a feature which has been seen to favour the use of CAN. Interestingly, as will be seen, Sermons and Philosophical texts are also those which show the highest increase in the use of merged dynamic / epistemic values; undoubtedly this affects the overall frequency between the two periods.

3. Verb phrase structure

In both M3 and in E3 CAN mostly occurs in what is currently by far the most common verb phrase pattern, consisting of two verbal elements, the modal and the bare infinitive of the main verb:

(14) For now I se here na felaw, / Ne no man þat I *can* knaw. (NHOM: II, 205)

(15) whether such Pipe or other Conveyance may or *can* convey any Wash […] fitt for Distillation out of one Back or Vessell into another (STAT7: VIII, 457)

This structure is evenly distributed across the different text types of both subperiods, accounting for 78% of the occurrences in M3 and for 81% of those in E3; this testifies to its relative stability over the centuries, as can be seen in Table 4, showing the raw data of all the verb phrase patterns occurring with CAN.

The most interesting change between the two subperiods is in the use after CAN of the passive infinitive, which has not been recorded at all in M3, while in E3 it reaches 9% of all uses. This pattern has been found in all text types; it is particularly common in Handbooks, Educational treatises, Philosophical texts, Sermons and Letters, largely in combination with dynamic possibility values with epistemic nuances, where the passive form perhaps aims to give a certain objectivity to the subjective utterance.

Verbal complementation	*M3*	*E3*
active infinitive	63	335
passive infinitive	-	38
to-infinitive	-	1
second modal	3	-
Ø	15	41
Total	*81*	*415*

Table 4. Verbal complementation of CAN (absolute numbers).

The data from E3 also exhibit a fairly unusual pattern which again was not recorded in M3: CAN in collocation with a *to*-infinitive:

(16) you saw him within four or five Days after at Tixhall?
LORD ASTON. To name particular Days, I *cannot*; but that I saw him several Days at Tixhall, I am sure. (OATES: IV, 75.C2)

This use is to be accounted for by the peculiar syntactic structure of the sentence itself, its main verb being at the very beginning, thus partly losing the direct dependency on the modal.

The relative decrease of elliptical verb phrases – 18% in M3 as opposed to 10% in E3 – is not associated with any particular text type. In (17) *recomende* is implied after *can*, *oughte*, *shulde* and *may*, all of which are introduced by the correlative *as*. CAN in elliptical verb phrases also occurs in comparative clauses, which appear to be relatively frequent in M3, since 8 of the total 15 cases of elliptical CAN are in this context, as in (18).

(17) to the Soueragn highnesse of your kyngly mageste with all maner of Lowenesse and reuerence mekly we recomende vs, Nat oonly as we oughte and shulde, but as we best *can* and may. (LLETT: 74)

(18) for to declaren the entente of my billes for the kynges auantage and for fortherynge of his trewe lieges better than I *can* in this heye Court of rightwisnesse (PET3: 199)

Double modal constructions were recorded only in M3, three cases all in *The Cloud of Unknowing*:

(19) Bot now it is so blendid wiþ þe original synne þat it may not *kon* worche þis werk bot it it be illuminid by grace. (CLOUD: 116)

(20) Do þis werk euermore wiþ-outyn cesyng & wiþ-outyn discrecion, and þou schalt wel *kun* beginne & ceese in alle þin oþer werkes wiþ a grete discrecion. (CLOUD: 81)

(21) And forþi þat þou schalt *kun* betir wite how þei schul be conceyued goostly, þees wordes þat ben spoken bodely. (CLOUD: 114)

This pattern, though no longer observed in standard PDE, was frequent in OE and ME, where syntactic units like SHALL MAY, SHOULD MAY, SHALL WILL, and also – as in (19), (20), and (21) – MAY CAN and SHALL CAN were possible.[3]

4. Time reference

In both subperiods CAN regularly occurs most of all with present time reference (54% of M3 cases vs 50% in E3), followed respectively by timeless and, though to a very limited extent, future time reference; understandably, there are no instances of past time reference in either period.

The slight increase of CAN in E3 timeless contexts (from 37% in M3 to 45% of cases), at the expense of present and future time reference, does not bear any statistical significance, particularly when

3 For discussions and bibliographical references concerning the origin, history, and development of modal combinations, see Butters (1991), Nagle (1993, 1994, 1995, 1997), De la Cruz (1994, 1995), Battistella (1995), Fennell / Butters (1996) and Facchinetti (1997), *inter alia*.

considering the limited number of occurrences recorded in M3 (30). With reference to textual categories, timeless reference is preferred in M3 Sermons and Religious texts, while in E3 it is favoured by Handbooks, Scientific samples, and Philosophical texts. In all such cases, general truths or states of fact are expressed, particularly in collocation with inanimate subjects or abstract entities:

(22) For the Bodies being each of them so very hard, the puls cannot be far communicated, that is, the parts of each *can* yield but very little, and therefore the violence of the concussion will be exerted on that piece of Steel (HOOKE: 13.5, 45)

(23) þe mercy of þis fadur kan we not telle fully, for he ys þe moste worchere þat may ben in þis world; and he *can* not worche but ȝif he medle mercy, for he wrohte by mercy wan he made þis world (WSERM4: I, 236)

Indeed, unsurprisingly, in both subcorpora timeless reference is mostly linked to dynamic possibility values, thus showing that circumstances lead to a specific state, and to the E3 epistemic and dynamic/epistemic contexts, expressing the speaker's degree of commitment to his utterance. In contrast, present time reference is more directly linked to ability values, in collocation with animate, preferably human, subjects and referring to the moment of speaking; consequently, it was traced more frequently in the questioning typical of E3 Trials, where the speaker expresses his (in)ability, as in (24):

(24) I cannot charge my Memory, my Lord, that he did, so as particularly to swear it: But there he came into my Company sometimes at Tixhall; but I *cannot* tell the particular Days. (OATES: IV, 75.C1)

Fiction and Letters from both subperiods, but also E3 Drama, exhibit a more diversified framework, including future time reference as well; this is largely due to the fact that they include direct conversations, reports and narration. These future meanings were frequently recorded in conditional or temporal clauses, as in (26).

(25) I will go up stairs, and see what I *can* do with her (PENNY: 271)

(26) Beth war [...] with lordes how ye pleye. / Syngeth Placebo, and 'I shal, if I *kan*' (CTSUMM: 133.C2)

5. Type of modality

In M3 the original value of 'being intellectually able to', deriving from the OE 'to know, to know how', gradually gave way to meanings more directly related to physical ability. This shift is confirmed by the occurrences recorded in the corpus under scrutiny; indeed, the overwhelming majority of CAN-forms in M3 convey dynamic values expressing physical ability and this type of modality is the prevailing one in the E3 subsection as well, as shown in Table 5.

While the M3 subcorpus exhibits only clear-cut instances of dynamic modality, in E3 we witness a high incidence of 'merger' (Coates 1983), whereby one occurrence can be interpreted according to more than one type of modality. This is the case of dynamic / epistemic possibility, and of dynamic / deontic possibility. Clear-cut epistemic values are also present in E3, though to a very low extent (5%), as opposed to dynamic modality (88%).

Modality	*M3 %*	*E3 %*
dynamic	100	88
dynamic / epistemic	-	7
epistemic	-	5
dynamic / deontic	-	0.5
Total	*100*	*100*

Table 5. Modality types expressed by CAN in M3 and E3.

5.1. Dynamic modality

Within dynamic modality, ability is the most recurrent semantic value in both subperiods. However, as previously anticipated, in E3 CAN widens its semantic scope, thus leading to an increased number of occurrences where two types of modality merge, and producing two equally acceptable interpretations. In contrast, bleached values – where CAN conveys little or no modal meaning – disappear totally, while up to 6 cases were recorded in M3, like the following:

(27) For now se here na felaw / Ne no man þat I *can* knaw. (NHOM: II)

These uses are almost exclusively in collocation with *know* and *wite*, and Visser suggests that they might be the survival of the empty, periphrastic *gan / can*, whose instances with preterite values were previously discussed. Hence, in (27) the paraphrase 'I (do) know' seems more appropriate than 'I can know'.

Let us now view the overall distribution of all the values expressing dynamic modality either fully or partly, in concomitance with epistemic or deontic modality in both subperiods (Tables 6, 7).

	ability		*poss*	*abil/poss*	*bleached*		
	No.	*o/ooo*	*No.*	*No.*	*No.*	*Tot*	*o/ooo*
FICTION	21	*15*		1	1	23	*16*
LETTERS	4	*8*				4	*8*
REL TR	24	*6*	1	2	1	28	*8*
DOCUMENTS	8	*5*			1	9	*6*
SERMONS	6	*4*		2		8	*6*
HOMILIES	1	*1*			1	2	*3*
PHILOSOPHY	2	*2*	1			3	*2*
RULES	1	*2*				1	*2*
TRAVELOGUES					1	1	*2*
HANDBOOKS	1	*1*				1	*1*
HISTORY					1	1	*0,4*
SCIENCE						-	
BIBLE						-	
All texts	68	*4*	2	5	6	81	*5*

Table 6. Distribution of CAN conveying dynamic modality in M3 (ranked in order of total frequency).

Dynamic possibility values are extremely limited in M3 (only 2 examples, 0.1 per 10,000 words) and increase in E3 (82 examples, 5 per 10,000 words). In fact, dynamic ability values cover the majority of cases in both M3 (84% of cases) and E3 (64%); their frequency increases from 4 per 10,000 words to 15, with frequency increasing for all text types except Fiction[4] (which falls from a normalized 15 to 10). In the earlier period this type of meaning for CAN is found most frequently in Fiction (15 per 10,000 words), Letters (8 per 10,000 words) and Religious treatises (6 per 10,000 words). In the later period it is found most frequently in Trial transcripts (36 per 10,000 words), Philosophy (34 per 10,000 words), Drama (28 per 10,000 words) and again Letters (28 per 10,000 words). All these text types share interactional features, which seem to favour the use of CAN, as previously remarked. As shall be illustrated, such interactional features also favour the diversification of the uses of CAN in terms of their pragmatic implications. Let us now consider in detail each of the different values conveyed by CAN.

	dynamic					*mixed*			
	ability		*possibility*		*illoc. ov.*	*dy/ep*	*dy/de*		
	No.	*o/ooo*	*No.*	*o/ooo*	*No.*	*No.*	*No.*	*Tot*	*o/ooo*
PHILOSOPHY	30	*34*	7	*8*		27		64	*73*
TRIALS	50	*36*	3	*2*	2	1	1	57	*41*
LETTERS	53	*28*	16	*8*	1	2	1	73	*38*
SERMONS	20	*16*	16	*13*		12		48	*38*
DRAMA	35	*28*	6	*5*	6			47	*37*
EDUC TR	16	*14*	7	*5*	1			24	*21*
HANDBOOKS	13	*11*	5	*4*	1	3		22	*19*
FICTION	12	*10*	5	*4*	1			18	*15*
DIARIES	5	*5*	8	*7*				13	*12*
BIOGRAPHIES	6	*5*	2	*2*				8	*7*
SCIENCE	5	*4*	2	*2*		1		8	*7*
TRAVELOGUES	4	*4*	2	*2*		1		7	*7*
LAW	3	*2*						3	*2*
HISTORY	1	*1*	1	*1*				2	*2*
All texts	253	*15*	80	*5*	12	47	2	394	*23*

Table 7. Distribution of CAN conveying dynamic modality and mixed values in E3 (in order of total frequency; 'illoc. ov.' = 'illocutionary overtones').

4 Law texts are not covered in M3, hence no comparison can be made between the two subperiods.

5.1.1. Ability

Ability values can be illustrated in the following examples:

(28) þe sutilte of Poulis wordis may make me and foolis schame, whenne we *konnen* not vndurstonde sutilte of his schorte wordis. (WESERM1: I, 479)

(29) and I *can* tell you that Pigeons will fly forty miles for a breakfast, but Sir, I am sure the Otter devours much Fish (WALTON: 211)

Paraphrases of (28) and (29) might be 'we are unable to understand' and 'I am able to tell you'. Similar instances account for 68 of the 81 occurrences recorded in M3 and for 263 of the total 415 in E3. Not all instances, however, are clear-cut, as shown in the following discussion.

5.1.1.1. Illocutionary overtones of ability values

In E3 dynamic ability CAN gains additional pragmatic meaning from its use, so as to exhibit considerable overtonal variety. This is the case of the following illocutionary acts:

1) *Request*

(30) FOIG. Come, my dear Joy, I vill secure your Body and your Shoul too; I vill make you a good Catholick, and give you an Absolution.
GIB. Absolution! *can* you procure me a Pardon, Doctor?
FOIG. No, Joy.
GIB. Then you and your Absolution may go to the Devil.
(FARQUHAR: 62)

In this context, the speaker performs a request by ostensibly 'asking' about the addressee's ability to do something. This request is a way to avoid the imperative and consequently combines with an interrogative form; there is also one case in a declarative sentence with positive polarity:

(31) LORD FOP. Why, Faith, Madam – I can't tell. A Man must have very little to do there, that can give an Account of the Sermon.
BER. You *can* give us an Account of the Ladies, at least. (VANBR: I, 38)

These indirect requests have become quite frequent in PDE and are explained as a typical aspect of English culture-specific background (Wierzbicka 1991: 44). Searle (1975: 74-75) explains this linguistic feature as follows: "Firstly X does not presume to know Y's abilities, as he would if he issued an imperative sentence; and, secondly, the form gives – or at least appears to give Y the option of refusing, since a yes-no question allows no as a possible answer. Hence, compliance can be made to appear a free act rather than obeying a command".

2) *Proposal / offer*

In a total of 3 cases, with 1st person singular subjects, the person proposes to act in a certain way:

(32) Y. FASH. Why then my dear little Bedfellow, if you'll call her hither, we'll try to perswade her presently.
MISS. O Lord, I *can* tell you a way how to perswade her to any thing.
(VANBR: I, 62)

3) *Promise*

There is only one occurrence expressing promise in the corpus:

(33) [do you think you can prevail with him?] NURSE. Prevail with him – or he shall never prevail with me, I *can* tell him that. (VANBR: I, 64)

4) *Reprimand*

This use suggests some form of irritation and dissatisfaction and is recorded in two occurrences:

(34) MRS. SULL. How *can* you, after what is past, have the Confidence to ask me?
ARCH. And if you go to that, how can you after what is past, have the Confidence to deny me? – Was not this Blood shed in your Defence, and my Life expos'd for your Protection. (FARQUHAR: 65)

5) *Refusal*

There is one occurrence with this meaning:

(35) [A] Man was cheapning her Fish, says she to him, as you intend to Have some of my Fish in your Belly, so I would fain have some of your Flesh in my Belly; no says he, I *can't* spare my Flesh to such an ugly Puss as you
(PENNY: 160)

5.1.2. Ability / possibility

In 5 instances from M3 and in 19 from E3, it is hard to tease out whether the possibility/impossibility of the action should be ascribed to the subject or to an external circumstance; hence in such occurrences, dynamic ability merges with dynamic possibility values, as in the following:

(36) þe mercy of þis fadur *kan* we not telle fully, for he ys þe moste worchere þat may ben in þis world; and he *can* not worche but ȝif he medle mercy, for he wrohte by mercy wan he made þis world. (WSERM4: I, 236)

(37) But thou mayst say, what greater Confusion can there be, that both prosperous and adverse things should by times happen to good Men, and that evil Men can enjoy what their Hearts *can* desire, and yet be afflicted too with things which they hate? (BOETHPR: 195)

In (36) *kan* is easily paraphrased by 'we are (not) able to', while *can* expresses the lack of capability on the part of the subject of the verb phrases (God), but it can also be viewed as dynamic possibility, conveying the lack of possibility due to an external circumstance, which prevents the carrying out of the action. However, as it is hard to consider God 'unable to do something', it seems more feasible to consider that the very nature of God prevents him from working without mercy (it is not possible for him to...). Similarly, in (37), both paraphrases of 'what is possible for their hearts to desire' and 'what their hearts are able to desire' would seem acceptable.

5.1.3. Dynamic possibility

Only 2 cases in M3 and a total of 82 in E3 have been found to express dynamic possibility values, as in the following:

(38) þere one haþ smylyng semelaunt / And behetyþ þe to holde cunnaunt, / kepe þe þan fro losengrye, / For feyre spekyng man *kan* weyl lye. (HS: 121)

(39) the gloves of an Otter are the best fortification for your hands that *can* be thought on against wet weather. (WALTON: 210)

All these occurrences can be paraphrased by 'it is not possible for X to', thus implying that external circumstances, rather than the subject's power or disposition, allow for the occurrence of a situation, a state of fact, or an action.

On the basis of the evidence drawn from the Helsinki Corpus, Rissanen remarks that, in the early 16th century, CAN "is favoured, in particular, in texts close to spoken language, such as Diaries, private correspondence, Trials and, to some extent, Sermons. It gains ground, at the expense of MAY in the sixteenth and seventeenth centuries." (Rissanen 1999: 239). This speech-related feature of a few E3 text types has been seen to correlate with use of CAN in the present study as well; indeed, in the E3 data, dynamic possibility CAN is particularly concentrated in Sermons, where the preacher frequently presents situations in life as uncontroversial, unalterable states of fact, which no man, despite his will, can change, due to his lack of choice, rather than lack of ability, as in (40):

(40) a Controversie concerning an infallible Judge *can* never be ended. (TILLOTS II: ii 446)

Letters, mostly private ones, also exhibit a comparable high frequency of possibility values (8 per 10,000 words), together with Diaries (freq. 7); moreover, this type of modality gains ground in Philosophical samples (freq. 8) – which have been seen to be purely dialogic – and in Educational treatises (freq. 6). In contrast, E3 Trials do not show the high concentration of possibility values Rissanen had recorded for ME, since they exhibit a frequency of merely 2 per 10,000 words; indeed, in these contexts CAN is frequently found in collocation with the private verbs *remember, recollect* and *tell*, which refer to the subject's ability rather than to external circumstances.

5.1.3.1. Illocutionary overtones of possibility values: suggestion

The following examples have been qualified as dynamic possibility with an overtone of suggestion: the first (41) has been interpreted as 'it is not possible for a carp-angler to be too early or too late when he wants to fish carps'; that is, 'the circumstances do not allow him to do so (otherwise he will not catch any carp)'. However, in both cases the speaker also seems to express his suggestions.

(41) let me tell you, that in hot weather [...] you *cannot* be too early or too late at it. (WALTON: 297)

(42) obstinancy being an open defiance you *cannot* overlooke, and since the occasions of punishment, espetially beating, are as much to be avoided as may be, I would not have it often brought to this point. (LOCKE: 57)

5.2. Epistemic modality

The epistemic occurrences recorded in E3 are always either in interrogative or in negative contexts, as in (43) and (44):[5]

(43) Sure this Addition of Quality, must have so improv'd this Coxcomb, he *can't* but be very good Company for a quarter of an Hour. (VANBR: I, 35)

(44) Let me ask thee, *can* that, dost thou think, which needeth nothing want Power? (BOETHPR: 124)

Indeed, out of the total 21 epistemic tokens, 8 are in the interrogative form, while 13 are negative. They are particularly frequent in Sermons and Philosophical texts, both involving some kind of interpersonal interaction, and both aimed at expressing one's opinion on a specific topic of discussion. In contrast, in the less interactional Legal texts, Handbooks, Scientific texts and Educational treatises no occurrence of epistemic modality was recorded.

5.3. Dynamic / Epistemic possibility

A good number of occurrences cannot be classified easily as purely dynamic possibility, since they also seem to express a subjective view of the speaker with reference to the truth of the proposition expressed:

---

5 The acceptability of epistemic CAN is a matter of great debate still nowadays, and not all scholars acknowledge the epistemic uses of CAN particularly in interrogative contexts. Palmer, for example, posits that the modal is used for epistemic modality "only when negated" (Palmer 2001: 77). Papafragou (2000: 92, 106-107) rejects any epistemic value of CAN. In contrast, Coates (1995: 63) admits its existence in affirmative contexts as well, particularly in American English, and to a lesser extent in British English.

(45) Ph. Thinkest thou that any thing on this side Heaven can confer that Good of which thou speakest.
Bo. I think not indeed; and thou hast already shewed me, that nothing *can* be desired beyond such a State of Perfection. (BOETHPR: 128)

These cases were recorded only in Philosophical texts (23 per 10,000 words), in Sermons (2 per 10,000 words) and in Letters (1 per 10,000 words), for a total of 28 instances, and largely contribute to increasing the overall frequency of dynamic possibility values.

5.4. Dynamic / Deontic possibility

Deontic values for CAN are generally said not to occur until the 19th century. Indeed, in a research based on Shakespeare's works, Kakietek (1972) recorded no occurrence of deontic modality. Similarly, Ehrman remarks that "the greatest difference beween PDE and EModE CAN is the total absence of 'permissive' CAN from the earlier material. (Ehrman 1966: 80). Traugott confirms this view and charts the use of CAN to express permission as a substitute for MAY from the 19th century onwards (Traugott 1972: 170-172, 198); similarly, Kytö (1991: 121) points out that in a study carried out on a section of the Helsinki Corpus "since no clear instances of COULD could be found, MAY NOT seems to be the form used for negated permission". Finally, Rissanen (1999: 237) remarks that in the period 1476-1776 "MAY is the sole auxiliary in contexts related to permission (in negative contexts prohibition); the use of CAN in expressions of the type *You can go now* is a nineteenth century development" (Rissanen 1999: 237). Nevertheless, in E3 two tokens have been noticed that appear to be close to deontic values:

(46) If ye Liberty of twenty ships should be granted wch is insinuated as ships of small Burden, they would easily be furnish^{t} wth ships of Greater Burden from ye New England men, & others who have found ye encouragem^{t} from ye farm^{rs} of Ireland to ye ruin of ye fair Trader here. Nor *can* it be duly kept to a Limited number of Ships considering ye convenience & number of their Ports, but it would in time amount to a gen^{ll} Liberty. (COMMISS: I, 56)

This occurrence can be considered an order emanating not from the speakers, but rather from a rule, although there is an implication that the speakers agree with such order. However, there is no clear boundary between deontic regulation and circumstantial possibility, as is clear in (47), in which a paraphrase might easily be both 'it is possible for you to' and 'you are allowed to':

(47) Dost thou take the God of Heaven not to be a God of Truth, and that he is not a Witness of all thou say'st? Dost thou think because thou prevaricatest with the Court here, thou *can'st* do so with God above, who knows thy Thoughts, and it is infinite Mercy, that for those Falshoods of thine, he does not immediately strike thee into Hell? (LISLE: IV, 114 .C2)

6. Concluding remarks

All the occurrences of dynamic modality expressing illocutionary overtones in E3 have been recorded in interactional contexts, as shown in Table 7. Indeed, the majority of these occurrences have been found in Drama (6 cases) and Trials (2 cases).

The grammaticalization process of CAN is still incomplete in M3, as shown by its 32 occurrences as a lexical verb, totalling 27% of all the tokens recorded in the corpus; however, the modal appears to have reached an advanced stage of grammaticalization in E3, where only modal meanings have been recorded.

The M3 instability of CAN is mirrored in its semantic values as well; indeed, in M3 it has not totally abandoned its original OE sense 'to know' or 'to know how to', but at the same time it intrudes more and more into the dynamic field which had been typical of OE *magan*, to denote the general sense of possibility. These dynamic values get consolidated in E3 and the modal takes on a wider range of semantic and pragmatic meanings, now closer to those of PDE.

III. Could

COULD is less than half as frequent as CAN in both M3 and E3, with a total of 46 occurrences in M3 and 196 in E3. As in the case of CAN, all E3 instances of COULD have modal values,[1] while 13 (28%) of the M3 tokens are non-modal lexical verbs meaning 'to know, to have discrimination or knowledge' – cf. (1) and (2). This leaves a frequency for modal COULD of 2 per 10,000 words, against 11 in E3.

(1) Of remedies of love she knew per chaunce, / For she *koude* of that art the olde daunce (CTPROL: 31.C1)

(2) for these greete doctouris weren noon English men, neither thei weren conuersaunt among English men, neithir in caas thei *kouden* the langage of English (WYCPROL: I, 59)

In (1) both *knew* and *koude* are employed as synonyms, with the value 'to have knowledge'; however, while *knew* expresses mere intellectual knowledge, COULD also partly implies ability; in (2), for example, "these greete doctouris" 'did not know English', which can also mean 'they could not understand or speak English'. Hence, even in these instances of COULD + object, the preterite form of CAN seems to be shifting steadily towards its PDE semantic values.

Though the limited number of COULD-forms renders difficult any generalization of results, these non-modal uses seem to prevail in verse rather than in prose (10 instances were recorded in verse and only 3 in prose):

Prose	RELT	*The Cloud of Unknowing*	1 (*couþe*)
	RELT	Purvey, *The Prologue to the Bible*	1 (*kouden*)
	HIST	Trevisa, *Polychronicon*	1 (*couþe*)
Verse	FICT	Gower, *Confessio Amantis*	2 (*couthe*)

1 However, instances of COULD as a lexical verb have been traced up to the 19th century, as testified to by the OED: a1875, Kingsley Poems, Little Baltung 82 That cunning Kaiser was a scholar wise, And could of gramarye.

FICT	Chaucer, *Prologue to the C.T.*[2]	4 (*koude*)
HIST	*Cursor Mundi*	4 (*cuth*)

1. Spelling variants

The spelling variants in M3 belong to two groups: (i) *koude* (61% of cases) and *coude* (21%) (together with *cowde* and *coudest*) and (ii) a total of 6 tokens (18%) ending *-th(e)* or *-þe*. None of these are found in E3, where only *could(e)* is recorded – <l> is present in 85% of cases, while it is implied by an apostrophe (*cou'd*) in 15% of cases.

The apparent rarity of ME forms with *-en* ending (Burrow / Turville-Petre 1992: 32) cannot be proved one way or another as our corpus contains no cases of COULD with a plural subject. Similarly, no third person singular in *-es*, which is typical of Northern dialects, has been recorded, while the forms found for 3rd person singular are *coude, couþ, couthe, cowde, koude* and *kouth.* These, though apparently more typical of Southern or South Midland dialects, are found in the M3 corpus in Northern and East Midland texts as well.

As for the 2nd person singular form ending in *-est*, this was already rare in M3 (only 1 token present) and disappears completely in E3. Finally, while a few negative contracted forms have been recorded for CAN, none have been recorded for COULD: all the negative forms with *not* are written as two separate words.

2. Distribution according to text type

Little can be said of COULD with reference to text type distribution in M3, due to the scanty data available, as shown in Table 1.

2 As pointed out with reference to CAN (cf. Chapter 2), Chaucer often employs COULD both with a modal and a non-modal meaning.

Text Type	*No.*	*o/ooo*
FICTION	17	12
HOMILIES	2	3
RELIGIOUS TREATISES	7	2
DOCUMENTS	3	2
LETTERS	1	2
PHILOSOPHY	1	1
HANDBOOKS	1	1
HISTORY	1	0.4
All texts	33	2

Table 1. Distribution of COULD-forms in M3.

The distribution of COULD is very similar to that recorded for CAN, where Scientific texts and the Bible exhibit no occurrence at all, and Fictional texts have the highest concentration of this modal (51.5% of the total), all represented by the variant *koude*. A closer look at these Fictional occurrences reveals that, as with CAN, they are found exclusively in Chaucer's *Canterbury Tales*. Concerning the second most frequent M3 form, *coude*, 3 of the 5 tokens are from Robert Mannyng's *Robert of Brunne's Handlyng Synne*, suggesting once more that the author's idiosyncratic usage largely accounts for the relationship between variant forms and text type distribution in M3.

Let us now consider E3 data. As shown in Table 2, Law is the only text type where COULD does not occur. As a matter of fact, Legal texts are typically direct and uncompromising and generally avoid tentative expressions associated with hypothetical COULD; in addition, they refer to future actions rather than to past events, so have no need of narrative COULD. The same considerations account for the very reduced number of COULD forms in Handbooks as well, where the writer invites the reader to act according to his indications and employs COULD almost exclusively with hypothetical value, when remarking on a situation different from what he envisages:

(3) That which is every bodies business, is no bodies business. If it were otherwise, there *could* not be so many Nets and Fish that are under the Statute size, sold daily amongst us (WALTON: 213)

(4) yet by this means you will make advantage of such portions of your Wall, as otherwise you *could* have had little benefit from. (LANGF: 128)

Text Type	*No.*	*o/ooo*
BIOGRAPHIES	37	32
FICTION	34	28
SCIENCE	25	22
LETTERS	25	13
HISTORY	15	13
TRIALS	15	11
EDUCATIONAL TREATISES	9	8
DRAMA	9	7
TRAVELOGUES	7	7
PHILOSOPHY	5	6
DIARIES	7	6
SERMONS	5	4
HANDBOOKS	3	3
LAW	0	0
All texts	196	11

Table 2. Distribution of COULD in E3.

In contrast, Fiction still has a very high incidence of COULD (28 per 10,000 words), as do Science (22) and Biographies (32). This is largely due to the fact that all of them contain many narrative sequences, as in Scientific writings, where the author often reports on his experiments:

(5) and each look'd almost like a prety bright Iron-Ball, whose Surface was prety regular, such as is represented by the Figure A. In this I *could* perceive the Image of the Window prety well, or of a Stick (HOOKE: 13.5, 44)

3. Verb phrase structure

In M3 COULD is used in 26 verb-phrases featuring positive polarity (78%) and in 7 (22%) negative verbal groups; in contrast, in E3 a total of 88 tokens of COULD are negative, representing 44% of all the occurrences (cf. Figure 1). No instance of COULD has been recorded in interrogative contexts in either M3 or E3.

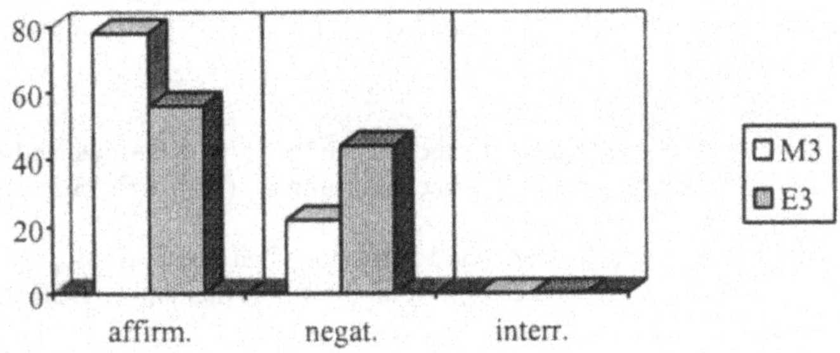

Figure 1. Percentage distribution of COULD in M3 and E3 by sentence type (affirmative, negative, interrogative).

In M3 COULD negation is realized by *non ne*, *not*, *ne ... nat*, *no*, *ne ... no*, or by *noght*, as exemplified in (6) and (7), while in E3 *not* is the only adverb employed, as in (8):

(6) Thomas, contynuyng his falsnesse and disceit aboueseyd, wityng wel þat he might ne *cowde* nat perfourme þat he hadde benight, delaied her forth fro day to day (JUDG: 95)

(7) Bot his sekenes he *kouth* noght se. (NHOM: III, 128)

(8) And I said att once hearinge over a paper att a great distans from mee: I *coulde* not aunswer. (FOX: 83)

Within the verbal group, the lexical verb which collocates with the modal is almost always expressed, except for 4 elliptical cases in M3 and 8 in E3:

(9) But for to teche ȝow how ȝe schul kepe an hors þat he ne take no suche manere harme. y wold if y *cowþe* (HORSES: 117)

(10) This made me afeared, so I got home as fast as I *could* – and hearing of no present hurt, did go to Sir Robt. (PEPYS: VII, 415)

The missing lexical verb is implied in the context, within a subordinate clause which is mostly either of the comparative or of the temporal kind. When expressed, the verb in M3 is always a bare active infinitive, and no instance of perfective or progressive aspect has been recorded. In contrast, in E3, though bare active infinitives are still the large majority of cases (77%), passive and perfect infinitives are also present:

(11) and indeed this contrivance of the feet is very curious, and *could* not be made more commodiously and compendiously (HOOKE: 13.5, 212)

(12) if the king himself (God bless him) had come ashore, there *cou'd* not have been greater expectation by all the whole plantation (BEHN: 186)

Let us now view in detail the distribution of COULD with reference to verbal complementation, as expressed in Table 3.

	M3		*E3*	
	No.	*o/ooo*	*No.*	*o/ooo*
bare infinitive	29	2	150	9
Passive infinitive			24	1
perfect infinitive			11	1
perfect passive infinitive			3	0.2
Ø	4	0.2	8	0.5
Total	33	2	196	12

Table 3. M3 and E3 – Verbal complementation after COULD.

The data show an increased frequency of COULD followed by bare infinitive and the emergence of COULD with passive infinitive (12% of tokens in E3, not found in M3). Such passive contexts do not appear to favour any specific text type, but typically co-occur mostly with inanimate subjects (71% of all passive occurrences):

(13) for she express'd her sense of the present the prince had sent her, in terms so sweet, so soft and pretty, with an air of love and joy that *cou'd* not be dissembled (BEHN: 158)

Interestingly, in one case COULD is followed by active infinitive + gerund, with the gerund taking on an adjectival function:

(14) and yet yo^{u} will horkkin to thim that doe wish nether yo^{u} nor yor any good but thim silfes, in henderinge yo^{u} to com, why cannot yo^{u} com as will as mr dadge hee *could* bewanttinge to mounthes (JPINNEY: 39)

Within the verb phrase, COULD mostly collocates with *be* (28 tokens); private verbs indicating knowledge do not seem to be very frequent, with *perceive*, *see*, *know*, *wish*, and *imagine* being exploited to a very limited extent.

Unlike CAN, M3 COULD frequently occurs in verb-phrases featuring inversion; yet this is largely due to the idiosyncrasy of the writer, specifically Chaucer, since 11 out of the 12 recorded in the corpus are from the *Canterbury Tales*, the most frequent pattern, with 9 tokens, being the WELL + COULD + SUBJECT, as in:

(15) Wel *koude* she carie a morsel and wel kepe / That no drope ne fille upon hire brest. (CTPROL: 25.C2)

In contrast, in E3 there is only 1 instance of inversion, featured in the protasis of a conditional sentence:

(16) Now *cou'd* we find him out, the Money were ours. (FARQUHAR: 8)

4. Time reference

The large majority of COULD forms both in M3 and in E3 have past time reference, referring to events which took place before the moment of speaking, as in (13) above. This concerns almost all text types, particularly Scientific, Historical and Fictional texts, but also Biographies and Letters, all of which make large use of narration or description of past events.[3] No deontic or epistemic value has been recorded with these occurrences,[4] which, in contrast, exclusively exhibit dynamic ability or possibility values. Tokens of use with non-narrative, hypothetical value are scanty and occur mostly in Drama and Trials:

(17) MISS. Shall I? (Aside.) O Lord, I *cou'd* leap over the Moon.
FASH. Dear Nurse, this goodness of yours shan't go unrewarded.
(VANBR: I, 64)

(18) I cannot say positively that, Mr. Attorney; [...] Nor *could* I testify this so positively, I say, but by Notes that I have (OATES: IV, 75.C1)

Reference to future time has been recorded to a very limited extent in both subperiods, and again is mostly featured in narrative contexts by instances of 'future in the past':

(19) He disguised himself, so that his nearest Friends *could* not have known him, and set up in Tower-street for an Italian Mountebank (BURNETROC: 27)

As for instances expressing timelessness, Philosophical samples account for 4 of them, while in the other categories it is either totally absent or ranging from 1 to 2 occurrences:

(20) Reason then doth so clearly demonstrate that God is good; that at the same time it evinceth the sovereign Good to be in him. For if it were not so, he *could* not be the Ruler of all things (BOETHPR: 134)

5. Type of modality

In M3 COULD has been found to express only dynamic modality, while epistemic and deontic values start to emerge in E3 (cf. Table 4).

3 Such past uses of COULD are now much less exploited, since they have been overwhelmed by hypothetical conditional senses (Bybee 1995: 504)

4 Indeed, I did not record any occurrence of 'obligation' in the past or of epistemic meanings framed in a context of reported speech.

Modality	*No.*	*o/ooo*	*M3 %*	*No.*	*o/ooo*	*E3 %*
dynamic	33	2	100	180	11	92
dynamic / epistemic			-	3	0.2	4
epistemic			-	7	0.4	2
deontic			-	6	0.4	3
Total	33	2	100	196	11	100

Table 4. Modality types for COULD in M3 and E3.

	dynamic									
	ability		*possibility*		*ab/poss*	*dy/ep*	*de*	*ep*		
	No.	*o/ooo*	*No.*	*o/ooo*	*No.*	*No.*	*No.*	*No.*	*Tot*	*o/ooo*
BIOGR.	27	*23*	8	*7*	1		1		37	*32*
FICTION	24	*20*	5	*4*		3	2		34	*28*
SCIENCE	18	*16*	5	*4*		2			25	*22*
LETTERS	8	*2*	14	*7*	1		1	1	25	*13*
HISTORY	10	*9*	5	*4*					15	*13*
TRIALS	10	*7*	2	*1*	1	1	1		15	*11*
EDUC	9	*8*							9	*8*
DRAMA	5	*3*	2	*2*				2	9	*7*
TRAV.	3	*3*	4	*4*					7	*7*
DIA.	2	*2*	5	*4*					7	*6*
PHIL.	3	*3*	2	*2*					5	*6*
SERM.	2	*2*	2	*2*			1		5	*4*
HAND.	1	*1*	1	*1*		1			3	*3*
LAW									-	-
All texts	122	*7*	55	*3*	3	7	6	3	196	*11*

Table 5. Types of modality expressed by COULD in E3.

The dynamic occurrences in M3 convey almost exclusively ability values (29 tokens), with only 4 of them expressing possibility. In E3, ability is still the most widespread type of modality (122 tokens), but dynamic possibility is now more common (55 tokens). The analysis has shown the presence of deontic and epistemic values as well, some of which merge with dynamic modality, so that two readings are available and perfectly acceptable for a given utterance. Unlike PDE, where merger occurs quite frequently in formal texts and particularly in academic writing (Coates 1995: 61), neither CAN nor COULD seems to favour merger in formal text types, although Science texts have a few rare instances already, as shown in Table 5.

Though infrequent, these instances of merger are a hint of the widened semantic scope of COULD in E3; in some cases, as for wish and prohibition, they even embody pragmatic values which are totally absent in the M3 subcorpus.

Table 5 also shows that COULD is used with above-average frequency in Biographies, Fiction, Science, Letters and History. The dominant dynamic value is ability with the interesting exception of Letters (mostly private), where dynamic possibility is more important.

5.1. Dynamic modality

5.1.1. Ability

As previously anticipated, in M3 the large majority of the occurrences (88%) express ability values, referring either to a general ability in the past or to a particular action, as in (21). Dynamic ability in E3 is found in more tokens and with greater frequency, though the category accounts for only 62% of cases, due to the emergence of ther semantic values. In Educational treatises this is the only use of COULD, as in (22):

(21) Wel *koude* he dresse his takel yemanly (CTPROL: 25.C1)

(22) He had the will of his maid before he *could* speake or goe (LOCKE: 51)

This exclusive presence of ability COULD in Educational treatises is largely due to the samples from Locke's *Directions Concerning Education*, where the author enriches his teachings with anecdotes of past events on the one hand, and proposes his educational theory on the other; this accounts for the presence of both past time values and of hypotheticality in these occurrences.

5.1.2. Ability / Possibility

Overall, ability and possibility meanings are clearly distinguished in the corpus, except for the following 3 E3 instances, where the writer seems to be remarking either on the (lack of) objective possibility – due to external circumstances – to carry out the action, or on the (lack of) ability of the subject:

(23) had hee let mee pleade to my Indictment I *coulde* have proved ye Courte forsworne men againe: by there Almanackes & ye Indictment. (FOX: 85)

(24) He said he *could* not stay, because he was to go into the Country upon Saturday. (OATES: IV, 73.C1)

(25) I sent a letter by the Tuesday and Fryday post whereby you may perceive that I *could* not come home without leaving my busines undon (HOXINDEN: 279)

5.1.3. Possibility

The 4 occurrences recorded in M3 which do not exhibit ability values are clearly of the possibility kind, and occur in Letters, Religious texts, and Fiction:

(26) Certein trewe liege man is þer non, ne feithful subgit *coude* þer non ne durste tarie or be lachesse in any wyse to the effectuell praier or comaundement of so soueraign (LLETT: 75)

(27) þey toke neuer gode at Pers hand; / Ne noun pore man neuer shal haue, / *Coude* he neuer so weyl craue (HS: 182)

(28) Therto he koude endite and make a thyng, / Ther *koude* no wight pynche at his writyng (CTPROL: 28.C2)

The fact that possibility is anchored to circumstantial situations allows COULD to be particularly frequent not only in Biographies and Letters, but also in Scientific extracts, whose overall discourse function is to qualify situations or states of fact which are objectively recognisable and do not depend on ability, power or disposition of the subject; this is the case of (29), where Hooke claims that it was not possible for a guinea-pig frog to take in any more food:

(29) and the Creature was so greedy, that though it *could* not contain more, yet it continued sucking as fast as ever (HOOKE: 13.5, 213)

The same goes for non-technical text types, like the following Historical sample:

(30) leaving part of his Army for the defence of his Ships, with the rest sped him to the West-Saxons, ere Edmund *could* have time to assemble all his powers (MILTON: X, 271)

Above-average frequencies are also found in other narrative text types: Fiction, Travelogues and Diaries.

5.1.4. Dynamic / Epistemic possibility

Finally, 7 instances of dynamic possibility also exhibit epistemic overtones:

(31) and the sweetness of her words and behaviour while he stay'd, gain'd a perfect conquest over his fierce heart, and made him feel, the victor *cou'd* be subdu'd. (BEHN: 155)

This could be paraphrased as 'it was possible for the victor to be subdued', suggesting a dynamic interpretation; on the other hand, it could also be paraphrased as 'it was possible to subdue the victor'; this would place the instance in a superordinate epistemic frame, strengthened by the presence of the harmonic verb *feel*, showing the point of view of the writer.

5.2. Epistemic modality

Epistemic modality was recorded in 3 instances like the following:

(32) Now all things being Sign'd, and Seal'd, and Agreed, I fancy there *cou'd* be no great harm in practising a Scene or two of Matrimony in private (VANBR: I, 64)

The writer posits his point of view with reference to the truth of the proposition expressed, rather than merely remarking on a state of fact.

The harmonic lexical verb *fancy* in the superordinate clause further contributes to qualifying the epistemic environment.

5.3. Deontic modality

5.3.1. Prohibition

In a few E3 instances in negative polarity contexts, COULD expresses deontic prohibition, the source of the authority in each case not being a single subject, but official authority or regulation. The following quotations thus include reported illocutionary acts of prohibition:

(33) and therefore the Romans forbad any Donations to be made between Man and Wife, because neither of them *could* transfer a new Right of those things, which already they had in common (JETAYLOR: 17)

(34) Though when he told me this, he *could* not but acknowledge, it was as unreasonable thing for him, to think, that Beings in another State were not under such Laws and Limits, that they *could* not command their own motions (BURNETROC: 18)

(35) as by the laws he *could* not [...] take from any man his wedded wife; so she believ'd she shou'd be the occasion of making him commit a great sin, if she did not reveal her state and condition; (BEHN: 159)

5.3.2. Wish

Both (36) and (37) have been categorised as instances of deontic modality, since they express a person's willingness to do something. In both cases, COULD is used in collocation with a 1st person singular subject, with present time reference. In (36), taken from Trial transcripts, the subject expresses the wish to die if what he has just said is not true and in so doing he emphasizes his utterance:

(36) I never knew he was Nelthorp, I *could* die upon it, nor did not know what Name he had, till after he came into my House (LISLE: IV, 122.C1)

The following has also been placed in this category, since the speaker regrets his past behaviour and wishes he had behaved differently:

(37) I *could* hang myself for being such a sot (PENNY: 270)

6. A comparison between CAN and COULD

CAN and COULD exhibit a similar percentage of non-modal values in M3 (27 for CAN and 28 for COULD) and a complete disappearance of such uses in E3. In addition, both modals have a similar sixfold increase in normalized frequency between the two periods: from 4 to 24 per 10,000 words for CAN, from 2 to 11 for COULD. However, E3 COULD has been found in very few cases with hypothetical values; this suggests that, while CAN has reached a fully grammaticalised status by E3, for COULD, with its overwhelming narrative uses, the process is still far from completion.

CAN has also been recorded to a much higher extent than COULD throughout the corpus in both subperiods, as shown in Figures 2 and 3:

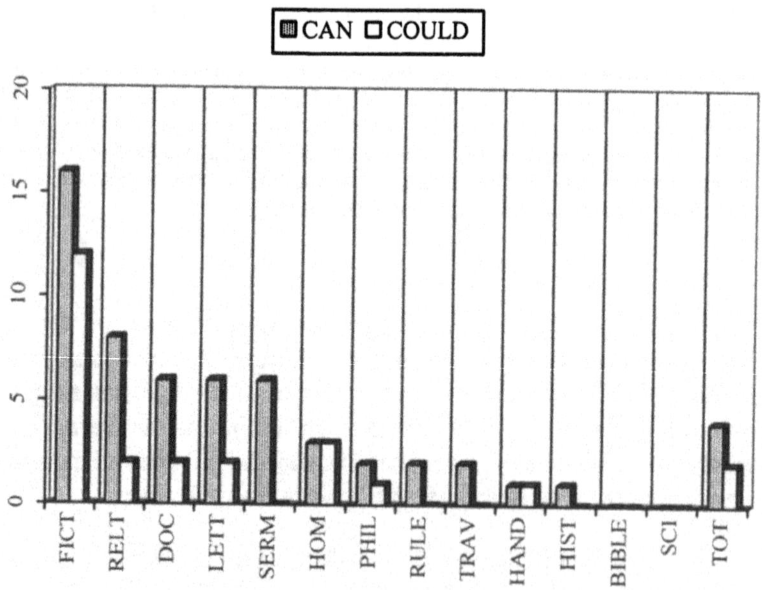

Figure 2. Comparison between CAN and COULD in M3 (normalized figures).

In M3 CAN is used more frequently than COULD, except in Homilies and Handbooks, where it has the same frequency per 10,000 words.

Both modals are absent from Scientific writings and the Bible. Perhaps this is because Science texts are generally formal, while CAN and COULD have been seen to favour informal, speech-related samples. As for the Bible, its archaic language in this period largely favours MAY in dynamic values, which were gradually being taken over by CAN in more progressive texts.

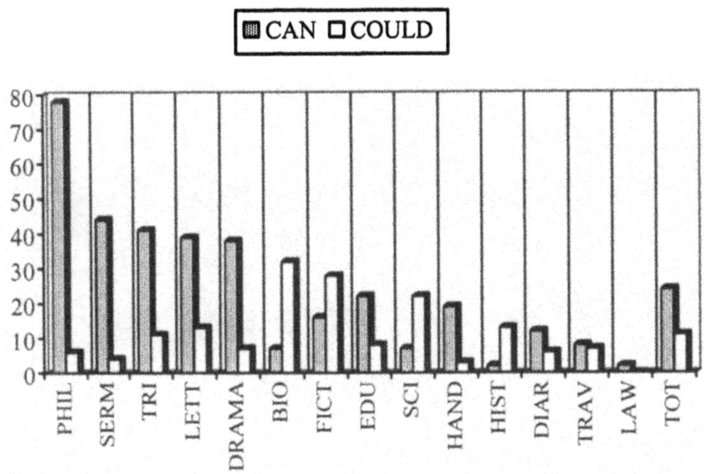

Figure 3. Comparison between CAN and COULD in E3 (normalized figures).

In E3 COULD is more frequent than CAN in Biographies, Scientific writings, History samples, and – to a more limited extent – Fiction, due to the wider use of narrative past time forms in all these samples. In contrast, CAN is more frequent than COULD in all other text types, especially in Philosophy, Sermons, Drama and Trials, where present and future time reference are widely exploited.

Finally, with reference to modality types, while in M3 both modals exhibit only dynamic modality, it is interesting to notice that in E3 they also show a very similar semantic extension to deontic and epistemic uses in a small number of cases.

Additionally, in E3 some instances of CAN and COULD are difficult to categorise according to one single type of modality, since they occur in contexts of merger or embody pragmatic values in a few contexts. This further testifies to the gradual widening semantic area covered by the two modals in E3, which are more and more associated with new meanings and enriched with new illocutionary force.

IV. May

The M3 part of the Helsinki Corpus contains 693 examples of modal MAY, against 477 in the E3 part. Hence, MAY clearly declines in frequency between the two periods: from 38 occurrences per 10,000 words in M3 to 28 in E3. In the M3 translation of Boethius it occurs 78 times, but in the parallel E3 translation only 44 times.

While the E3 corpus contains no non-finite forms or lexical-verb uses, the M3 corpus contains a small number of the former, all with a clear dynamic meaning (cf. Plank 1984: 314): (i) 8 gerunds (*mowynge* 'power' or 'ability' found only in one East Midland text – Chaucer's Boethius translation), and (ii) 8 infinitives (*mow, mowe, mowen*),[1] one of them with a possible lexical-verb meaning (cf. 6.2.1.1).[2] A verbal complement of the gerund is a *to*-infinitive, while infinitive MAY is followed by a bare infinitive:

(1) but I desire gretly that [...] schrewes weren despoyled of *mowynge* to don yvel (BOETHCH: 446.C2)

(I wish that wicked people were deprived of *the power* to do evil)

(2) if ony man may noumbre the dust of erthe, also he schal *mowe* noumbre thi seed (WYCOLD: XIII, 1G) (then he shall *be able* to number your seed)

Examples of adverbial *maybe*, *mayhap* and *may hap* have been excluded from the E3 corpus. Eight examples of *it may be* without further complementation (e.g. *It may be hee was out of purse*) and eight of *as may be* (e.g. *as near as may be to the Church*), which could be regarded as adverbial, have nevertheless been included in the calculations.

---

1 Found only in three East Midlands texts (BOETHCH, CLOUD, WYCOLD); apart from one example of *to mowe* (BOETHCH: 446.C2), other examples are all verbal complements (without *to*) after other modals: 3 times after SHALL, 3 times after SHOULD, once after CAN.

2 These non-finite tokens have been excluded from the total number for calculations where their inclusion would be inappropriate.

1. Spelling variants

76% of all M3 forms are plain uninflected *may* (64%) and *mai* (12%) – found for all persons – and a further 8% are 2nd person singular forms derived from these (*mayst*, *maist*). The *mow(e)n)* or *moun* forms[3] are found with plural subjects, in particular the 3rd person plural (48% of examples with 3rd person plural subjects). Three examples of *þu mi /t* or *my /t* seem to be present-tense forms (<OE 2nd person singular present *miht, meaht*). The 15 *mow(e)* forms after singular subjects have been taken as subjunctive morphology.[4] There is a clear text type preference for *mou*-forms in M3 Documents (the only text type with more *mou*- than *may*-forms: 24 to 21).

As might be expected, dialect correlates closely with the spelling forms: Northern dialect texts have only the uninflected forms *may* and *mai*, while the other dialect texts, in particular the Southern, also have plural forms like *mowen* as well as *mayst* forms for the 2nd person singular.

In the E3 corpus *may* and derived forms represent 100% of all cases. In this later period, *thou* and *-st* morphology are more clearly associated: 15% of 2nd person singular subjects are without *-st* morphology in M3, half of them of the levelled type *thou may*; there are no such examples in E3.

2. Distribution according to text type

Table 1 shows the distribution of the various forms in the different text types included in the M3 section. Religious treatises and Philosophy show the most frequent use of MAY; in contrast, the one Science text (PHLEBOTOMY) contains no examples at all.

---

3 *Mowe* is found in numerous cases, though not listed by the OED (A. 2c.χ) as a variant spelling before the 16th century.

4 OED MAY 2.c.g (indic. pl forms) and 3.b (subj. sing. forms), 2.a and b (indic. sing. forms).

	M3	*E3*
PHILOSOPHY	71	50
LETTERS NON-PRIVATE	46	39
FICTION	40	17
TRAVELOGUES	33	5
SERMONS	28	29
HANDBOOKS	19	79
HISTORY	14	3
SCIENCE	0	43
RELIGIOUS TREATISES	70	-
RULES	58	-
HOMILIES	41	-
DOCUMENTS	29	-
BIBLE	16	-
EDUCATIONAL TREATISES	-	64
LAW	-	31
LETTERS PRIVATE	-	29
DRAMA	-	27
BIOGRAPHIES	-	10
TRIALS	-	6
DIARIES	-	3
All texts	38	28

Table 1. Normalized frequencies of MAY by text type.

In the E3 period it is Handbooks and Educational treatises, followed by Philosophy, that have the highest frequency of MAY. An interesting development is the way MAY-use in E3 is spread less evenly over text types than in the earlier period. Text types using the modal most frequently in M3 still have less than double the average frequency and only one has below 10 tokens per 10,000 words. In contrast, the top E3 categories have more than double the overall average and four text types slip below 10 tokens per 10,000 words.

In both periods, the formal texts of Philosophy and non-private Letters have higher than average frequencies of MAY, while History texts use the modal little. Science texts go from no occurrences at all in M3 to a clearly above-average 43 occurrences per 10,000 words; and Handbooks go from below-average 19 tokens per 10,000 words, to a top-of-the-list 79 in E3 (in the case of Science – cf. Table 6 below – the overall increase involves a frequent use of epistemic MAY). It is clear that the text types united in these categories were rather different in the two periods.

3. Sentence Structure

More tokens of MAY are found in subordinate than in main clauses in both periods (55% and 62% of tokens), with more frequent E3 use in noun clauses (from 13% to 26% of sub-clauses with MAY) and final clauses (from 18% to 28%),[5] and in the main clause of conditional sentences (from 7% to 13% of main clauses); and a decline in its use in conditional and causal clauses (from 8% to 3%, and from 8% to 2% of sub-clauses).

Word order in M3 is generally SVO, though there is commonly VS inversion after an initial adverbial, and occasionally the verbal complement is clause final:

(3) And thus Skarsnesse in every place / Be reson *mai* no thonk porchace (GOWER: II, 74)

After an indefinite pronoun *who* or *that* meaning 'whoever' or 'whatever' the modal may be clause-final:

(4) syn we speke of God prynce of alle thynges, feyne who so feyne *mai* who was he that hath conjoyned thise divers thynges togidre (BOETHCH: 432.C2)

This is rather like *catch who catch can* (OED Kingsley 1855), *come what come may* (OED Shakespeare 1605). It seems to be a favourite construction of the author of *Cloud of Unknowing* since we find it in

5 These clause types probably increased in general in the E3 texts, due to stylistic changes.

two other examples using MAY (with *gete* and *see*) as well as in two examples using WILL (cf. Chapter 9, examples 55, 56):

(5) Gete þat þou gete *mayst*. (CLOUD: 581)

In both periods we occasionally find long adverbial expressions between the auxiliary and the infinitive:

(6) in so moche þat þou [...] *may* soþfastly, bi witnes of Scripture, be clepid a God (CLOUD: 120)

(7) an Antimonial Glass *may* without an addition of other Ingredients be made (BOYLE: 23)

In the only negative interrogative sentence in M3, the negative particle comes after the subject, while in all three examples in E3 it comes immediately after the modal,[6] in one case in a reduced form:

(8) *may* man *nat* see... (CTPARS: 300.C2)

(9) *Mayn't* we hope...? (VANBR: 1, 38)

Clauses containing MAY are declarative and affirmative in 70% of M3 cases and 95% of E3 cases. An interesting development is the clear decline in the number of declarative negative examples of MAY, from 27% in M3 to a mere 4% in E3.[7] Interrogative clauses represent only 3% and 2% of cases respectively.

A clue to the decline in frequency of MAY in negative contexts may be found by comparing the two parallel Boethius translations: the M3 text has 36 examples (32 with clause negation, 4 with a negative subject), representing 35% of all MAY occurrences in the text; in contrast the parallel E3 text has only one single example. Table 2 shows the different choices made by the E3 translator for M3 occurrences of MAY in both negative and affirmative contexts.

---

6 According to Plank (1984: 329-330), this is the more typical position when the finite verb is one of the evolving auxiliary elements, such as (pre-)modals.

7 Mindt (1995: 106) found MAY in negative contexts in 12% of cases in his PDE corpus study.

MAY in M3 Boethius	*M3 tokens*	*transl. in E3 by:* *MAY*	*CAN*	*COULD*	*ABLE*	*others*
neg. contexts:						
No.	36	0	23	1	2	10
% M3 tokens	100	0	64	3	6	28
affirm. contexts:						
No.	67	8	34	2	2	21
% M3 tokens	100	12	51	3	3	31
all clauses:						
No.	103	8	57	3	4	31
% M3 tokens	100	8	55	3	4	30

Table 2. M3 and E3 Boethius translations: E3 equivalents of M3 MAY (excluding MAY in added M3 glosses).

It is remarkable that of the 36 examples of M3 MAY in a negative context, not a single one is translated in the same way in the E3 version. On closer inspection, it turns out that all the examples of negative-context MAY in the M3 Boethius translation express dynamic modality, so we can suppose that MAY NOT shared the declining fortunes of dynamic MAY. Not entirely, however: though all M3 MAY NOTs are dynamic and none 'survive' into E3 (mostly being replaced by CANNOT), out of the 8 M3 affirmative MAYs that 'survive' in the E3 translation, three are dynamic, e.g.:

(10) a fewe thingis of the devyne depnesse, the whiche that mannys resoun *may* undirstonde (BOETHCH: 453.C1)

(11) few things concerning the Depth of the Divine Knowledg, which humane Reason *may* comprehend (BOETHPR: 196)[8]

It seems that dynamic MAY NOT disappeared first, leaving affirmative dynamic MAY a slightly longer life into the E3 period.

The proportion of inanimate subjects increases from 32% of all subjects in M3 to 51% in E3. Contributions to this gain seem to have come from epistemic MAY and MAY with a bleached meaning (both

8 4P6, 32: quae ratio *ualet* humana, 'which human reason is capable of'; Watts (1969: 138) has 'such as human reason *can* grasp'.

categories larger in E3 and with more inanimate subjects). The number of 'existential subjects' (*it* or *there*) also increases from 1% of the total in M3 to 9% in E3.

As far as text types are concerned, non-private Letters and Handbooks in both periods have a higher-than-average proportion of inanimate subjects. Science and Law texts are obviously very different in the two periods: both show a great increase in inanimate subjects between the M3 and E3 periods.

In the E3 corpus there are also 8 cases of MAY with no formal subject, in the expression *as... as may be* (see below §6.2.2.2).

4. Verb phrase structure

4.1. Verb complementation

Verb complementation after MAY is basically unchanged in the two periods, with the bare infinitive[9] as the most common complementation in both (75% of cases in M3, 78% in E3).[10] The perfect infinitive is rare: only two examples in E3, and in M3 we have only the following single example, where, however, HAVE *-en* clearly does not indicate tense:

(12) And ȝit, in o steryng of alle þeese, he *may* haue sodenly and parfitely forȝeten alle create þing (CLOUD: 22)
(And yet in just one of these soul-stirrings, he *may* suddenly and completely forget all created things)

9 There is no sign of the *to*-infinitive (except after the gerund *mowing*). Also no sign of the progressive infinitive.

10 These numbers are similar to those of Mindt's PDE corpus: MAY followed by bare infinitive 72%, followed by passive infinitive 13%. In PDE, however, the perfect infinitive is quite common: 15% of Mindt's corpus (Mindt 1995: 169). These numbers are close to those in Biber *et al.* (1999: Figs. 6.15-6.18), though the latter reveals clearly lower frequencies of 'marked aspect or voice' after MAY in their conversational corpus.

There is also a single example of a second modal after MAY in M3:

(13) it is so blendid wiþ þe original synne þat it *may* not kon worche þis werk bot ȝit it be illuminid by grace (CLOUD: 116)
(that it *cannot* have the power to perform this work)

In contrast, the passive infinitive is found quite frequently: in about 20% of cases in both periods. Above-average percentages of passive infinitives are found in M3 Documents (36% of MAY tokens in the text type), in the related genre of non-private Letters (30%) and in Religious treatises (28%). In E3 (ignoring text types with small numbers of tokens), most passive infinitives after MAY are found in Law (34%), possibly related to the top two M3 text types, followed by Educational treatises (28%); Science has a close-to-average 21%.

Passive complementation does not seem to correlate very clearly with modal meaning, except that the two mixed categories, dynamic/deontic and dynamic/epistemic, have a large proportion of passive complementation (respectively 50% and 45% in M3) – the mixed categories may therefore simply reflect our difficulty in classifying modality when passives are involved.[11]

Ellipted complementation declines from 4% of cases in M3 to 1% in E3. Of the 30 M3 occurrences, over half are in comparative and *all that* clauses (cf. 6.2.1.1 and 6.2.1.2).

4.2. Combination with verbs

The most common verbs following M3 MAY are *be* (excluding *be* in the passive infinitive) and *see* (52 and 50 tokens, representing about 7% each of MAY complementation). The next most frequent verbs are *do*, *come* and *have* (32, 32 and 26 tokens). In the E3 period there is an interesting increase of MAY + *be* to 88 cases (18%), followed by *see* and *make* with 19 cases each (4%). Over a third (35%) of occurrences of MAY + *be*, and two-thirds of MAY + *seem* (67%, 6 out of 9 occurrences) have epistemic meaning. In contrast, *see* is dynamic in 95% of cases.

11 'Examples with the passive voice are sometimes difficult to place into notional [= modal meaning] categories' (Kytö 1987: 155).

The dynamic/stative classification of the verb complementation shows a clear tendency for deontic and dynamic modality to be associated with dynamic verbs (between 64 and 73% for both categories in both periods), and for epistemic modality to be associated with stative verbs (53% and 58% of cases in M3 and E3 respectively, against an average incidence of around 35% of these verbs after MAY in the two periods).

If we now examine the correlations between modal type and subject and complement type, we see that there is a clear similarity to the correlations noted in PDE.[12] Table 3 shows how deontic and dynamic modality resemble each other in both periods regarding a tendency to combine with an animate subject and a dynamic verbal complement. It is true that epistemic MAY in M3 combines with inanimate subject and stative verb in only 16% of cases, corresponding to only 3 examples:

(14) Ðat *may* be ment on þis manere (NHOM: III, 137)

However, this low number is still above average for the whole M3 corpus, just as the 32% of epistemic MAY with complementary animate subject and dynamic verb is below average. The pattern of association for epistemic MAY becomes clearer in the E3 period, when we find only 18% of examples associated with the animate-dynamic pattern and 42% with the inanimate-stative pattern. Table 3 also shows a general increase in the inanimate-stative pattern between the two periods (from 11% of the sub-corpus to 22%). Here are a few of the 35 examples from E3 of epistemic MAY with an inanimate subject and stative verbal complement:

(15) perhaps also the white spot I I *may* be the liver or pancreas (HOOKE: 13, 5, 213)[13]

---

12 'There are two typical structural correlates of modal verbs with intrinsic [i.e. deontic] meanings: (a) the subject of the verb phrase usually refers to a human being (as agent of the main verb), and (b) the main verb is usually a dynamic verb, describing an activity or event that can be controlled. In contrast, modal verbs with extrinsic [i.e. epistemic] meanings usually occur with non-human subjects and/or with main verbs having stative meanings' (Biber *et al.* 1999: 485).

13 'I I' = 'marked on the diagram by the line I – I'.

(16) But it *may* more probably be an Invention to fright Passengers into the right Way (FRYER: II, 184)

(17) the Reason *may* possibly be, that… (BOYLE: 38)

	M3 (% of mod. type)		*E3 (% of mod. type)*	
Subject:	*animate*	*inanimate*	*animate*	*inanimate*
verb comp:	*dynamic*	*stative*	*dynamic*	*stative*
Deontic	*62*	0	*52*	20
Dynamic	42	*12*	*42*	12
Epistemic	32	(16)	18	*42*
All modality types	42	11	34	22

Table 3. Percentage of main modality types of MAY corresponding to subject-complement correlates (above-average percentages in italics; percentages referring to absolute numbers of 4 or less in brackets).

5. Time reference

In the M3 period future, present and timeless orientation of MAY seem to be about equally represented (32%-35% of uses for each time category).[14] In E3, 62% have been classed as future, 23% as present and 16% as timeless. This increase in future reference could be associated with the rise of epistemic MAY, since the future, being unknown, is naturally associated with a subjective interpretation.

In expository prose, meta-argumentative references to what 'may be said' or 'may be concluded' are considered to have present time orientation, since they refer to the present processes of thought and to the present text. For example:

(18) Here *may* we see þat… (WSERM: I, 238)

14 These numbers are open to question as the concept of 'present', like the concept 'here', can be understood as a precise point or as a larger area.

(19) these following particulars *may* be considered (TILLOTS: II, ii, 445)

If the subject is indefinite (*a man, whoever, anyone* etc.) then a timeless orientation is more probable:

(20) *may* a man speken and determinen of atempraunce in corages (BOETHCH: 452.C2)

(21) it is possible that some one *may* be able to distinguish betwixt the Good and the Bad (BOETHPR: 195)

6. Type of modality

6.1. Modal categories and text types

As Table 4 shows, the principal phenomenon in the evolution of MAY is the decline of dynamic uses, from 80% in M3 to (a still substantial) 45% in E3, associated with the rise of other uses: epistemic, from 3% to 17%; deontic, from 3% to 13%; and – surprisingly – periphrastic subjunctive uses (i.e. periphrastic subjunctive combined with a bleached meaning), from 8% to 17%. Clearly the PDE default epistemic meaning of MAY has not yet been established. The two mixed categories contain a total of not more than 5% of the examples, though it is perhaps in these uses that some of the migration of MAY towards deontic and epistemic uses takes place.[15]

Table 5 shows the distribution of M3 modal meanings by text type. The latter have been ranked in order of increasing dynamic modal uses, in an attempt to isolate those genres where the non-dynamic uses may be developing. This shows that the most 'conservative' texts at the bottom of the Table are Bible translations,

15 The author of the present section has preferred to class ambiguous cases in 'mixed categories', as it was felt that this might help in tracing the evolution of epistemic MAY. However, the proportion of cases in these categories is small and similar to the numbers of 'uncertain cases' that are placed in square brackets elsewhere in this study.

Handbooks, History and Sermons. In contrast, Rules and Documents at the top are the most 'advanced' in their low proportion of dynamic MAY tokens, both of them using MAY very frequently as a bleached periphrastic subjunctive (48% and 33%).

		M3			*E3*		
Modal cat.	*Meaning*	*No.*	*o/ooo*	*%MAY*	*No.*	*o/ooo*	*%MAY*
dynamic	possibility	357	19	53%	167	10	35%
	ability	130	7	19%	28	2	6%
	prediction	51	3	8%	16	1	3%
	prediction/possibility	4	0.2	1%	1	0.1	0.2%
	necessity				2	0.1	0.4%
	habit	1	0.1	0.1%	1	0.1	0.2%
	Dynamic total	543	29	80%	215	13	45%
epistemic	possibility	18	1	3%	83	5	17%
	necessity	1	0.1	0.1%			
	inference						
	Epistemic total	19	1	3%	83	5	17%
deontic	possibility	14	1	2%	31	2	6%
	necessity	6	0.3	1%	29	2	6%
	(wish)	1	0.1	0.1%			
	Deontic total	21	1	3%	60	4	13%
dy/de	possibility/permission	10	1	1%	2	0.1	0.4%
	Dy/de total	10	1	1%	2		0.4%
dy/ep	possibility	20	1	3%	22	1	5%
	prediction/poss.	1	0.1	0.1%	1	0.1	0.2%
	ability/poss.	1	0.1	0.1%			
	Dy/ep total	22	1	3%	23	1	5%
bleached	with private verb	9	1	1%	15	1	3%
	periphrastic subjunct.	53	3	8%	79	5	17%
	Bleached total	62	3	9%	94	5	20%
TOTAL		677	37	100%	477	28	100%

Table 4. Distribution of MAY by modal category and modal meaning.

	dyn	*epist*	*deon*	*mixed*	*pte vb*	*p. subj.*	Tot.
RULE	48			(3)		*48*	100
DOCUMENTS	53	(2)	(7)	(2)	(2)	*33*	100
HOMILY	67	(3)		(10)	(3)	*17*	100
TRAVELOGUES	67		(17)		(6)	(11)	100
LETTERS N-P	78					*22*	100
REL TREAT	*81*	*4*	*4*	*8*	(1)	2	100
PHILOSOPHY	*84*	*5*	(4)	(3)	(1)	(3)	100
FICTION	*88*	(2)	(4)	(2)	(4)	(2)	100
SERMON	*89*	(3)	(3)	(5)			100
HISTORY	*91*	(3)				(6)	100
HANDBOOKS	*94*			(3)		(3)	100
BIBLE	*100*						100
All texts	80	3	3	5	1	8	100

Table 5. M3: Distribution of modal meanings of MAY by text type: occurrences as percentage of total MAY-forms in each text type (ranked by increasing frequency of simple dynamic modality, the horizontal dotted line dividing text types with below average frequency of simple dynamic uses from the others; percentages corresponding to fewer than 5 tokens in brackets; above-average frequencies for substantial numbers in italics; omitting Science with no MAY tokens).

Tracing the early evidence for deontic and epistemic MAY is difficult because of the small M3 numbers in these categories: M3 Travelogues use MAY deontically 17% of the time and Documents 7%, but for each this only represents 3 cases. The only substantial collection of 'new' uses in M3 is in Religious treatises: 9 tokens classed as deontic and 7 as dynamic / deontic; 10 as epistemic and 14 as dynamic / epistemic.

The E3 text types that adopt above-average epistemic meanings (Table 6) are headed by the unlikely couple of Science and private Letters, which probably adopted the new meaning for different reasons: the tentativeness of modern scientific styles on the one hand, and politeness on the other. The periphrastic subjunctive category also shows a clear generic polarisation, with Philosophy having 39% attributed to this category (8 of the 17 cases being in purpose clauses). Deontic MAY is found especially in Law texts (54% – the only text type where the largest category is not dynamic).

	dyn	*epist*	*deont*	*mixed*	*pte vb*	*p. subj.*	Tot.
TRIAL	(13)	(25)	(25)			(38)	100
TRAVELOGUES	(20)	(60)				(20)	100
LAW	22	(7)	*54*			*17*	100
LTR N-P	30	*30*	(13)	(9)	(13)	(4)	100
DIARY	(33)	(33)				(33)	100
FICT	35	(15)	*25*	(10)		(15)	100
PHIL	39	11	(2)	(5)	(5)	*39*	100
DRAM	41	*26*	*18*	(3)		12	100
SERM	42	*19*	*19*	(3)	(3)	14	100
LTR PR	42	*32*	11	(8)		(8)	100
SCI	44	*33*	(4)	*8*	(6)	(4)	100
H/B	*53*	12	6	8	(3)	*18*	100
EDU	*63*	(4)	3	(4)	(4)	*22*	100
BIOG	*83*	(8)	(8)				100
HIST	(100)						100
all texts	45	17	13	5	3	16	100

Table 6. E3: Distribution of modal meanings of MAY by text type: occurrences as percentage of total MAY-forms in each text type (ranked by increasing frequency of simple dynamic modality, the horizontal dotted line dividing text types with below average frequency of simple dynamic uses from the others; proportions for text types with small totals in brackets; text types with above-average frequencies and substantial numbers in italics).

We have already seen that dynamic CAN increases in texts with interactional features (cf. Ch. 2 §2); a glance now at the frequencies for dynamic MAY among texts identified by the Helsinki Corpus as having such features[16] shows a decline from 49 to 9 tokens per 10,000 words between the two periods, while such use in the other texts declines only from 28 to 15. This suggests that text types with

16 For M3 these are only non-private Letters and one of the Philosophy texts (the dialogue-based Boethius); for E3 they are the same as for M3 plus Trial proceedings, Drama, private Letters, a part of Fiction (the part of PENNY with dialogue) and one of the Handbook texts (ANGLER); the calculations for interactional texts are not shown on the tables published here.

interactional features adopt dynamic CAN and abandon dynamic MAY more quickly than others.[17]

6.2. Dynamic meanings

6.2.1. Dynamic ability[18]

6.2.1.1. 'To have the power to'

There is perhaps only one example of non-modal MAY ('to be strong', 'to have power') in M3:

(22) yif so be that it be wrecchidnesse to wilne to doon yvel, thanne is it more wrecchidnesse *to mowe* don yvel (BOETHCH: 446.C2)

The case is not clear, since the following verb is a bare infinitive (unlike the complement of the preceding *to wilne*), and 'have the power to' could be seen as close to 'be able to'. There are also traces of the older meaning in other examples:

(23) wel is hym þat *may* stoonde! (WSERM: I, 435)

(24) This thyng [i.e. God] [...] that *may* don alle thynges by hise strengthis (BOETHCH: 429.C2)

The second example, however, has the explicit adverbial "by hise strengthis", suggesting that MAY by itself no longer expresses the lexical meaning strongly enough and needs to be given lexical support by an adverbial.

The collocation *if I may* with no following verb appears three times in the M3 corpus. It might be classed as a non-modal use ('if I have any power in the matter'), or could be seen (as here) as dynamic

17 All texts abandon dynamic ability MAY in a similar (almost total) way; the abandonment of dynamic possibility MAY is greater among interactional texts (declining from a very high 39 to 6 per 10,000 words) than among other texts (declining from 18 to 12).

18 No examples have been found in M3 or E3 of dynamic ability MAY with illocutionary overtones (request etc.) as for CAN (cf. Ch. 2 §5.1.1.1).

ability with an implied verb of accomplishing or preventing.[19] In each case the truncated *if*-clause follows a main clause with SHALL expressing deontic volition[20] (so the overall meaning is: 'I promise / intend to do something, if I have any power in the matter'):

(25) Thou shalt abye this fart, if that I *may*! (CTSUMM: 134.C2)

One possible echo of this use is found in the E3 corpus:

(26) I see thy care and vigilance and thank Thee; mine is not wanting wherein I *may* (HOXINDEN: 272)
(my care and vigilance are not lacking, where I *have the power*)

6.2.1.2. 'To be able to'

Closely connected to the concept of 'to have the power to' is that of 'to have the inherent ability to', 'to have the capacity to':

(27) I *ne mai* my wit unfolde / To finde o word of that I mene (GOWER: I, 319)

(28) take a rasor & pare it as ney as þou *maist* (HORSES: 123)

There is a fall in use of this meaning, from 20% of examples in M3 to 6% in E3. The closeness of meaning with the emerging meaning of CAN is shown by the way the formulaic *may or can* in formal contexts (two examples in both sub-corpora) is lacking in any distinctive meaning between elements:

(29) in as meke wyse and lowely maner as any symple officers and pouuere lieges best *may or can* ymagine and diuise (LLET: 72)

---

19 The OED classes *if I may* with the non-modal meaning, yet adds the gloss 'if I have any power in the matter… if I can avoid or prevent it', where the second half of the definition could be interpreted as dynamic ability followed by an implied verbal complement. The MED places the collocation in section 6(h) and (i), in sections that seem to be implicitly parts of the treatment of the modal auxiliary.

20 The striking association of SHALL-MAY in this construction is also true of the 2 OED examples (under MAY 1) and 10 of the 11 examples (the other having *wol*) in MED 6(h) and (i).

Here, in the context of 'binomial phrases' (*meeke wyse and lowely maner, officers and lieges, imagine and deuise*), the paired modal verbs form part of a politeness strategy via prolixity. The same features can be used to suggest a need to make careful legal distinctions:

(30) Be it further enacted That [...] it shall and may be lawfull to and for the Gaugers [...] to turne any Cock or Cocks to try and examine whether such Pipe or other Conveyance *may or can* convey any Wash (STAT7: VIII,457)

An interesting set of collocations associated with dynamic ability are comparative clauses like (with varying subject persons) *as...as I may* (13 examples) and the similar *all that I may* (3 examples):[21]

(31) to come vp as fer as they *may* in to the riuer of seyne (LLETT: 75)

(32) Þat wyl serue þe to pay, Peyneble, al þat he *may* (HS: 188)
(who will wait upon you to pay, scrupulously, all that he *is able to*)

6.2.2. Dynamic possibility

The most frequent M3 meaning of MAY is dynamic possibility (representing 53% of all cases). It occurs in all text types (especially History, Fiction and Handbooks), though with relatively few examples in Rules. Here are a few short examples from a range of text types:

(33) the bok in which is rased The lettre, and *mai* nothing be rad (GOWER: I, 317)

(34) bothe these thinges *may* causen errour (ASTR: 671.C2)

(35) it is gret meruayle how it *may* be (MAND: 143)

Although in some cases MAY in a result clause has a predictive meaning, there are numerous examples where it expresses possibility:

(36) They been so knyt ther *may* noon harm bityde (CTMERCH: 156.C1)
(They are so closely joined that no harm *can* befall them)

---

21 *All that + may/might* is not listed among OED phrases but can be found in CD-ROM searches, e.g. 'speed us in al that ye may' (1386, SPEED), 'A surgian muste þanne be bisy in al þat he my | te' (1400, WAX).

Dynamic possibility is also the single largest category in E3 (35% of cases) and is well represented in Handbooks and Educational treatises. It is less frequent in Law, Trial transcripts, non-private Letters and Philosophy texts. Here are some examples of this usage:

(37) Midsummer […] is the best time, though it *may* be done from the beginning of May (LANGF: 29)[22]

(38) as in ye folowinge paper *may* bee seene more at large (FOX: 159)

This meaning is clearest where there is some emphasis on the easiness or difficulty of the action:

(39) Glass of Antimony made without additament, *may* easily, as experience has inform'd us, be in part reduced to a Regulus (BOYLE: 23)

6.2.2.1. I doubt not but that

An interesting phraseological unit in E3, not listed as a phrase by the OED, is MAY in the subclause following *I doubt not but that* (cf. also below §6.3.1.3: *I do not know but that*):

(40) Now though quick Lime be the powder that this direction makes choice of, yet I doubt not, but that there *may* be much more convenient ones found out, one of which I have made tryal of, and found very effectual (HOOKE: 13.5, 47)

The gloss 'I'm sure a more convenient one *can* be discovered' has been accepted here, though '*will* be discovered' is another possibility, and simple prediction is the best gloss for the only other example of the collocation in the sub-corpus:

(41) though itt bee very difficult to steere amongst so many rocks of faction, without striking upon some; I doubt not but yr Excellency by yr great prudence *may* bee soe happy as to do itt (OSBORNE: 22)

22 Such examples with inanimate subject and passive complement have been classed as dynamic possibility where the 'possible for' paraphrase seems most apt, as in this case: 'though it is possible for it to be done from the beginning of May'.

6.2.2.2. As...as may be

A collocation that occurs eight times in the E3 corpus, though not listed in the OED, is *as...as may be*, where *may be* having no subject has a quasi-adjectival status:[23]

(42) that they may have as much of the summer heat at ripening time as *may* be (LANGF: 126)

6.2.2.3. Ironic understatement (MAY = 'can – and how!')

There are three problematic M3 examples of MAY used in a construction that might be summarized as 'well may he [lament], who x':

(43) Wel *may* the sike man biwaille and wepe, / Ther as ther nys no wyf the hous to kepe (CTMERCH: 156.C1)

Opinions on the modal meaning of these examples seem to be divided, depending on the interpretation given to *wel may*: deontic,[24] dynamic,[25] epistemic,[26] mandative subjunctive.[27] From the MED examples we see that the relative clause is not essential but the verbal complement is often in the same semantic area as the examples above: e.g. "O Troye allas! wel maistow mourne & weepe". We have interpreted them as dynamic possibility used in an ironic understatement: 'the man can certainly lament who...', 'Oh Troy,

---

23 An OED on CD-ROM search for 'as may be' reveals about 50 examples among the quotations, including the following early citations: 1577 (*as riche as may be*), 1594 (*as farre from excesse of drinke as may be*). Kytö (1987: 160) glosses this collocation as 'as circumstances allow' and sees it as close to deontic permission. The examples here seem to be all closer to dynamic possibility, so that 'as fast as may be' means 'as fast as possible'.

24 The MED puts such examples in section 7c.(c) 'senses resembling those of ME ouen and shulen'; another member of the present group also sees them as deontic.

25 The present writer.

26 Visser (1963-73) deals with these examples in §1667, implicitly as epistemic modality, with epistemic sections before and after; another member of the present group sees them as epistemic.

27 Another member of the present group. The OED lists similar examples under WELL but does not discuss the meaning of MAY.

there is certainly no impediment to your weeping now', similar to examples of litotes in OE poetry:

(44) A *mæg* gnornian se ðe nu fram this wigplegan wendan thenceð (*Maldon*: 315-6)
(He *can* forever mourn / he is free to mourn forever who thinks now to turn from this war-play)

The following famous outburst is a different case, having an inanimate subject, no verb of lamenting and no categorizing relative clause, and seems to be more a case of epistemic necessity:

(45) Thow seyst we wyves wol oure vices hide / Til we be fast, and thanne we wol hem shewe / Wel *may* that be a proverbe of a shrewe! (CTBATH: 108.C2)
(That *has to* be the proverb of a wicked man!)

6.2.2.4. Dynamic possibility with illocutionary overtones of advice or suggestion

As for CAN (cf. 5.1.3), we find a number (26) of examples in the E3 corpus of dynamic possibility MAY used in a context where advice is being given, to mean 'one possibility is for you to do this',[28] as in the following (where the suggestion is immediately qualified):

(46) KA.: Who shall be my Father to give me.
JO.: Thou *mayest* ask Jack Wheeler, but I know he had rather had thee himself (PENNY: 119)

All but one (the example just given) come from two texts (HOOLE and LANGFORD) on the growing of fruit-trees and the creation of a model school:

(47) But this work [Inoculating] *may* be done in the middle of the day, if the heat be not violent [...] And for all that hath been said before, the afternoon may be as good a time as any; (LANGF: 39)

28 This use seems close to that of dynamic CAN used 'to suggest, by implication, that what is possible will, or should, be implemented' (Palmer 1979a/1990: 86).

(48) There should likewise be a place provided for a School-Library, and the rest *may* be made use of as Lodging roomes (HOOLE: 225)

The few potential M3 cases (6) of this use of dynamic possibility MAY mainly come from the same text type of Handbooks but most of them are not clear cases.

6.2.3. Dynamic prediction

The MED has over one and a half columns dedicated to MAY "expressing futurity", adding, however, that the examples are "usually with vestiges of the older senses". We have classed as prediction examples that translate convincingly into PDE as WILL and where any translation as CAN/MAY has only a small difference in meaning.

6.2.3.1. In final clauses

Purpose and result clauses and relative clauses with a final meaning often have a bleached subjunctive use of MAY, but in other cases this can be seen more as neutral prediction, as in the following relative clauses:

(49) He es þe brede of God ful euyn Þat lastand life euer more *may* gif Vntill þam þat will lely lif (NHOM: II, 76)
(the bread of God [...] which *will* give lasting life to those who live in faith)

(50) To plant such [Grapes] as ripen soonest in the Year, that they *may* have as much of the summer heat [...] as may be (LANGF: 126)

Here the predictive meaning could be considered to be totally belonging to the syntactic and semantic context, though we have preferred to place them in the category of 'prediction' when WILL is a possible gloss. Predictive MAY in purpose clauses is found only in M3 (15 examples):

(51) And hys [i.e. the dragon's] power, lorde, þou bynde, þat þe folk *may* knowe and se þe mercy and þe myȝt of þe (HS: 64)
(so that people *will know* / *know* and see Thy mercy and power)

Projection into the future is also a characteristic of result clauses:

(52) [the soul] es swa sutil, þat aftir þe dede, It *may* occupy na stede. (PRICK: 83)

Independent clauses can also have a final meaning with respect to a preceding clause if they contain an adverbial such as *thus*, *therefore* or *thereby* (or the equivalent *by þat*):

(53) And bi þat þou *maist* it knowe if þou it touche it wol gladli blede
(And by this you *will* know it: if you touch it, it will bleed readily)
(HORSES: 123)[29]

6.2.3.2. Reference to the act of reception of the text

MAY is found in M3 (9 times) in introductory sections (of both narratives and expositional prose), announcing what is to come or what the reader will learn:[30]

(54) And þat *may* y shewe apertly By a tale of seint Gregorye (HS: 321)

(55) The fifthe partie shal be an introductorie [...] in which thou *maist* lerne a gret part of the generall rewles of theorik in astrologie (ASTR: 663.C2)

Sometimes a dynamic possibility meaning is present:

(56) þe whilk es declared in a stede, In þe thred part þat spekes of þe dede. Alle þis matere men *may* se þare, þarfor here I wil spek þar-of na mare. (PRICK: 81)
(All this one *can* read there, so I won't say more of it here.)

Interestingly, similar formulas are also found at the end of the text in what looks like a kind of summary of the expected effects:

(57) þis tretice [...] may be cald Prik of Conscience als men may fele, For if a man it rede and understande wele, And þe materes þar-in til hert wil take, It *may* his conscience tendre make (PRICK: 257)

---

29 This use is very similar to SHALL in such examples as 'And þat þou schalt knowe by þese signus. Loke þat he be hardi & coragious of herte' (HORSES: 87).

30 Cf. Visser (1963-73: 1658), OED 3f, MED 7b. This is similar to the use of SHALL (§5.1.1): "to introduce an exposition or concept [...] and thus guide the reader's decoding activity."

Although the author is referring here to an unknowable future effect on the reader, we exclude epistemic meaning since the author seems to be making a confident prediction about the effect of his work. We have found seven examples that seem to continue this usage into EModE prose texts:[31]

(58) He that shall view the [...] Statutes [...] *may* see several provisions made against the destruction of Fish (WALTON: 213) (He...*will* see...)

(59) affirmed by S. Richard Baker, in whose Chronicle you *may* find these Verses (WALTON: 292)

6.2.4. Prediction / Possibility

There are a few examples (4 in M3, 1 in E3) where MAY certainly has a predictive use but where there is an uncertain element of dynamic possibility:

(60) who-so-euer to þys ys custummable, hys amendment *may* neuer be stable (whoever is accustomed [to do] this [folly], his reformation *will / can* never be stable) (HS: 121)

Here the consequence of instability seems to follow without impediment, which would lead us to a classification as 'prediction'; at the same time, however, the attainment of stability is not easy, and this would incline us to a classification as 'possibility'.

There are also examples of dynamic/epistemic modality where the uncertainty involves dynamic prediction or epistemic possibility. These are cases of future reference in a subordinate clause after a matrix clause that already expresses epistemic modality (*It is possible that* or *I think that*). We have classed examples in subclauses after *It is possible that* (and similar, as in 61) to be mere dynamic prediction (effectively bleached); in other cases, such as after *I think that* (62), we have taken MAY as reinforcing the matrix epistemic modality:

31 Visser (1963-73: 1658) gives only ME and mainly verse quotations; OED (MAY 3f) says that the use of MAY to refer forward to the text is found 'in ME poetry' and has a last citation from c1425.

(61) This is all the news that I heare our parts afford, but it is possible I *may* send you word of another wedding when I write next (EOXINDEN: 333)
(it is possible that I *send / will send*)

(62) he doth think that the King sees that he cannot never have much more money or good from this Parliament, and that therefore he *may* hereafter dissolve them (PEPYS: VII,411)
(he thinks that… *it is possible that he will* later dissolve them)

In one case of timeless orientation we have classed a potentially epistemic MAY as bleached, because it seems to add no further epistemic modality within a heavy epistemic frame:

(63) I shall adde the Recital of a surprising Phaenomenon, which […] may help to make it probable, that Electrical Attractions […] *may* be the effects of unheeded […] Causes (BOYLE: 26)
(it is possible that [this recital] will make it appear probable that Electrical Attractions *are* the effects)

6.2.5. Habit

In one case from each sub-corpus it was thought that MAY refers to the permanent properties of a phenomenon, hence the classification as dynamic habit:

(64) For byfor ar þai may God se Byhoves als thre thynges brinned be, þat es at say, als wodde, and hay, And stubble, þat *may* sone *wast away*; […] þe lest veniel syns sal brin sone, Als stobble, þat son brinnes and son es done
(For before they can ever see God, three things should be burned away, like wood and hay and stubble that *quickly burns* away […] The least venial sins will burn quickly, like stubble, that quickly catches fire and is quickly burnt away) (PRICK: 87)

(65) the higher [walls] may be reserved for such Fruit-trees as will not do well without them: of a Tarras-walk *may* do well for Vines, and the Gravel-walk under the Wall will mightily encrease the heat about them (LANGF: 127)

6.2.6. Dynamic necessity

Two examples only have been classed as dynamic necessity:

(66) Then we *may* well grant that such are always in a State of Joy
(it is necessary for us to grant that…) (BOETHPR: 125)

Here, the Latin is *necesse est confiteri* (3P9: 15), and the M3 translation *mote we graunten* (BOETHCH: 126),[32] while the modern translation by Watts (1969: 95) also uses deontic modality *it must be admitted*.

6.3. Epistemic meanings

6.3.1. Possibility

The semantic shift of MAY from objective to subjective possibility meanings is undoubtedly one of the most interesting episodes in the modal saga. Unfortunately, for any suspected epistemic MAY in M3, a dynamic meaning can almost always be substituted, with perhaps a slightly forced meaning – to us, but who knows how M3 Man thought about possibility? We decided that the only examples we could legitimately class as epistemic are those where the surrounding context supplies sufficient confirmation. Such contexts may provide us with a clue to those where the semantic change was taking place.

6.3.1.1. Harmonic verbal complement: reference to private events

We have already seen above (6.2.3.2) how MAY is found in metatextual references to the reception of the text with a bleached predictive meaning. There are cases of similar contexts where, however, the act of reception is presented as less certain (as a paperback blurb might say "this book will change the rest of your life" or, less confidently, "this book may change the rest of your life"). An example is the following:

(67) Tis same subieccion of þe body to þe spirit *may* be in maner verrely conceiued in þe preof of þis goostly werk of þis book by hem þat worchen þerin
(This subjection of the body to the spirit *may* (to some degree, indeed) be understood by the experience) (CLOUD: 112)

---

32 In the next sentence of the Latin, *necessarium est* is again translated by *mote we graunten* in the M3 translation, and again by MAY in the E3 translation: *may we also grant*.

Here, the author is making a claim as to the effect of his text on the reader's understanding so cannot be too confident. In addition, the modal verb is followed by two adverbials *in maner* ('in a way', or even 'perhaps')[33] and *verrely* ('indeed'), one a hedge implying uncertainty, the other an emphasizer at risk of losing intensity from extended use.

Other aspects of the reader's reaction to the text also fall into the same category of unknowable events and suggest an epistemic interpretation (as in PDE *you may wonder at this point…*):

(68) Bot now *may* som say here agayne And aske how þe saul may fele payne (PRICK: 82)

Somatic states like hunger being just as private as mental states, we can easily appreciate the epistemic nature of the following:

(69) and as for your Bride, tho' you *may* be sharp set [= hungry] before she's quite ready, I'll engage for my Girl, she stays your Stomach at last (VANBR: I, 61)

6.3.1.2. Harmonic verbal complement: reference to eventualities

Verbs like *happen* (*befall*, *fall*, *chance*) focus attention on the uncertain reality of events. Though such 'eventualities' can be presented as objectively as possible, they are inevitably open to interpretation as having the possibility of happening according to the speaker. The evolution can be seen in the way MAY + *hap* and MAY + *be* come to have an adverbial meaning of 'perhaps' (with the first OED quotation for the former dated at 1300); even the word *(h)appen* itself is used adverbially in modern Northern dialects to mean 'perhaps'. We should not be surprised, therefore, to find these verbs associated with epistemic MAY, as in the following examples:

(70) þa er veniel synnes þat *may* falle, Bathe grete and smale (PRICK: 87)

(71) But now I shall add, that, not onely there *may* happen some variations in the success of Trials […], but that it is not so certain as many think, whether some particular Bodies be or be not Electrical (BOYLE: 35)

33 Cf. also "whi þof al it *may* be seide in maner þat…" (CLOUD: 120), also classed as epistemic possibility.

(72) You *may* chance to have Suckers of an old Vine which will be sure to grow (LANGF: 129)

6.3.1.3. Harmonic matrix clause (I think that etc.)

Epistemic MAY is also found in a subordinate clause dependent on a matrix verb like *I think that*, *I believe that* and *I don't know but that*:[34]

(73) I rather think, in a day or two longer, we *may* have 1000 supernumeraryes (RHADDSR: 15)

(74) Y. FASH.: O no, they study how to spend Money, not to save it.
MISS.: I'Cod, I don't know but that *may* be better Sport than t'other, ha, Nurse (VANBR: I, 63)

6.3.1.4. Reference to unknowable future time

Explicit reference to the future will often have a subjective and epistemic meaning, and 71% of examples classed as epistemic were also classed as referring to future states of affairs (against 58% for dynamic MAY):

(75) Love will account that to be well said, which it may be was not so intended; and then it *may* cause it to be so, another time (JETAYLOR: 28)

(76) Past Pleasures, for ought I know are best, such as we are sure of, those to come *may* disappoint us (FARQUHAR: 6)

6.3.1.5. Tentative explanations

Mental events, future events and even remembered past events are fugitive phenomena often associated in the E3 period with epistemic MAY; equally difficult to pin down are the causes of phenomena, and there are several examples that show the modern tendency to 'modesty' in the forwarding of claims to explanations:

---

34 This construction is noted by the OED (BUT 19), though the common use of MAY in the subordinate clause (when referring to the present or future) is not noted. The collocation *I doubt not but that* (see § 6.2.) has been taken to mean 'I am sure that' and is not associated with epistemic MAY. Epistemic MAY in the subclause is also found after an interrogative *Who knows but that* (meaning 'Perhaps'), cf. HYDROSTATICKS, p. 212, in the Helsinki Corpus of Older Scots (my thanks to Marina Dossena for this reference).

(77) it seems, Iron does contain a very combustible sulphureous Body, which is, in all likelihood, one of the causes of this Phaenomenon, and which *may* be perhaps very much concerned in the business of its hardening and tempering (HOOKE: 13.5, 46)

(78) And that this *may* be so, seems with great probability to be argued from the strange Phaenomena of sensitive Plants, wherein Nature seems to perform several Animal actions with the same Schematism or Orginization that is common to all Vegetables (HOOKE: 13.5, 116)

The emphasis (through repeated epistemic expressions) is on the opinion of the speaker – not a declaration of objective but of subjectively perceived possibility, to be confirmed by other subjects and other observations. The scientist is giving a personal interpretation to explain the phenomena without claiming this *is* the case.

Where however the writer refers to the qualities of the observed phenomena (rather than suggesting explanations), MAY has its dynamic meaning:

(79) from the foregoing Instances [...] we may learn, that when the form of a Body seems to be destroyed by a fiery Analysis [...], the remaining substance *may* yet be endowed with Electricity (BOYLE: 25)

6.3.1.6. Respectful relativizing of statement or request

In contexts where the speaker is trying not to impose on the listener, epistemic MAY is appropriate as it places a statement in the area of personal interpretation, so leaving the way open for the other person to disagree. An amusing example is John Stripe's letter to his mother in which he asks for more money and for some cloth to make a winter coat:

(80) The season beginning now to hasten towards Winter, and a Coat I shall have great occasion for. It *may* be you *may* meet with a piece of black cloth, either in the chest my uncle Bonnell sent, or among the Broakers, which *may* serve my turn (STRYPE: 182)

This use of epistemic MAY is associated with polite formulas:

(81) your Ladyship *may* please to take notice, that (VANBR: I, 38)

6.3.1.7. In a concessive clause

It is only in E3 that we find quasi-subjunctive epistemic MAY in concessive clauses as in three PDE cases: (i) 'although you may not believe this,...' ; (ii) 'you may not believe this, but...';[35] and (iii) 'however difficult it may be to believe this,...':

(82) though the inconveniences arising from the ill use of it *may* be very great, yet the mischief on the other hand is intolerable (TILLOTS: II: ii 451)

(83) it [wife-beating] [...] *may* proceed from wrath and folly, but can never end in vertue (JETAYLOR: 26)

(84) How plausible soever this Objection *may* appear, I do not despair [...] to make it abundantly evident, that (TILLOTS: II: ii, 445)

Further evidence that the use of MAY in these contexts is a recent phenomenon comes from the parallel Boethius translations: the Latin (4P6: 6) has "quodsi te musici carminis oblectamenta <u>delectant</u>" (a present indicative), and the M3 translation (85) has a similar indicative yet the E3 translation (86) now uses MAY:

(85) although the noryssynges of dite of musyk *deliteth* the [...] (BOETHCH: 451.C1)

(86) And although the Charms and Musick of my Verse *may delight* thee, yet [...] (BOETHPR: 191)

However, the classification of MAY in concessive clauses is a problem[36] and even Palmer is undecided: at first he suggests that they may be classed as epistemic (1990: 52), but then later says these uses may be only marginally epistemic and resemble the 'non-factive' subjunctive in other languages (Palmer 1990: 111). Indeed, in a few

---

35 Quotation (83) is the only example in this class (cf. Traugott / Dasher 2002: 115-116) on the late development of this modal use).

36 In a similar case to the one above, the Latin has present subjunctive (*uideas*), M3 this time has bleached MAY *whatsoevere thou mayst seen* (BOETHCH: 453 C.1), while E3 and Watts have present indicatives *whatsoever thou seest*' (BOETHPR: 197) and *Whenever....you see* (Watts 1969: 138).

examples we have classified the MAY in concessive clauses as having a bleached subjunctive meaning.

6.3.1.8. With an indefinite subject

Statements with a generic or indefinite subject are concerned with 'virtual reality' not actuality and so will tend to be statements of likelihood or probability, not descriptions of actual events or situations:

(87) a man *may* be constreyned so, by som cause (BOETHCH: 436.C1)

(88) And it is to be fear'd, that some *may* have so far feared their Consciences [...] that (BURNETROC: 149)

(89) because the Nature of some Men *may* be so forward and importunate, that Poverty, and the want of Necessaries, would rather urge them to do ill (BOETHPR: 199)

In the last example, MAY corresponds to epistemic adverbs in other versions: Latin *fortisan*, M3 *peraventure* and the modern translation (Watts 1969: 140) *perhaps*.

6.3.1.9. Uncertainty conveyed by an adverbial

It is possible that the evolution of epistemic MAY was aided by accompanying adverbs that originally meant the top point on a scale or a high point on it (amplifiers) but then lost their 'impact' over time. One of the most common adverbs associated with the modal in M3 is *well* (in 19 examples, 5 of them with epistemic MAY), which functions originally as an amplifier but then is "used to denote the possibility or the likelihood of an occurence or fact" (OED, WELL 9b, with citations from c1400). Here are some examples with epistemic MAY:

(90) it [concupiscence] *may* wel wexe fieble and faille by vertu of baptesme and by the grace of God thurgh penitence, but fully ne shal it nevere quenche (CTPARS: 297.C2)

(91) But lat us graunten, I pose, that som man *may* wel demen or knowen the good folk and the badde (BOETHCH: 452.C2)

Other M3 adverbials that accompany and reinforce an epistemic modal are: *in maner* ('to some extent'), *by som cause* ('for some reason'), *li /tli* ('probably'), *perauenture* ('perhaps').

The E3 period is notable for the presence of three epistemic adverbs, almost unknown before the 15th century: *probably* (11 occurrences in E3, 3 times associated with MAY), *possibly* (10 occurrences, twice with MAY),[37] and *perhaps* (40 occurrences, 10 with MAY):

(92) And this *may* probably be one reason why... (TILLOTS: II: ii 420)

(93) but it has proved longer than I intended, and possibly *may* not to you be considerable (WALTON: 294)

(94) perhaps there *may* be Hopes (VANBR: I, 40)

6.3.1.10. It may be

There are eight examples of epistemic *it may be* with no following complement in the E3 corpus.[38] It can occur in clause-initial, -final and -medial position:

(95) Love will account that to be well said, which it *may* be was not so intended (JETAYLOR: 28)

6.4. Dynamic / Epistemic modality

As dynamic possibility MAY evolved into epistemic possibility MAY, many examples are 'mergers' (Coates 1983): ambiguous to both interlocutor and linguistic observer (indeed, it is this ambiguity that allowed the evolution). For Nuyts (2001: 181-2) this would be because the epistemic meaning began as an invited inference from a dynamic meaning. However, the ambiguity continues into PDE:

---

37 *Possibly* has the only earlier quotation: 1391 in Chaucer's Astrolabe treatise, included in the M3 corpus, used with *might*.

38 For Nuyts (2001: 194-5) the German and Dutch equivalent of 'it can / may be that...' is 'a perfect prototype' for epistemic modality deriving from dynamic modality: stative predicate and a lack of a controlling participant in the state of affairs.

according to the OED, the dynamic use still exists but mixed with epistemic: "Expressing objective possibility [...] Now with a mixture of sense 5 [subjective possibility]" (MAY 3). Hyland (1998: 117) says that often in PDE formal texts both interpretations "are equally possible and do not conflict".

Visser (1963-73: 1756) sees the matter more in terms of strict observer 'ambiguity' (ideally distinguishable, though often not so) when he says: "Since this shift in meaning [from objective to subjective possibility] is not formally expressed, the correct interpretation of quite a number [i.e. a substantial number] of the later quotations is problematic, and the placing of them in this section [1654, objective possibility] instead of in section 1663 [subjective possibility] is purely arbitrary".

Where the meaning seemed 'merged' or so unknowable as to make a clear assignment 'purely arbitrary', we have preferred to assign the example to a small mixed dynamic/epistemic category.[39] Here are a couple of typical examples:

(96) whanne scripture speketh oonly bi counceil, men *moun* be sauid, thouȝ thei do not the counceil (WYCPROL: I, 56)
(it is *possible for* men to be saved though they do not follow the advice / it is *possible that* men will be saved though they do not follow the advice)

(97) A sharp wit *may* find something in the wisest man whereby to expose him to the contempt of injudicious people (TILLOTS: II: ii 428)
(it is *possible for* a sharp wit to find something / it is *possible that* a sharp wit will find something)

Adverbs, though helping to interpret modal meaning, may be open to more than one interpretation themselves. This is the case of *lightly* and *wel*:

(98) but if so be that he somtyme descharge hym of hem [venial synnes] by shrifte, they *mowe* ful lightly amenuse in hym al the love that he hath to Jhesu Crist; (CTPARS: 298.C1)

39 Equivalent to Kytö's 'indeterminate' possibility category (1987: 150). Ambiguity may well be normal in this area of modality: Nuyts (2001: 189) finds over 70% of his Dutch and German epistemic examples of *kunnen* and *können* are ambiguously dynamic / epistemic.

(it *is* easily *possible for* them to lessen his love for Jesus Christ / it *is* most *probable* that they will lessen his love for Jesus Christ) [40]

(99) My wit is short, ye *may* wel understonde. (CTPROL: 35.C1)
(as it is *possible for* you to *easily* understand / as it is *possible that* you *perfectly* understand)

We even find two examples of a familiar ambiguous hedging formula:

(100) Byneþe þi God þou arte: for whi þof al it *may* be seide in maner þat in þis tyme God & þou ben not two bot one in spirit (CLOUD: 120)
(although *it is possible for* it to be said in a way that / although *it is possible that* it can in a way be said that)

(101) the taking Fish in Spawning time, *may* be said to be against nature (WALTON: 213)

6.5. Deontic meanings

6.5.1. Deontic possibility

6.5.1.1. Legal and moral authority

Uses of MAY for granting or requesting legal permission are only found in the E3 corpus:

(102) if any Prisoner [...] shall [...] be arrested [...] hee or she *may* plead the General Issue (STAT7: VII,77)

Equally, the use of MAY to grant or request permission on the basis of moral law is rare in M3, though we have an example in the following (a self-justifying answer to the question why the speaker was so fond of music that he had a harper playing in the next room):

(103) ȝyf ȝe do þus [yn harpe [...] wurschepe God], y sey hardly, ȝe *mow* here ȝoure mynstralsy (HS: 159)

---

40 Two other records in this category of meaning contain the same adverb, *lightly*, though it seems more associated with dynamic modality (7 records).

There are more examples in the E3 corpus; in the following, "have a Charter for lying" is presented as equivalent to 'may lie', so the 'permission' meaning ('granted by charter') is clear:

(104) It seems the Saints have a certain Charter for Lying; they *may* lye and cant, and deceive, and rebel, and think God Almighty takes no notice of it (LYLE: IV, 114.C2)

The moral permission may be simply that of 'good manners' 'good sense' or 'the rules of our community' which allow us to do or say something:

(105) Yet some [town pleasures] there are we *may* speak kindlier of (VANBR: I, 32)

6.5.1.2. Permission on the authority of the speaker

A clear example of permission given directly by the speaker is where the maid Mary consents to seduction by her Quaker master:

(106) thou *mayest* proceed (PENNY: 148)

Other examples occur in the context of giving advice or instructions:

(107) Also whanne oo word is oonis set in a reesoun, it *mai* be set forth as ofte as it is vndurstonden, either as ofte as reesoun and nede axen (WYCPROL: I, 57)

or in a formula of politeness or sarcastic politeness:

(108) Y. FASH.: [...] I have something of Importance to speak to you about.
MISS.: Sir, (my Lord, I meant) you *may* speak to me about what you please (VANBR: I, 62)

(109) you and your Absolution *may* go to the Devil (FARQUHAR: 61)

6.5.1.3. Request for permission:

We find requests for permission with MAY only in the E3 corpus:

(110) My Lord, *may* I speak one word more? (LISLE: IV, 123.C1)

(111) let me [...] beg a courtesie of you [...] that from henceforth you *would allow* me to call you Master, and that really I *may* be your Scholar (WALTON: 216)

A request for permission used as a hedge is found three times in scientific texts:

(112) effluviable matter, if I *may* so call it (BOYLE: 11)

6.5.1.4. Permission from the argumentation or from the intellectual community

The authority for an act of saying, concluding etc. may come from the argumentation of the text itself. These cases resemble PDE hedges that usually mix a tentative epistemic meaning with the deontic meaning. The following is a good example of a pure deontic meaning:

(113) Thanne *mowen* we concluden sykerly, that… (BOETHCH: 434.C1)

In confirmation of this classification, we see that the modal corresponds to *licet* ('it is allowed') in the Latin original (*securo igitur concludere licet*).

6.5.2. Deontic necessity

Apart from permission / prohibition and legalistic MAY meaning 'must', other deontic uses of MAY are not mentioned in either Visser or the OED, but the MED entry for MOUEN has not only sections 7 a and b (permission and prohibition) but also 7c ('should', 'be advised', 'must', 'to have good reason to').

6.5.2.1. Deontic necessity (prohibition)

Prohibition, an extension of negated permission, is found in two cases in M3 and two in E3:

(114) Whoso shal telle a tale after a man, [...] / He *moot* reherce as ny as evere he kan […] He *may nat* spare, althogh he were his brother; / He *moot* as wel seye o word as another (CTPROL: 35.C1)

Here, the impediment to action derives from strict social convention to the point of becoming deontic prohibition, indeed the clause with

MAY is in a parallel structure with clauses containing *moot* (here clearly meaning 'must') both before and after. A clear E3 example is the following:

(115) My Text expresly bids Christians to try the Spirits, which to any man's sense does imply that they *may* judge of these matters: But the Church of Rome says they *may not*; because if this liberty were permitted... (TILLOTS: II: ii 444)

6.5.2.2. Deontic necessity (advice)

The category of deontic advice (two examples in M3, nine in E3) has been reserved for examples where the interlocutor is clearly indicating the appropriate behaviour (and not cases where there is dynamic openness about the advice: 'you can or not, as you prefer'):

(116) Bot ȝif þei wil proue whens þis steryng comeþ, þei *mowe* proue þus, ȝif hem likyþ. First lat hem loke ȝif... (CLOUD: 131)
(if they desire to ascertain where this stirring comes from, they *can / should* test it as follows, if they wish)

(117) QUAKER: Satan is departed for this time, and thou *mayest* thank thy Hand-maid too, for she, like a pious Sister, has been very diligent since thy departure.
DAME: Yea, I say unto thee, I shall thank her (PENNY: 151)

Sometimes *you may* seems close to a softened imperative:[41]

(118) And you *may* note, that though this may seem a curiosity not worth observing, yet others have judged it worth their time and costs, to make Glass-hives, and order them in such a manner as to see how Bees have bred (WALTON: 295)

The following example is problematic:

(119) T'is shee that must do mee what kindnes is to be done when all comes to all; and therefore *may* observe her what you can, as indeed *wee ought*.
(HOXINDEN: 281)

41 The verb *note* seems be associated with deontic modality in this period: in the same text we have *and you are to note, that*; and in the earlier E2 corpus, the only examples with *note* are three examples with the imperative.

It is not clear if the letter-writer has accidentally omitted *you*; if not, then MAY is being used here in an interesting way without a subject, perhaps an unusual imperative not noted by the OED or the MED.

Examples of deontic advice come principally from the prototypical text types of secular instruction, e.g. from a Handbook on fruit-trees or a (handbook-like) Educational treatise. A special case is the following:

(120) God hath of late years manifested himself in a very dreadful manner [...] And now that those judgments have done no good upon us we *may* justly fear that he will appear once for all (TILLOTS: II, ii, 430)

Glosses that fit the context well are 'we would do well to fear', 'we really ought to fear' – and for this reason it has been placed in the category of deontic necessity (advice).

6.5.2.3. Deontic necessity (order)

As remarked in the chapter on SHALL (§3), in legalistic contexts MAY can be interpreted as SHALL or MUST. This occurs not only in the formula 'shall and may' in Statutes, but also in other legalistic texts such as official letters:

(121) to require M^{r}. Attorney and M^{r}. Solicitors opinion, as to the several persons who are in custody, what *may* be done with them. (SOMERS: IV, 327)
(what *shall / must* be done with them)

6.5.3. Deontic volition (wish)

The one example in this category has explicit subjunctive morphology, yet it seems to have additional meaning deriving from the modal auxiliary itself. It is an enigma:

(122) ȝyf þou wendest oute of cuntre, Aȝens þy wyuys wyl to be, But she *mow* wone yn þat stede To haue þy fleshly felawrede, ȝyf þou do hyt aȝens her wyl Certeynly þou synnyst ful yl. ȝyf þou hyt do to holde þe chaste wyþ-oute here wyl, þou werchyst waste. For but hyt be for grete resun, ȝyf she mysdo, þou art enchesun. (HS: 68)

(If you travel outside of your home area (? interrupt marital relations)[42] contrary to your wife's will, but she *would remain* in that state of fleshly communion with you, [and] if you do it against her will then you certainly commit a grave sin. If you do it to remain chaste against her will, then you do wrong. Unless it [your choice] be for an important reason, if she [subsequently] does wrong, it is you who are responsible)

The use of MAY here seems to be close to 'want to', not corresponding to any of the senses listed in the OED or MED or by Visser. The use is not like that of MAY for a wish in an independent clause (*may the best man win!*), since in those cases it is the speaker / writer who is publicly expressing his or her desire for the future, while here it is a private desire of a third person.[43]

6.6. Dynamic / Deontic modality

Typically, *one may say* can be interpreted as dynamic 'it is possible for us to say' or deontic 'it is permissible for us to say'.[44] These uncertain cases are marginal uses, representing very few examples in both periods. In some cases it is the clause itself that contains elements of different modality, for example the two adverbials in (123). Here, *soþfastly* goes best with a dynamic interpretation ('is truly able to be called'), while *bi witnes of Scripture* mentions a source of deontic authority:

(123) God & þou ben not two bot one in spirit – in so moche þat þou or anoþer [...] *may* soþfastly, bi witnes of Scripture, be clepid a God (CLOUD: 120)

42 John Donne refers to sexual pleasures as 'country pleasures' in 'The Good Morrow' and Hamlet refers to sexual matters as 'country matters' (III.ii.119).

43 See also the discussion of possible deontic volition uses of MIGHT (§ 6.5.3).

44 Cf. Kytö (1987: 156), who refers to 'problematic' examples of uncertain 'permission' or 'external circumstances', though she finally places such examples in the category of dynamic possibility.

6.7. Bleached uses

6.7.1. Use with 'private verbs'

Of the verbs following MAY, 119 in the M3 corpus are 'private verbs' of sensation or mental state (about 19% of the total), and 61 in the E3 corpus (about 13% of the total), including *see*, *hear*, *feel*, *behold*, *know*, *think*, *conceive*, *imagine*, *seem*, *understand*, *doubt*, *wit*, *forget* etc. Often a dynamic ability modal (CAN in PDE) used with such a 'private verb' has no modal meaning at all (and so has been classed here as having 'bleached meaning'). Here are some examples from M3 and E3:

(124) she Coveiteth every man that she *may* se (CTBATH: 108.C2)

(125) there was a time [...] when there were no Carps in England, as *may* seem to be affirmed by S. Richard Baker, in whose Chronicle you may find these Verses (WALTON: 292)

Elsewhere, the modal verb followed by a private verb can still have a modal function (e.g. dynamic ability). Predictably, with MAY this will be where there is some emphasis on the difficulties involved or on the process of thought or perception, as in the following, where the achievement is emphasized by two intensifiers (*certes*, *wel*) and the process of achievement is focalised by *thus*:

(126) And thus certes *maistow* wel seen how greet is the diligence of nature (BOETHCH: 435.C2)

6.7.2. Periphrastic subjunctive

There is no doubt that the uses of the subjunctive are a part of modality in the broad sense.[45] The closeness of subjunctive and the modality of modal auxiliaries is shown by the fact that OE subjunctive-use is partly replaced by later use of modal verbs (plus adverbs, collocations, intonation etc.).

---

45 For Visser (1963-73: §834) the explicitly marked subjunctive (the 'modally-marked form') is associated with 'a modality of non-fact (wish, imagination, contingency, doubt, diffidence, uncertainty, supposition, potentiality, non-reality, etc.)'.

The authors of this study see the subjunctive as having a broad 'root modality' meaning or a general non-assertive meaning, but do not wish to assign it to any of the modal categories used in the study since they assume any more precise meaning to derive exclusively from the context. The real problem is that modals were used originally as subjunctive substitutes – subjunctivally inflected themselves – in contexts where their own modal meaning 'supported' the modal meaning of the subjunctive, but in some cases the modal auxiliary came to be a mere 'subjunctive substitute' or 'subjunctive equivalent', hence with that very broad context-dependent meaning that we have decided to exclude from our study. Such examples in the present section have been classed as 'periphrastic subjunctive'. The problem is essentially similar to that of MAY and CAN followed by a private verb: it is necessary to distinguish between those cases where the modal auxiliary retains some of its own meaning and those where it has lost it.[46]

6.7.2.1. In object clauses after a verb of petition, desire or emotion

Subjunctive-like MAY is found in noun clauses after verbs of direct petition like *pray, beseech* with first-person subjects and also after other verbs that similarly look forward to a desired future, such as *wish* and *hope* (cf. Visser 1963-73: §1678; OED MAY 8a(c); MED 4 (c); Fischer 1992: 326). There are two cases of a clear subjunctive after the verbs of petition[47] in the M3 corpus:

(127) we <u>prayen</u> [...] that the Statut [...] *mowe* stonde in strengthe (PET3: 197)

and similar examples in E3:

(128) Now God <u>grant</u> that we *may* all know and do in this our day, the things that belong to our peace. (TILLOTS: II: ii 453)

---

46 Kytö (1987: 154), however, does not distinguish between bleached and other uses: she considers all examples of MAY in final clauses and after a verb of volition as dynamic possibility.

47 Besides those illustrated here, the corpus also contains examples with an imperative *suffer that* (allow that), *lend* (grant), *give* (grant), all of which can also be followed by a subjunctive-like MAY with bleached meaning.

There are examples where the modal auxiliary retains its own meaning. The following use seems to be dynamic ability (request for permission being ruled out by the fact that this is the King writing to a Mayor):

(129) we pray you specially þat we *mow* haue it at such tyme and in such wyse as our broþer of Bedford shal moor pleinly declare vnto you on our behalue (HENRY5C/L: 82)
(we ask you especially that we *be able to* have it at such a time)

After verbs of wishing, the only example in the M3 corpus is the following (notice the clearly subjunctive *be* in the coordinated clause):

(130) þe Kyngus wille is, þat [...] þe ordre of Knyghthode, [...] be al brouȝt to nouȝt [...] and þat alle *may* take ensample by þe, her lord aftirward trewely forto serue (BRUT: 227)

More examples are found in the later section:

(131) I hope it *may* be certain and clear enough That there is a God (TILLOTS: II: ii 446)

6.7.2.2. In the protasis of a conditional sentence[48]

The three very similar M3 examples with *but* ('unless') that have explicit subjunctive morphology are a legal formula and have been judged to have a bleached meaning:

(132) it schal be payd, but he *mowe* fynde a verrey encheson (RET: 55)

There are also examples of subjunctive-like use with little modal auxiliary meaning where the morphology is non-distinctive:

(133) If mi fader [...] *Mai* mi fallace oght vnderfind, (CURSOR: 217)
(if my father [...] *discover / discovers* my deception in any way)

48 "Modal verbs in protases [...] sometimes have only pure grammatical function" (Molencki 1999: 212).

In the following, MAY seems to function like the subjunctive-like auxiliaries in PDE as an indicator of a subordinate conditional clause:

(134) Thou seyst men may nat kepe a castel wal, / It *may* so longe assailled been overal. (CTBATH: 108.C2)
(You say that one cannot defend a castle wall, *were it attacked* for so long)

Only one example of MAY in the protasis of a conditional sentence in the E3 period has been classed as bleached periphrastic subjunctive, though it is different from the above:

(135) For so things are always best governed, if that pure Simplicity or Singleness, dwelling in the Divine Nature, *may* produce that unalterable Order of Causes (BOETHPR: 194)

MAY is clearly being used as a translation of the Latin subjunctive mood (*promat*) and its bleached meaning is suggested by the choices of other translators: *scheweth forth* (M3) and *produces* (Watts 1969), with no indication of modality.

6.7.2.3. In clauses with a final meaning

The M3 corpus contains five cases of final clauses (some purpose, some result) with explicitly-subjunctive MAY. Two have a bleached meaning:

(136) Let þer be fair peynture [...] þat þe faymesse of o vertu [...] *mowe* make þe mor brit in schynyngge (AELR3: 33)
(so that the fairness of one virtue [...] *make / may make* you more bright)

Other cases, with non-distinctive morphology, are found both in M3 and E3:

(137) Lauerd, þu do vs sua at liue, þat we *may* <u>deliuir</u> vs of al vre fautes (BENEDME: 12)

(138) let the Scion be six inches long with several buds that they *may* <u>shoot</u> forth many branches (LANGF: 40)

A common construction is that of 'Verb of petition + object / non-finite object clause + final clause' where MAY often has a bleached meaning:

(139) lauerd gif us sua meke at be, þat we *may* halde ure ordir (BENEDME: 10)

Relative clauses with a final meaning resemble purpose clauses[49] and can be associated with similarly bleached uses of MAY. A relatively clear M3 example is the following:

(140) Let faire lynnene towayles ligge vppon þyn awter [...]; þe whiche for here whitnesse and clennesse *mowe* signefie and schewe to þe þe whitnesse of chastete and simplenesse (AELR3: 34) (which signify / aimed at signifying)

There are four cases in the E3 corpus:

(141) whilst I in order weave together my Reasons, which *may* tend to the Solution of thy Doubts (BOETHPR: 191)

(142) whether there may be any one amongst them which *may* compleat the Substance of it (BOETHPR: 138)

Here, *may compleat* corresponds to a present subjunctive in both the Latin ("aliquid quod… compleat") and the M3 translation ("swich that it acomplise").

6.7.2.4. In relative clauses after an indefinite relative pronoun or antecedent subject

In legal texts, a typical formula is 'any / all x that may y', where the modal auxiliary has a bleached meaning:

(143) any Person that *may* be otherwise injured by the enlargeing of the said High-ways (STAT7: VII, 210)

Here, the legal draftsman is not interested in any kind of possibility but in a clear category: 'anyone who *is* otherwise injured'. An

49 E.g. *considerations that may / might / should / will put your mind at rest* (= 'aimed at putting your mind to rest'); *an act that may / might / could frighten the inhabitants* (= 'that might have the result of frightening').

apparently related use is the following, where 'the ability to be suitable' is taken to be identical to 'to be suitable':

(144) set the minde right, that in all occasions it may be disposed to doe noething but what *may* be suitable to the dignity and exellency of a rationall creature (LOCKE: 49)

6.7.2.5. In temporal clauses (with future orientation)

An apparent case of MAY used as a subjunctive substitute in a temporal clause is found in the following:

(145) þei [...] gon be see & be londe .xj. monethes or .xij. or more sumtyme or þei *may* come to the yle of Cathay (MAND: 140)

We know that OE *ǣr* "prefers the subjunctive" (Mitchell / Robinson 1964/1986: §174) and this seems to be a ME preference for a periphrastic subjunctive in the same syntactic context. The justification for this marking of 'unreality' would be that the time in the subordinate clause does not yet exist from the point-of-view of the earlier time in the main clause.[50] A confirmation of the use of a subjunctive-like MAY after *ere* comes from the following:

(146) So hid þai sines foul and rogh, Als stinkand cors es vnder throgh, Or þai *may* mene men sins sertaine Ðat beres þe saule to endles paine. (NHOM: III.135)
(They hide foul sins like a stinking corpse underneath sooner than mention[51] certain wicked sins that bear the soul to endless pain)

6.7.2.6. Subjunctive-like uses in independent clauses

Main-clause MAY with quasi-subjunctive use is found in E3 used to translate a Latin subjunctive (*coherceat*):

(147) for this Order, by its own Unchangeableness and Constancy, *may* restrain those things which in their Nature are mutable (BOETHPR: 194)

---

50 Cf. Shakespeare, *Romeo & Juliet* I.2.iii.10-11: "Let two more summers wither in their pride / Ere we *may* think her ripe to be a bride". Fischer (1992: 356) says that a subjunctive in a ME temporal clause can indicate uncertainty, a non-fact or a prospective event.

51 OED MEAN v 6a.

or to express a wish (as in PDE *may the best man win!*):

(148) trust us together this once; and if I don't shew my Breeding from the head to the foot of me, *may* I be twice Married, and die a Maid (VANBR: I, 61)

or in a polite formula:

(149) *May* it please yr Ma^{ty} (CAPEL: 88)

The following M3 example is problematic:

(150) þus *may* þis tretice, with þe sentence, Pryk and stirre a mans conscience, And til mekenes and luf and drede it dryfe (PRICK: 257)

We have classed this as periphrastic subjunctive used for an exclamatory wish with some reserves: (i) Visser has only three pre-16th century quotes and says it is "extremely rare" before then, (ii) the didactic texts in the M3 corpus often refer (using MAY) to the future reception of the text with an apparently neutral predictive meaning (see § 6.2.3.2) and the quotation above could be an example of this usage. The following E3 example has Subject-Verb ordering, but seems a more certain example:

(151) he was one of them that rifled and plunder'd my House [...] and if I should not be convicted, he and the rest of them *may* be call'd to account for what they did, for they ought not to have meddled with my Goods (LISLE: IV, 123.C1)

Lady Alice Lisle, defending herself against the accusation of treason (therefore in no position to give an order), seems to be using a periphrastic subjunctive form to express a wish: '[I pray that] the rest of them (may) be called to account', 'let the rest of them be called to account'.

6.7.2.7. May be able

The E3 corpus contains five interesting examples of *may be able*, all of which seem to be periphrastic subjunctives (the need to add *be able* therefore supports the idea of the bleached meaning of MAY in these cases). Two are in a result clause, one in a purpose clause, a fourth in a relative clause with indefinite subject, and the last in a noun clause corresponding to a subjunctive in the original Latin:

(152) the Masters Chaire should be so raised at the upper end of the Schoole, as that he *may* be able to have every Scholar in his eye (HOOLE: 224)

(153) But let us grant, that it is possible that some one *may* be able to distinguish betwixt the Good and the Bad (BOETHPR: 195)
(Boethius 4P6: 26 concedamus ut aliquis *possit* [pres. subj.] bonos malosque discernere).

7. Concluding remarks

MAY declines in frequency between M3 and E3 and shows a tendency to concentrate in certain text types, especially formal texts less influenced by the spoken language. Lexical-verb uses can still be seen in M3 in scattered instances: a few gerunds, infinitives, possible residual uses with the meaning 'to have the power to', and a single negative interrogative sentence with the negative particle after the subject.

Dynamic MAY declines significantly between the two periods, especially dynamic possibility use in texts with interactional features, while dynamic MAY in negative clauses virtually disappears. Epistemic MAY, rare in M3, becomes a more important (though still minority) use in E3 (associated especially with Science and Letters), when its PDE association with inanimate subject and stative verb also appears more clearly. Deontic MAY is found especially in E3 Law texts. Bleached periphrastic subjunctive use increases between the two periods and is found especially in formal texts (M3 Rules and Documents, E3 Philosophy).

V. Might

The M3 part of the Helsinki Corpus contains 228 tokens of modal MIGHT-forms,[1] including one non-finite past participle ("they wolde [...] haue slayn hym [...], yf they had myght", USK: 29); in the E3 part there are only 142 examples. The frequency of MIGHT thus falls from 12 to 8 per 10,000 words, a decline that is also visible in the use of MIGHT in the parallel Boethius translations: 13 in M3, but only 5 in E3.

1. Spelling variants

84% of all M3 forms have the front vowel /i/, the remainder having a back vowel, /o/ or /u/. These latter are only found in Northern texts, where they are a distinctive form (accounting for 82% of the 44 Northern-text tokens). The front vowel is spelt <y> in 65% of cases and <i> in the remainder. The fricative is represented by <gh> in 51% of cases, by <|> in 38% of cases, and <h> in 11%.

There seems to be little correlation between *-t* and *-te* forms (such as *might* and *mighte*) and any person, singular or plural: 1st person singular tokens split 9:7 between *might* and *mighte* forms (with various spellings of the vowel and fricative); 3rd person plural tokens split 19:16:14 between *-t:-te:-ten*. Only the 3rd person singular shows a preference for *-t* forms (88, against 54 *-te* forms).

The *-en* forms are plural (though only 16 of the total of 60 forms after plural subjects have this distinctive morphology, and none

---

1 Although the MED lists *mot* and *mote* as past forms of MAY, all the examples in the corpus can be interpreted as present forms of MOTE ('may', 'must').

among the Northern texts); the *-est* forms are 2nd person singular (and are found in 4 of the 9 forms following a 2nd person singular subject).[2]

E3 tokens are all *might*-forms, with 3 cases of *thou mightst* and a clearer association (as we have seen for MAY) of *thou* and *-st* morphology than in M3 (there are 5 examples of *thou might* (etc.) in M3, but no such examples in E3).

2. Distribution according to text type

Table 1 shows the distribution of the various forms in the text types included in the M3 corpus. History and non-private Letters show the most frequent use of MIGHT; in contrast, the Science text contains no examples at all and very low frequencies are found in a series of other text types.

In the E3 period it is Biography (with some generic similarity with History, also with above-average E3 scores) and Educational treatises, followed again by non-private Letters, that have the highest frequency of MIGHT. Fiction slips from above- to below-average frequency (a reflection no doubt of the falling frequency of 'narrative past' MIGHT and the adoption in Fiction texts of COULD, cf. Ch. 3 §2) and the reverse trend is seen for Science texts[3] (though this is not due to any contribution from new epistemic uses in this case, see Table 7 below). As for MAY, there is a less even spread over text types in the E3 period: the number of text types with scarce use of the modal (under 10 tokens per 10,000 words) rises from 5 in M3 to 10 in E3.

---

2 The OED (MAY A.4.b) gives only *-st* forms for the 2nd person singular past of MAY and omits to indicate when the *-t(e)* forms spread to this person. In the M3 corpus 5 of the 9 tokens of MIGHT with a 2nd person singular subject end in *-t*, and a search of the OED on CD-ROM gives an example with an earlier date of c1314 (*Guy of Warwick*): "Al bi times þou *mi /t* wende".

3 The change between M3 and E3 from below- to above-average frequencies in Science texts is also found for COULD and WOULD, cf. §2 in Ch. 3 and 11.

	M3	*E3*
HISTORY	24	11
LETTERS NON-PRIVATE	22	12
FICTION	17	5
SERMONS	15	5
PHILOSOPHY	12	6
TRAVELOGUES	2	7
HANDBOOKS	1	6
SCIENCE	0	11
RELIGIOUS TREATISES	16	-
HOMILIES	10	-
DOCUMENTS	10	-
RULES	7	-
BIBLE	3	-
BIOGRAPHIES	-	21
EDUCATIONAL TREATISES	-	14
LETTERS PRIVATE	-	8
DIARIES	-	7
DRAMA	-	6
TRIALS	-	5
LAW	-	3
All texts	12	8

Table 1. Normalized frequencies of MIGHT by text type.

3. Sentence Structure

Table 2 shows an increase between M3 and E3 in the proportion of MIGHT tokens in subclauses (increasing from 74% to 82%),[4] represented in particular by a growth in its use in noun clauses. The

4 PDE MIGHT (Mindt 1995: 114) is much less frequent in subordinate clauses: 44% of all clauses.

same table also shows how MIGHT declines in relative frequency in relative and conditional clauses between the two periods, while it increases significantly in noun clauses (from 19% to 44% of subclauses) and in the main clause of conditional sentences (from 7% to 17% of all tokens).[5]

	MAY				*MIGHT*			
	M3		*E3*		*M3*		*E3*	
clause type	*No.*	*%*	*No.*	*%*	*No.*	*%*	*No.*	*%*
relative	116	31	80	27	53	32	22	19
result/purpose	68	18	83	28	32	19	27	23
noun	47	13	77	26	31	19	52	44
conditional	31	8	10	3	22	13	3	3
cause	31	8	6	2	9	5	1	1
comparison	30	8	21	7	12	7	9	8
other adv. clauses	46	12	20	7	8	4.8	3	3
Total subclauses	*369*	*100*	*297*	*100*	*167*	*100*	*117*	*100*
main cl. of cond. sent.	22	3	24	5	15	7	24	17
Subclauses	369	54	297	62	167	74	117	82
Main clauses	308	46	180	38	61	26	25	18
Total all clauses	*677*	*100*	*477*	*100*	*228*	*100*	*142*	*100*

Table 2. Distribution of MAY and MIGHT forms by clause type (numbers for use in main clauses of conditional sentences expressed as percentage of all tokens).

Word order in M3 is generally SVO, though there is commonly VS inversion after an initial adverbial, and occasionally the verbal complement is clause final:

(1) *Moght* i euer wit me wit him ming Suld he neuer aftur ber cron, I suld him sla (CURSOR: 431)

(2) First þai sal in helle about þam se Mare sorow þan ever in þis werld *mught* be (PRICK: 253)

5 Though we do not know how much of this is due to stylistic evolution: to a general increase in subclauses and in certain types of subclause.

As we saw for MAY, we find long adverbial phrases between the modal and the verbal complement in both periods:

(3) But þe Scottes […] tariede þe Englisshe-men fro day to day, þat þe Kyng *myght* for no maner þing ham fynde in pleyn felde (BRUT: 225)

(4) He *my /t* no lenger for sorow stande, but | ede home ful sore gretand (HS: 186)

(5) Then I guessd that [...] he *might* in time by a constant application bring it to be habituall (LOCKE: 46)

(6) a very acute and scholastical man [...] *might* by the very same way of Reasoning conclude (TILLOTS: II: ii 445)

Table 3 shows how the incidence of MIGHT in declarative negative clauses falls dramatically from 29% of occurrences in M3 to 6% in E3 texts.[6] It is probable that dynamic MIGHT in negative contexts declined in favour of dynamic COULD (cf. Ch. 3 §3). Although no less than 95% of the 65 declarative negative cases of M3 MIGHT have been classified as dynamic modality, only one of the 8 cases in E3 has been so classified, the others being classed as epistemic or as periphrastic subjunctive.

	M3		*E3*	
clause type	*No.*	*%*	*No.*	*%*
declar + affirm	158	69	130	92
declar + neg	65	29	8	6
interrog + affirm	5	2	1	1
interrog + neg	0	0	3	2
Total	228	100	142	100

Table 3. Distribution of MAY and MIGHT forms by declarative/interrogative and affirmative/negative clause type (absolute numbers and percentages).

An interesting pair of E3 examples suggest a complementary distribution of negative-context COULD and affirmative MIGHT:

6 Mindt (1995: 113) found MIGHT in negative contexts in 9% of cases in his PDE corpus study.

(7) And I said att once hearinge [...] I coulde not aunswer: but if they woulde lett mee see it [the Indictment] [...] I *might* aunswer (FOX: 83)

(8) he acted his part so naturally, that even those who were in the secret [...], could perceive nothing by which he *might* be discovered (BURNETROC: 28)

The typical subject is animate in both periods: 76% of cases in M3; 59% in E3.[7] The proportion of inanimate subjects therefore increases from 24% in M3 to 41% in E3, some of this represented by the subjects of the increasingly-frequent epistemic MIGHT (37% of inanimate subjects in E3 are associated with epistemic modality). 'Existential subjects' (*it* and *there*) are infrequent (1% and 4% of tokens in the two periods).

As far as text types are concerned, and as with MAY, non-private Letters, Philosophy and Handbooks (and the similar Educational treatises) in both periods have a higher-than-average proportion of inanimate subjects with MIGHT.

4. Verb phrase structure

4.1. Verb complementation

MIGHT is followed by the bare infinitive in 79% of cases in the M3 corpus, though only in 65% of cases in E3, when we find larger numbers of passive infinitives (increasing from 11% in M3 to 20% of cases in E3)[8] and perfect infinitives (4% in M3, 11% in E3). There are a few other types: perfect passive infinitives (numbering 2 in M3, 6 in E3), progressive infinitive (1 example in E3). Ellipted (or zero) complementation is found in the M3 texts in 14 cases (6%), in E3 in 6

7 The latter is closer to the 62% of cases in Mindt's PDE corpus (Mindt 1995: 113).

8 In Mindt's PDE corpus, the frequency of the bare infinitive after MIGHT is 70%, about the same as in the E3 texts; the perfect infinitive is more frequent than in the E3 texts (17%), and the passive infinitive much less frequent (included in the small group of 'others').

cases (4%), slightly more frequently than in the case of MAY (4% in M3 and 1% in E3).

In M3, there are two cases of a perfect infinitive not used in a counterfactual statement:

(9) Before er man synned, *mi /t* reson haue done al þis by kynde (CLOUD: 116)

(10) byfore hene of the persones that weren [...] Commissioners vp on myn enditement [...]: I *myghte* not haue ben remedied ne myne neyghebores nother so sone at that tyme lyk as we oughten to haue ben of right: and that was for cause of meyntenance that was a | eyns vs and | it is (PET3: 198)

The other 8 perfect infinitives in M3 are all counterfactuals and correspond to perfect infinitives in PDE; the 10 E3 examples of impossible conditions all conform to PDE usage:

(11) If Mr. John Andrews had been in Town [...], something considerable *might* have been don with Mr Billop (HOXINDEN: 275)

4.2. Combination with verbs

The most common verbs following both M3 and E3 MIGHT are *be* (excluding *be* in the passive infinitive) and *do* (about 7% each of MIGHT complementation in both periods). The next most frequent verbs are *have* and *see* (about 5% and 4% of verb complementation in both periods). About 40% of E3 cases of *be* are associated with epistemic modality.

As with MAY, the dynamic / stative classification of the verb complementation shows a clear tendency for deontic and dynamic modality to be associated with dynamic verbs (60% or more for both categories in both periods), and a less marked tendency for epistemic modality to be associated with stative verbs (stative verbs represent 27% of verbal complements after MIGHT in M3 but 31% of cases after epistemic MIGHT; in E3, stative verbs represent 31% of verbal complements, but 47% of cases after epistemic MIGHT).

Table 4 shows the tendency in both periods for deontic and dynamic MIGHT to combine with animate subject and a dynamic verbal complement (cf. the top two lines of the table), and for epistemic modality (third line of the table) to combine with inanimate subject and stative verb, with this pattern becoming clearer (partly due to more examples of non-dynamic modality) in the later period. The epistemic percentages associated with the inanimate-stative pattern are not high but are clearly higher than average for all tokens of MIGHT (bottom line of table). There is a general increase of the inanimate-stative pattern in E3 (from 8 to 15% of cases).

	M3: %		*E3: %*	
subject	*anim.*	*inan.*	*anim.*	*inan.*
verb comp	*dyn.*	*stat.*	*dyn.*	*stat.*
Deontic	(40)	(0)	*100*	0
Dynamic	*60*	5	*43*	14
Epistemic	(15)	(0)	19	*28*
whole sub-corpus	49	8	40	15

Table 4. Correlation of main modality types of MAY with type of subject and type of verbal complement, (above average percentages in italics; percentages referring to absolute numbers of 4 or less in brackets).

Here are a couple of the 10 examples of the inanimate-stative pattern with epistemic MIGHT from the E3 period:

(12) I hope you will pardon my endeavour to rectify any mistake which *might* remaine (OSBOURNE: 47)

(13) SULL: This is a languishing Hour, Sister.
DOR.: And *might* prove a Critical Minute, if the pretty Fellow were here.
(FARQUHAR: 58)

5. Time reference

As for MAY, future reference for MIGHT increases between the two periods (40% to 61%), possibly associated with the growth of epistemic modality. Also in a similar way to MAY, timeless reference falls (from 14% to 8% of cases).

MIGHT is used (1 example in M3, 21 in E3) as a back-shifted tense in representations of past speech or thought, with present, future or timeless reference, as in the three following examples:

(14) And seide hou thanne wel sche wiste / That sche his wordes *mihte* triste (GOWER: II, 221)

(15) I told him [...] he *might* come upon Tuesday in the Evening (LISLE: IV, 123.C1)

(16) he thought a king who *might* be checked [...] was but a king in name (BURNETCHA: 1, I, 167)

MIGHT is also found in the subclause after superordinate clauses with a past-tense verb referring less directly to speech or thought (with less guarantee of the closeness of the subclause words to the actual words used), again with varying future, present or timeless reference:

(17) he desired me to call the Person to him, that he *might* ask him forgiveness (BURNETROC: 154)

(18) I knew an Apricock graffed in the cleft. as likely as *might* be to grow, but failed (LANGF: 35)

MIGHT (like all the past-tense modal verbs) is associated with real (or factual) and unreal (or hypothetical) uses: the former is found in narration and reports of past speech, while the latter (corresponding to a vague 'modality of non-fact'[9] that is not captured in our main categories) is found in two main syntactic environments: (i) in the main clause (apodosis) of an unreal conditional sentence (counterfactual or merely hypothetical) and in derived uses: with only an implied conditional clause, or with a pragmatic 'tentative' meaning, associated with only a vague conditionality; (ii) in an unreal conditional clause and in other subclauses where a 'hypothetical past tense' ('modal past', 'past subjunctive') is required or possible. In this last case, the modal meaning distinguished by our categories may be very weak, and numerous examples have been assigned to our category of (bleached) periphrastic subjunctive.

---

9 An imagined possibility, a state of affairs not presented as actually possible (James 1986: Ch. 3)

In non-past contexts, MIGHT always has a hypothetical meaning. Here are some hypothetical uses in main clauses with implied conditional clauses or with a more independent 'tentative' use (where the conditional clause is less easy to supply):

(19) And other folk dreden more than thei oughten the whiche thei *myghte* wel beren (BOETHCH: 453.C2)

(20) I am sure the regulation of these defects *might* be easily mended (WALTON: 213)

(21) wher-fore we preye yow yf we *myght* haue the kynges writ to go to a Newe eleccion (USK: 28)

(22) Much more *might* be said [...] but it *might* rather perplex than satisfie you (WALTON: 296)

A past context, on the other hand, can be associated with either real or hypothetical MIGHT, though the distinction is formally neutralized, so that the following:

(23) this Man came to me from Mr. Hicks to know if he *might* be receiv'd at my House (USK: 28)

could correspond to a present-context 'he wants to know if he *may* be received' or a tentative 'if he *might* be received'. In these cases we have classified uses as real unless there are other contextual markers of tentativeness.

Factual narrative MIGHT in main clauses and past-tense context falls from 41 examples (8% of occurrences) in M3 (e.g. example 24) to only one in E3 (example 25):

(24) And whan he rood, men *myghte* his brydel heere (CTPROL: 26.C1)

(25) sailing by Trumbay. where we receive Custom, we *might* see a comely Church and Aldea. At Noon we reached Tanaw (FRYER: I,190)

However, factual MIGHT in 'reported speech' subclauses, found in only one case in M3, is found in 21 cases in E3.

6. Type of modality

Table 5 shows the decline (but not the disappearance) of dynamic uses of MIGHT, which accounts for 79% of cases in M3, 49% in E3,[10] due in part to the virtual disappearance of dynamic MIGHT in negative clauses in E3 (as we have already seen in §3), in part to the collapse of dynamic ability MIGHT from 36% of cases in M3 to a single (uncertain) example in the later period, undoubtedly to the benefit of expanding COULD: dynamic MIGHT in general has a normalized frequency of 10 in M3 falling to 5 in E3, in neat specular contrast with dynamic COULD which goes from 2 per 10,000 words in M3 to 11 in E3.[11]

Other uses show a complementary rise in percentage of total uses: epistemic (from 6% to 25% of cases), deontic (a relatively modest increase from 3% to 7%), and the uses we have classed as periphrastic subjunctive (from 6% to 14%).

Table 6 shows the distribution of M3 modal meanings for MIGHT by text type. The ranking in terms of increasing dynamic modal uses shows that the most 'conservative' texts (at the bottom of the table) are Homilies, Bible translations, Fiction, History and Religious treatises. Text types with a lower than average proportion of dynamic MIGHT (at the top of the table) also use the modal with epistemic and periphrastic subjunctive meanings (though the absolute number of tokens is small in these cases).

In the E3 sub-corpus (Table 7) there are now some text types with substantial numbers of tokens for non-dynamic meanings and some text types where non-dynamic uses of MIGHT actually predominate: Trial transcripts (where MIGHT is deontic in 71% of cases), History and private Letters (where epistemic meanings represent about half the uses).

---

10 The M3 Boethius translation has 8 examples of dynamic MIGHT, which correspond to only 1 MIGHT and 1 MAY in the E3 translation, while 4 of them become CAN in E3.

11 Cf. Ch. 2, Table 4. In contrast with MAY, this fall in dynamic MIGHT is not associated with texts identified by the Helsinki Corpus as having interactional features: they show only a slight decline from 11 to 9 tokens per 10,000 words, while such use in the other texts declines from 10 to 5.

Modal cat.	*Meaning*	*M3 No.*	*o/ooo*	*%*	*E3 No.*	*o/ooo*	*%*
dynamic	possibility	90	5	39%	64	4	45%
	ability	83	5	36%	1	0.1	1%
	prediction	6	0.3	3%	4	0.2	3%
	prediction/possibility	2	0.1	1%			
	Total	181	10	79%	69	5	49%
epistemic	possibility	13	1	6%	35	2	25%
deontic	possibility	4	0.2	2%	7	0.4	5%
	necessity	1	0.1	0,4%	2	0.1	1%
	(wish)	1	0.1	0,4%	1	0.1	1%
	Total	6	0.3	3%	10	1	7%
dy/de	poss/permiss	3	0.2	1%	1	0.1	1%
dy/ep	possibility	7	0.4	3%	6	0.4	4%
bleached	with private verb	4	0.2	2%	1	0.1	1%
	periphr. subjunct.	14	1	6%	20	1	14%
	Total	18	1	8%	21	1	15%
Total		228	12	100%	142	8	100%

Table 5. Distribution of MIGHT by modal category and modal meaning.

	dyn	*epist*	*deon*	*mixed*	*pte vb*	*p. subj.*	*TOT*
HANDBOOKS	(50)	(50)					100
DOCUMENTS	63	(19)	(6)	(6)		(6)	100
SERMONS	65	(20)	(10)			(5)	100
LETTERS N-P	73			(9)		(18)	100
PHILOSOPHY	73	(27)					100
RULES	75	(25)					100
REL TREAT	*80*		(2)	(5)	(5)	(8)	100
HISTORY	*83*		(3)	(3)	(2)	*8*	100
FICTION	*88*			(13)			100
BIBLE	*100*						100
HOMILIES	*100*						100
TRAVELOGUES	(100)						100
All texts	*79*	*6*	(3)	(4)	(2)	*6*	100

Table 6. M3: Distribution of modal meanings of MIGHT by text type: occurrences as percentage of total MIGHT-forms in each text type.

	dyn	*epist*	*deont*	*mixed*	*pte vb*	*p. subj.*	*TOT*
FICT		(50)	(33)			(17)	100
TRIAL		(14)	*71*			(14)	100
SERM	(33)	(33)				(33)	100
HIST	(23)	*54*	(8)			(15)	100
LTR PR	(27)	*45*				(27)	100
LTR NP	(29)	(29)		(14)		(29)	100
LAW	(50)		(50)				100
EDU	*63*	(13)		(13)		(13)	100
H/B	(57)	(29)				(14)	100
BIOG	*60*	24		(4)		(12)	100
PHIL	(60)					(40)	100
DRAM	*63*	(25)				(13)	100
SCI	*67*	(17)		(17)			100
TRAV	*71*	(14)		(14)			100
DIARY	*88*			(13)			100
all texts	49	25	7	4	(0.7)	14	100

Table 7. E3: Distribution of modal meanings of MIGHT by text type: occurrences as percentage of total MIGHT-forms in each text type (ranked by increasing frequency of simple dynamic modality, the horizontal dotted line dividing text types with below average frequency of simple dynamic uses from the others; proportions for text types with small totals in brackets; text types with above-average frequencies and substantial numbers in italics).

6.1. Dynamic meanings

6.1.1. Dynamic ability

6.1.1.1. 'To have the power to'

A few uses that seem close to an original non-modal meaning of MIGHT, 'to have the power to', are still found in the M3 period (though they have all been counted as examples of dynamic ability):

(26) i-brend wiþ Grekkische fuyre, þat no water *myȝte* aquenche (TREVISA: VIII, 111)

(27) He *myȝt* no lenger for sorow stande, but ȝede home ful sore gretand (HS: 186)

6.1.1.2. 'to be able to'

More than a third of all M3 MIGHT tokens have been classed as dynamic ability:

(28) Quen þat dauid was armed sua, Forth a fote ne *moght* he ga (CURSOR: 434)

(29) he moste lete passe what he *myȝt* nouȝt take of ful wreche.
(he had to accept what he was unable to fully punish) (TREVISA: VIII, 85)

In complete contrast, in the E3 corpus, the only example found is not a clear case:

(30) It does not seem to have any eye-lids, and therefore perhaps its eyes were so placed, that it *might* the better cleanse them with its fore-legs
(HOOKE: 13, 5, 211)
(so that it *would be able* / so that it *would be possible* for it to clean them)

The interesting M3 collocations like *all that I may* with ellipted verbal complement noted in the previous chapter (§6.2.1.2) are found in equal numbers with MIGHT (9 examples with *all that I might*, 2 examples with *as many as I might*). The *all* (as in the first example below) can be emphasized by *ever*.

(31) And hath assembled him an host In al that evere he *mihte* most
(GOWER: I, 178)

(32) He hydde hys vysege al þat he *myȝt*, Out of knowlych of here syȝt (HS: 191)

(33) enarmyng of as many smale vessels as we *myght* (HENRY5C/L: 75)

6.1.2. Dynamic possibility

The disappearance of dynamic ability MIGHT does not greatly affect the frequency of dynamic possibility uses: 39% of cases in M3 and a similar 45% in E3 (with frequency of these uses falling from 5 to 4 per 10,000 words). We find it in all text types in M3 except the two with the smallest number of tokens (Travelogues and Handbooks):

(34) þe sister giuen was to þe broþer, þe lagh *moght* certayn be non oþer
(it wasn't possible for divine disposition to be otherwise) (CURSOR: 78)

(35) And trewely [...] gladder ne moor confortable tithinges *might* neuer haue come [...] for to satisfie [...] þe feruent desir of your poure lieges (HENRY5C/L: 79)

(36) I wolde selle Londoun, and I *myȝte* fynde a chapman þat myȝte wel paye. (TREVISA: VIII, 89)

One interesting example is the following:

(37) How *myhte* þe feend for schame cumbre men wiþ sich clowtyng?
(How *is it possible* for the devil – I protest – to distress men with such base additions?) (WSERM: I, 357)

Though the OED does not list *how might... for shame* (which seems similar to PDE 'How *could* you!') as a collocation, it contains another example among its citations:[12]

(38) How *might* ye for shame pray the pope undo that the Holy Ghost bit (Pol. Poems 1401)
(*Aren't you ashamed* to pray / How on earth *could* you pray the Pope)

In E3 dynamic possibility MIGHT is found in all text types except Trial transcripts and Fiction:

(39) but we had no Horse in the way on Suffolke side, otherwise we *might* have galled their Foot (PEPYS: VIII, 317)

(40) hee was askeinge Will Warwicke [...] how one *might* know ye Scriptures (FOX: 156)

(41) hopeing you *might* have gote away before an answer could arrive you, I forbore answering it (RHADDSR: 44-5)

6.1.3. Dynamic prediction

Six M3 examples in final clauses have been classed as neutral prediction (3 in final clauses), any 'possibility' meaning being judged to be bleached by the context (one generally does something in order that something else *will* happen, not in order that it *can* happen):

---

12 Also a similar "How *might* Robert Holonde fynde in his hert me to bitraye [...]?" (OED, Brut c1400)

(42) Gude werkes gladly we suld bigin, Þat vnto þat welth *might* vs win (NHOM: II, 206)

(43) And preide him [...] / That he hire holde covenant / So forth of al the remenant, / That sche *may* thurgh his ordinance / Toward the god do such plesance, / That sche wakende *myhte* him kepe / In such wise as sche mette aslepe (GOWER: II, 222)
(And begged him that he keep his promise concerning the rest so truly, in order that she *give* such pleasure to the god that as a result she *would welcome* him awake in the same way as she met him asleep)

Two examples have been classed as uncertain prediction / possibility:

(44) For þaire entent was for to be On hils whare God þaire werkis *might* se
(For their aim was to be on hills where God *could* / *would* see their deeds) (NHOM: II, 82)

In the E3 corpus only two examples have been classified as neutral prediction and none as mixed:

(45) that Licence of doing Evil, which thou prayedst *might* soon end (BOETHPR: 181)[13]

6.2. Epistemic meanings

6.2.1. Possibility

MIGHT seems to have had a longer association with epistemic meanings than MAY: its use with an (originally) implied conditional clause, with various meanings (including counterfactual dynamic and counterfactual epistemic), dates from the OE period, before the year 1000 (Visser 1963-73 §1672, 1673; OED: MAY 6b, 6c). In contrast, the earliest occurrences of epistemic MAY go back no further than 1200 (1205 for both Visser and the OED). In addition, final clauses in OE can refer to actual result or an eventuality (which will tend to be subjectively-viewed) and MIGHT lends itself to use as a metaphorically remote reference to indicate the latter.

---

13 The Latin is *cito finiri precabaris* 'you prayed to be finished quickly'.

In our corpus, epistemic MIGHT is slightly more frequent than epistemic MAY: 6% of cases in M3, compared with 3% for MAY; 25% in E3, against 17% for MAY. Epistemic uses may have spread especially where MIGHT has a non-narrative-past meaning, since, in most cases, any original objective possibility can easily be reinterpreted as subjective if the possibility is imaginary (the step from an imaginary *objective* possibility to an imaginary *subjective* possibility is a short one, since the foregrounding of imagination suggests a subjective view).

There is, however, no one-to-one relationship between hypothetical meaning and epistemic modality, its combination with dynamic modality being only slightly less frequent, as in the following example, where we have an epistemic frame ('I am sure (that)'), reinforced by the tentative form of the modal, which coexists with a dynamic possibility meaning:

(46) I am sure the regulation of these defects *might* be easily mended (WALTON: 213)

Unlike MAY, we have found no examples of MIGHT in non-past contexts for tentative explanations or to respectfully relativize a statement or request.

6.2.1.1. Harmonic verbal complement: reference to private events

Both parts of the corpus have one example similar to those with MAY referring to the reception of the text where hypothetical MIGHT rather than MAY is possibly chosen because the statement is denied:

(47) Ne this ne seie I nat now for that any man *myghte* thinke that the maneris of schrewes ben coriged and chastised by vengeaunce (BOETHCH: 447.C1)

(48) To excuse Austin of this bloodshed, lest some *might* think it his revengeful policy, Beda writes that [...] (MILTON: X, 149)

6.2.1.2. Harmonic verbal complement: reference to eventualities

The naturalness of an epistemic interpretation of fugitive eventualities has already been noted in the parallel chapter on MAY (§6.3.1.2). In the M3 sub-corpus, epistemic MIGHT is followed by a verb like *happen* in 3 cases, all of them in a non-past context where the hypothetical meaning further encourages a subjective interpretation:

(49) grete meschiefs that *mighten* by swiche wrongful cleymes: falle and turne to gret preiudice to the kyng (PET3: 24)

(50) But Crist denyeþ þis to hem for harm þat *myhte* come (WSERM: I, 375)

(51) we wile þat [...] þe maystres to non of hem, as it *miȝte* falle in cas for mede or be senguler profit, falle in affinite (RET: 57)

Strangely, these verbs occur less in the E3 sub-corpus: only 2 examples with MAY and none with MIGHT.

6.2.1.3. Harmonic matrix clause (I thought that etc.)

Especially in E3, epistemic MIGHT is also found in a subordinate clause in a past context and dependent on a matrix clause like *I thought that, I suspected that*, *it was possible that* and *I didn't know but that* etc.:

(52) I thought y[e] want of it *might* bee prejudicial (PHENRY: 341)

(53) I turn'd it into a Complemental Raillery, as suspecting there *might* be some trick in it (BOYLE: 27)

(54) among so many particulars he did not know but there *might* be some truth (BURNETCHA: 1, II, 158)

(55) L. C. J.: But you Blockhead, I ask you whether you did see any body else?
DUNNE: I do not know but I *might* see Goodman Carpenter
(LISLE: IV, 113.C2)

This last example could be glossed 'I think I saw Goodman Carpenter' (with a bleached MIGHT), but perhaps the evasive witness has succeeded in creating an utterance of unstable meaning, using *might see* both as periphrastic past and as a way to reinforce the epistemic meaning of the matrix verb: 'I think that it is possible that I see / saw Goodman Carpenter'.

6.2.1.4. Reference to unknowable future time

The use of MIGHT in the following non-past contexts with future reference adds a tentative (hence potentially subject-foregrounding) meaning:[14]

(56) alle the conclusions that han be founde, or ellys possibly *might* be founde in so noble an instrument as is an Astrelabie (ASTR: 662.C1)

(57) my Brother Richard should negociate the busines [...] and try what *might* be done that way (HOXINDEN: 280)

These two examples are both contained in relative clauses where the difference between dynamic and epistemic possibility is difficult to test[15] – indeed, this might be an indication that semantic differences could be neutralized in this type of context which might therefore provide a potential terrain for change.

6.2.1.5. In a concessive clause

There is one example in E3 of a reported-speech use of MIGHT in a concessive clause of the *though...yet* type, here with the epistemic meaning reinforced by *perhaps*:

(58) I told him, That [...] though perhaps the freedom formerly between us, *might* have excused it with those to whom it was known; yet it might have the appearance of so much Vanity, to such as were strangers to it
(BURNETROC: 136)

The concession of an imaginary possibility (together with the use of *perhaps*) places the statement in the realm of personal opinion.

---

14 In contrast with MAY, epistemic and dynamic examples with MIGHT referred to future states of affairs with equal frequency (63%, 64%).

15 The paraphrase test 'It is possible for...' (dynamic) and 'It is possible that ...' (epistemic) does not work for examples in relative clauses.

6.2.1.6. With an indefinite subject

An indefinite subject combined with future reference concerns 'virtual reality' and is associated with epistemic MIGHT in several cases in both periods:

(59) "I se nat," quod I, "wherfore that men *myghten* discorden in this." (BOETHCH: 434.C1)

(60) I hope you will pardon my endeavour to rectify any mistake which *might* remaine (OSBORNE: 47)

6.2.1.7. Uncertainty conveyed by an adverbial

In unexpected contrast with MAY, both M3 and E3 show only sporadic association of epistemic MIGHT with harmonic adverbials: 4 cases in M3 (with *rather*, *possibly*, *lightly* and *in cas*), 2 in E3 (with *rather* and *probably*):

(61) considering how such worthy persones [...], thurgh such falsnes in tyme comyng *myght* lightly and causeles renne in sclaundre (JUDG: 95)

(62) which constriction I was apt to thinke *might* probably be continued on in the guts (LOCKE: 46)

Perhaps MIGHT came with a built-in epistemic appropriateness in non-past contexts, so did not require the support of an adverbial as much as MAY did. In the following example, the epistemic adverb *possibly* in the first part of the sentence apparently does not need to be repeated in the parallel second part with MIGHT:

(63) It would but give us a fear of him, and <u>possibly</u> compel us to treat him so as I should be very loth to behold: that is, it *might* occasion his confinement (BEHN: 193)

6.2.1.8. In the apodosis of an unreal conditional sentence

An unreal conditional clause places the main clause in the virtual realm and it is natural to view this as subjective. 9 of the 35 cases of epistemic modality in E3[16] are in the main clause of conditional sentences:

(64) He was confident he should be happy if he died but he feared if he lived he *might* Relapse (BURNETROC: 146)

(65) And I was moved to aske ye children [...] if her husband had left any thinge to her for ye assistans of her children: which if shee marryed they *might* suffer losse therein (FOX: 153)

6.3. Dynamic / Epistemic modality

Mixed or unknowable combinations of dynamic and epistemic possibility represent 3 to 4% of cases in both periods:

(66) Of maistres hadde he mo than thries ten [...] able for to helpen al a shire / In any caas that *myghte* falle or happe. (CTPROL: 32.C2)
(able to help in any eventuality that *could* occur / *might possibly* occur)

(67) Þar defaut es of alkyn thyng Of wilk man *mught* haf lykyng (PRICK: 89)
(They lack everything which one *could* desire / *might perhaps* desire)

Following an epistemic matrix verb (*I thought that...*) it is often impossible to decide if the modality of the subclause containing an expression of possibility is epistemic or dynamic – an epistemic frame could be followed by a subclause expressing subjective or objective possibility, the whole with more-or-less the same meaning.

(68) I guessd that if a man [...] would presently solicit nature [...], he *might* in time by a constant application bring it to be habituall (LOCKE: 46)
(I guessed that [...] *it was possible* that he would render it habitual / *it would be possible* for him to render it habitual)

16 Only 2 out of 13 cases in M3, however. MAY is not found with particular frequency in this environment in either period (2 cases in M3, 3 in E3).

6.4. Deontic meanings

6.4.1. Deontic possibility

Although only MAY in a main clause is used for the speech act of granting permission, we have classed as deontic possibility (permission) a series of examples (mainly in E3) of granted or requested permission in reported speech, after a verb like *pray* or *beseech*, or in a narration (i.e. representations of the granting of permission):

(69) I asked her, *might* the Men be entertain'd? She said they *might* (LISLE: IV, 121.C1)

(70) þo ij eldest doughtren [...] hade ordeynede [...] þat he *might* worshipfully gone & ryde whider þat he wolde (BRUT: 18)

(71) Imoinda being his lawful wife [...], 'twas he was the injur'd man, and *might*, if he so pleas'd, take Imoinda back, the breach of the law being on his grandfather's side (BEHN: 160)

6.4.2. Deontic necessity

We have one example in the M3 corpus that has been classed as deontic necessity (weak necessity because of the tentative form in the non-past context), the particular context makes it unlikely that the meaning we are dealing with is a mere recommendation:[17]

(72) God [...] wole not þat men konnen only, but þat men do in deede þeraftur. And þus þe þridde gospel of Iohn *myȝte* be teeld on ȝol day
(And so the third gospel reading of John *might* / *could* / *should* be read on Christmas day) (WSERM: I, 590)

In the E3 corpus there are two examples in reported speech in a past context where *should and might* can be seen as a back-shifted version of legalistic *shall and may* (strong necessity; cf. Ch. 4 §6.5.2.3):

17 Cf. MED MOUEN 7c (a) 'ought (to do sth.), should (do sth.), be obligated, be advised', with examples 1225-1443.

(73) it was enacted [the first Act being ambiguous] That all Persons [...] who shall take the Oath [...] *should and might* bee released [...] in the same manner as Persons being Prisoners *might* have been by the said first mentioned Act (STAT7: VII, 75)

6.4.3. Deontic volition ('wish')

As for MAY, we also have two mysterious cases of MIGHT with an apparently deontic volition meaning, despite the fact that we do not find this among any of meanings in the OED or MED. The first is:

(74) Sua yod he forth, nan *moght* him der, þan he cried vnto þat her
(Then he went out – no one *wanted to* challenge[18] him – then he called out to that army) (CURSOR: 446)

Here the modal could simply be a bleached tense-marker ('no one challenged him'), and this would be supported by the observation of Molencki (2001: 17) that "In the southern manuscripts [of *Cursor Mundi*] *wolde* on many occasions replaces the northern bleached *mihte*". However, Molencki's examples can also be interpreted with a volitionary meaning in our scheme of categories.[19]

The E3 corpus also gives another example where MIGHT seems to mean 'would like to':

(75) up stairs she goes, admiring to the House, that her pretended Husband did not come; desiring to have a little Sack Posset, thinking he *might* eat some after his Journey (PENNY: 157)

This use is perhaps not surprising, when we remember that (i) COULD has the meaning 'to have an inclination to do something' (OED CAN 7), (ii) in German the *mogen* and *möchten*, cognates of MAY and MIGHT, evolve from 'can' to 'wish', (iii) in PDE *I could use* means 'I would like':

18 This is an interpretation dependant on an interpretation of *der* 'dare' as a transitive verb meaning 'to challenge', for which the OED only gives examples from 1580 (DARE II. 3, 4, 5).

19 E.g. Molencki's example (26) "þe man þat him *wald* fight a-gain" and "þe man þat *miht* fight him agayn" in two Northern manuscripts.

(76) "You'd probably like a shower too."Yeah," I answered. "I *could* really *use* one after that heat." (Bank of English: usbooks/09 Ref: <tref id=B9000001447>)[20]

It is likely (despite the silence of the OED) that MAY and MIGHT occasionally had this volitionary meaning too. Indeed the famous lines by Pope (1714):

(77) On her white Breast a sparkling Cross she wore, / Which Jews *might* kiss and Infidels adore ('Rape of the Lock' II: 7-8)

can be seen as gaining its effectiveness from its ambiguous range of meanings (i) 'which it would be *possible* or *permitted* for Jews to kiss', (ii) 'which – from the Jews' point-of-view – there *would be no impediment* to kissing' and (iii) 'which Jews *would like* to kiss'.

6.5. Dynamic / Deontic modality

There are a handful of examples (only one from E3) that have been included in the mixed or unknowable category of dynamic / deontic (uncertainly 'I could' or 'I was permitted'). While all of the M3 examples are in subclauses and in a past context, the sole E3 example (79 below) is in a conditional clause in a non-past context:

(78) þan ben we licnid to Beȝeleel, þe whiche *miȝt* not se þe arke er þe tyme þat he had mad it by his owne trauayle (CLOUD: 128)
(who *was not able / was not permitted* to see the ark)

(79) If therefore I *might* be heard I would advise that (LOCKE: 52)
(if I *had permission* to be heard / if it *were possible* for me to be heard)

6.6. Bleached uses

6.6.1. Use with 'private verbs'

We find parallel examples to those of MAY of bleached MIGHT (in a past context and in subclauses) before a private verb:

---

20 http://www.cobuild.collins.co.uk/form.html#democonc

(80) þai sal in helle about þam se [...] devels ful grym [...], Als men *mught* here me byfor say (PRICK: 253)
(as you *heard* me say before)

(81) A nedder was seitt up apon a tre, þat quen þe stanged men *moght* se þe nedder on þe tre þat hang, þai war all warist o þair stang (CURSOR: 1240)
(so that when the bitten men *saw* the serpent on the tree)

In the context of metatextual reference, while MAY (with the meaning of 'neutral prediction') is used with a private verb to talk about the future reception of the text, MIGHT is used in M3 effectively as a periphrastic past to refer back to past reception:

(82) Now es þe last part of þis buke sped, And alle þe maters þar-in haf I red, þat contenes, als yhe *mught* here, [...] ioyes sere [...] And sere schendshepes of helle (PRICK: 255)
(which includes, as you *heard*, the several joys of heaven and pains of hell)

The one example in E3 is in a main clause, again functioning as a periphrastic past:

(83) sailing by Trumbay. where we receive Custom, we *might* see a comely Church and Aldea. At Noon we reached Tanaw (FRYER: I, 190)

6.6.2. Periphrastic subjunctive

The periphrastic subjunctive (or 'subjunctive equivalent' use) with MIGHT is found in similar contexts (except that the temporal collocation is past) to those for periphrastic subjunctive MAY: in subclauses after verbs of requesting, commanding, wishing, hoping, fearing and believing; also as a 'hypothetical past' in unreal conditional clauses, as well as in concessive, temporal and purpose clauses. The modal, however, may retain its 'modal auxiliary meaning' in all these environments. In a way very similar to MAY, bleached periphrastic subjunctives with MIGHT double (from 7% to 15% of cases) between the two periods, possibly due to stylistic changes and preference for Latinate syntax in the E3 period.

In the corpus analysed there are no examples of bleached subjunctive-like MIGHT in temporal clauses (with future orientation) or in independent clauses.

6.6.2.1. In object clauses after a verb of petition, desire or emotion

We find MIGHT in subclauses after past forms of verbs of petition, desire or emotion (and related nouns in a past context):

(84) He [...] prayed with-alle Þat a drope of calde water *mught* falle Til his tung (PRICK: 84)

(85) I was spoke to, and desired, that Mr. Ireland *might* have the Opportunity of going in my Company down into Staffordshire. which I consented to. (OATES: IV, 75.C1)

(86) Grete merueyle had þey alle, Þat swych a chaunce *myȝt* hym *befalle* (HS: 183)

We also find hypothetical MIGHT in the same clause types but in a non-past context, used instead of MAY to make a request or wish more indirect:

(87) þou here nu mi praier, O þis wreche prisun þat es, þat he *moght haue* forgiunes (CURSOR: 550)

Here (as with similar expressions with MAY, cf. Ch. 4 §6.7.2.7) the bleached nature of the modal seems to be confirmed by the need to reinforce a dynamic meaning by means of the verbal complement *be capable*, though there is just one case in the corpus:

(88) All that I desire is that I *might* be capable of serveing you (EOXINDEN: 332)

6.6.2.2. In the protasis of a conditional sentence

There are five cases of bleached subjunctive MIGHT in M3 conditional clauses, but none in E3, partly due to the decline in use of this type of subclause:

(89) To þat waiour þey graunted alle, To ȝyue hym a ȝyft ȝyf so *myȝt* befalle (they all agreed to that pledge, to give him a gift if it *turn(ed) / might turn / should turn* out so) (HS: 182)

6.6.2.3. In clauses with a final meaning

Five purpose clauses in M3 and thirteen in E3 contain a bleached subjunctive MIGHT, mainly in past contexts (corresponding either to a present-context MAY or MIGHT):

(90) ther was made mochel ordinance [...] to make ful certein the comunes atte that day shulde chese the forseyde John Norhampton to be mair [...], to that entent that al hys ordinances *mighten* be confermed be our lord the kyng in hys statut (USK: 25)

(91) he desired me to call the Person to him, that he *might* ask him forgiveness (BURNETROC: 154)

6.6.2.4. In relative clauses after an indefinite relative pronoun or antecedent subject

The following bleached use seems related to the indefinite antecedent subject:

(92) And of alkyn noyse þat swete *mught* be, Ilkan sal here in þat cite (PRICK: 249)
(And every kind of noise that *is* / *were* sweet, everyone shall hear in that city)

7. A comparison between MAY and MIGHT

MAY (with a normalized frequency of 38 tokens per 10,000 words in M3, 28 in E3) is about three times more frequent than MIGHT in both periods (12 per 10,000 words in M3, 8 in E3); both modals decline in frequency in a very similar way between the two periods.

A comparison between frequencies of MAY and MIGHT in M3 (left side of Table 8) gives us some interesting information: (i) above-average frequencies of both modals are found in Religious treatises, Philosophy, non-private Letters and Fiction; (ii) below-average frequencies in Science, Bible translations, Handbooks, Documents and Travelogues; (iii) we find frequent MAY with less frequent MIGHT in Philosophy, Rules and Homilies, and (iv) the reverse configuration –

frequent MIGHT but infrequent MAY – for narrative-dominated History.

Comparing the frequencies of the two modals in E3 (right-hand side of Table 8), we find: (i) above average frequencies of both modals in Educational treatises, Science and non-private Letters; (ii) below-average frequencies of both in Diaries, Travelogues, Trial transcripts, Fiction and Drama – mostly text types influenced by speech norms of usage;[21] (iii) above-average MAY but below-average MIGHT in Philosophy, Law and Sermons; (iv) below-average MAY and above-average MIGHT in the narrative-based genres of Biography and History.

The same table also shows some interesting overall correspondences within the MAY-MIGHT system: (i) above-average frequencies of both modals in non-private Letters in both periods; (ii) below-average frequencies in Travelogues for both in both periods; (iii) above-average MAY but below average MIGHT in Philosophy texts in M3 and E3; (iv) the converse, below-average MAY but above-average MIGHT in History texts in both periods; (v) relative abandonment between the two periods of both MAY and MIGHT in Fiction; (vi) a contrasting rise in use of both modals in Science texts; (vii) relative infrequency in the use of both modals in Handbooks in both periods, with the puzzling exception of MAY in E3; (vii) both modals show a tendency in E3 for a greater contrast between text types that use the modals often and those that use them infrequently.

Table 2 illustrates the frequency of MAY and MIGHT in different clause types. Features of interest include: (i) the increase in subclause use of both modals between the two periods; (ii) more frequent use of MIGHT than MAY in subclauses in both periods; (iii) the decline in the frequency of both modals in relative and conditional clauses between the two periods; (iv) the increase in the frequency of both modals in result/purpose clauses, and their very great increase in noun clauses; (v) greater use of MIGHT in the apodosis of conditional sentences in the E3 period (17% of uses of MIGHT in the later period).

---

21 Where dynamic CAN has made most progress (cf. Ch. 2 §2).

	M3		*E3*	
	MAY	*MIGHT*	*MAY*	*MIGHT*
PHILOSOPHY	71	12	50	6
LETTERS NON-PRIVATE	46	22	39	12
FICTION	40	17	17	5
TRAVELOGUES	33	2	5	7
SERMONS	28	15	29	5
HANDBOOKS	19	1	79	6
HISTORY	14	24	3	11
SCIENCE	0	0	43	11
RELIGIOUS TREATISES	70	16	-	-
RULES	58	7	-	-
HOMILIES	41	10	-	-
DOCUMENTS	29	10	-	-
BIBLE	16	3	-	-
EDUCATIONAL TREATISES	-	-	64	14
LAW	-	-	31	3
LETTERS PRIVATE	-	-	29	8
DRAMA	-	-	27	6
BIOGRAPHIES	-	-	10	21
TRIALS	-	-	6	5
DIARIES	-	-	3	7
All texts	38	12	28	8

Table 8. Normalized frequency of MAY and MIGHT by text type.

Passive infinitives are found after both modal verbs in about 20% of cases and in both periods, with the exception of MIGHT in M3, where this complementation is rarer (11%). The two modals clearly contrast in the use of the perfect infinitive: rare for MAY (<1% in both periods), quite commonly found with MIGHT (4% of cases in M3, 11% in E3).

Both modals show a similar tendency, in both periods, for deontic and dynamic modality to combine with animate subject and a dynamic verbal complement, and for epistemic modality to combine with inanimate subject and stative verb, with this pattern becoming clearer (partly due to more examples of non-dynamic modality) in the later period. Both modals also show a general increase of the inanimate-stative pattern in E3 (from 11 to 22% of MAY occurrences, from 8 to 15% for MIGHT).

Aspects of modal meaning and the MAY-MIGHT system in the two periods are summarized in Table 9: (i) both modals show a decline in dynamic uses from about 80% of tokens to less than 50%; (ii) MIGHT is more frequently used than MAY for epistemic meanings and this use increases more between the two periods (from 17 to 25% of cases, against a growth from 3 to 6% for MAY), possibly due to a natural – though not inevitable – mutual reinforcement of tentative and epistemic meanings (cf. §6.2.1); (iii) deontic uses increase, with a greater increase for MAY; (iv) the bleached uses (principally periphrastic subjunctive) increase in both cases;[22] (v) dynamic ability uses decline greatly for both modals: from 19% to 6% of tokens for MAY, and a collapse from 36% to 1% for MIGHT; (v) there is also a parallel trend in the decline of MAY in negative clauses from 27% to 4%, and of MIGHT in the same context from 29% to 6%.

	MAY		*MIGHT*	
Modal cat.	*M3*	*E3*	*M3*	*E3*
Dynamic	80%	45%	79%	49%
Epistemic	3%	17%	6%	25%
Deontic	3%	13%	3%	7%
Mixed	5%	4%	4%	5%
Bleached	9%	20%	8%	15%
dyn. abil.	19%	6%	36%	1%
in neg. cl.	27%	4%	29%	6%

Table 9. Modal category meanings and other significant environments for MAY and MIGHT (as percentage of total MAY and MIGHT use in each period).

22 This increase in periphrastic subjunctive uses (from 8 to 16% for MAY, from 6 to 14% for MIGHT) could be related to a stylistic preference for certain types of subclause, though another factor is possibly the erosion of subjunctive morphology (Plank 1984: 358-361).

Table 10 gives us an idea of modal meaning distribution among text types in the MAY-MIGHT system in the M3 period: (i) the most conservative texts (with only dynamic meanings for both modals) are the Bible translations; (ii) the Science text lacks both of the modals; (iii) the 'official' genres of Rules, Documents, non-private Letters all have below-average numbers of dynamic uses for both modals; (iv) some text types seem to have a differing use of MAY and MIGHT (Homilies, Sermons); (v) substantial numbers of non-dynamic uses are only found for MAY, with the exception of periphrastic subjunctive uses for MIGHT in History texts.

	MAY				*MIGHT*			
	% dy	*% ep*	*% de*	*% subj*	*% dy*	*% ep*	*% de*	*% subj*
RULE	48			*48*	75	(25)		
DOC	53	(2)	(7)	*33*	63	(19)	(6)	(6)
HOM	67	(3)		*17*	*100*			
TRAV	67		(17)	(11)	(100)			
LTR NP	78			*22*	73	(9)		(18)
REL TR	*81*	*4*	*4*	2	*80*		(2)	(8)
PHIL	*84*	*5*	(4)	(3)	73	(27)		
FICT	*88*	(2)	(4)	(2)	*88*			
SERM	*89*	(3)	(3)		65	(20)	(10)	(5)
HIST	*91*	(3)		(6)	*83*			*8*
H/B	*94*			(3)	(50)	(50)		
BIBLE	*100*				*100*			
SCI								
All texts	80	3	3	8	79	6	2	7

Table 10. M3: Distribution of principal modal meanings of MAY and MIGHT by text type: percentages of total forms in each text type (ranked by increasing frequency of simple dynamic modality for MAY; proportions for text types with small totals in brackets; text types with above-average frequencies and substantial numbers in italics).

Table 11 gives an idea of the situation in E3: (i) Biography and Educational treatises are relatively conservative texts, with above-average proportions of dynamic meanings for both modals; (ii) more advanced texts, with below-average proportions (or very small numbers) of dynamic uses for both, are Trial transcripts, Law, non-private Letters, Fiction, Philosophy, Sermons and private Letters (a mixture of speech-influenced and more official and formal text types);

(iii) differing uses of MAY and MIGHT (the latter retaining more dynamic uses) are found in Science, Drama, Diaries and Travelogues; (iv) substantial numbers of non-dynamic uses are now in this later period found not only for MAY (Law, Letters, Fiction, Drama, Sermons and Science), but also for MIGHT (Trial transcripts, private Letters and History, the last of which seems to be abandoning narrative MIGHT in favour of epistemic uses in speculation about possible outcomes in the past).

	MAY				*MIGHT*			
	% dy	*% ep*	*% de*	*% subj*	*% dy*	*% ep*	*% de*	*% subj*
TRIAL	(13)	(25)	(25)	(38)		(14)	*71*	(14)
TRAV	(20)	(60)		(20)	*71*	(14)		
LAW	22	(7)	*54*	*17*	(50)		(50)	
LTR NP	30	*30*	(13)	(4)	(29)	(29)		(29)
DIARY	(33)	(33)		(33)	*88*			
FICT	35	(15)	*25*	(15)		(50)	(33)	(17)
PHIL	39	11	(2)	*39*	(60)			(40)
DRAM	41	*26*	*18*	12	*63*	(25)		(13)
SERM	42	*19*	*19*	14	(33)	(33)		(33)
LTR PR	42	*32*	11	(8)	(27)	*45*		(27)
SCI	44	*33*	(4)	(4)	*67*	(17)		
H/B	*53*	12	6	*18*	(57)	(29)		(14)
EDU	*63*	(4)	3	*22*	*63*	(13)		(13)
BIOG	*83*	(8)	(8)		*60*	24		(12)
HIST	(100)				(23)	*54*	(8)	(15)
All texts	45	17	13	16	49	25	7	14

Table 11. E3: Distribution of modal meanings of MAY and MIGHT by text type: percentages of total forms in each text type (ranked by increasing frequency of simple dynamic modality; proportions for text types with small totals in brackets; text types with above-average frequencies and substantial numbers in italics).

VI. Must

Comparing M3 and E3, we observe that the occurrences of MUST almost double between the two periods (from 118 to 226), and more than double in normalized terms (from 6 to 13 per 10,000 words).

1. Spelling variants

MUST, unlike the other English central modals, did not develop present vs. past tense forms (*can/could, may/might, shall/should, will/would*). As is well-known, the present tense form (*mot-*)[1] disappeared in the course of the ME period[2] and the past tense form came to have present and future meanings.[3] The M3 part of the

---

1 PDE MUST comes from the OE verb **motan* (the infinitive form is not attested), which had its origins in the Indo-European root **med-* and showed from the very beginning lack of non-finite forms. In fact, it is generally agreed that **motan*, together with **sculan*, represent the most prototypical member of the future class of modals (cf. Warner 1990: 537 ff). *Mote* belonged to the old class of preterite-present verbs, which derive from Indo-European formations and are well documented in Sanskrit, Greek and Latin (e.g. *oĩda, memini, odi*). In OE the other members of this class were *witen, owen, dowen, unnen, þarf, durren, schal, munen* and *mowen*. As is well known, these verbs soon lost their preterite sense and function (cf. Sweet 1891: 420-421) to acquire the meaning and function of the present connected to the semantic resultative value of the action which was primitively expressed by the preterite (cf. Mitchell 1985 and Mustanoja 1960).

2 According to the literature, in ME the preterite was frequently used with present meaning, and in EModE this usage became fixed – the present surviving only as an archaism, especially in poetry (cf. Spenser's verse: *as fair as fair mote be*).

3 Jespersen (1949) suggests that this use may have arisen from the practice of employing the 'preterite of imagination' *moste* as a present tense. According to Sweet (1891: 423) this shift began with the use of the preterite subjunctive, which was quite indistinguishable from the preterite indicative, to express

Helsinki Corpus includes 14 spelling variants, whose variety shows residual conjugation for the indicative and subjunctive moods.[4] The percentage of traditional present tense forms is still very high. In fact, present indicative forms (*mot, moot, mut, most, must, mustow, moten*) occur 70 times (59%) together with 20 instances (17%) of present subjunctive variants (*mote, moote* and *mute*). Preterite indicative and subjunctive forms (*moste, muste, mosten* and *musten*) amount to 28 (24%). The PDE form *must* occurs twice only in Chaucer, and in one of these the unstressed post-verbal pronoun subject is attached to the verb:

(1) Thou *must* worken in this wise (ASTR: 671)

(2) Thanne *mustow* graunten (BOETHCH: 435.C1)

The most common forms are respectively *mot* (22% of all tokens), *moste* (17%), the only one correlating to almost all subjects, *moot* (14%), *mote* and *most* (9% each) and *mut* (7%). The forms *moot* and *moote* appear only in Chaucer's works, where the widest range of forms is present (11 variants). It must be noted that *musten, mut* and *mute* never appear in Chaucer. Also the *Wycliffite Sermons* show a plurality of 8 forms. The forms *musten* and *mute* appear only in these Sermons, the others being *mot, mut, muste, mote, moten* and *moste*.

---

mild command, so that *thou moste* ('you would be able', 'you might') started to be pragmatically understood as 'you will have to' > 'you must'. Skeat, in his *Etymological Dictionary* (1884, s.v. *must*), suggests that the use of *must* denoting present necessity may be partly due to Scandinavian influence. Swedish *måste*, in fact, is used both as present and past tense. Traugott / Dasher (2002) see the following factors as playing a major role in the development of this modal: a. in the earliest examples, the obligation or epistemic conclusion is the result of a new condition, i.e. present state resulting from some action or condition such as God's or a king's command or will; b. *nedes* is a frequent collocate.

4 ME grammars generally give the following standard paradigm: Present indicative, 1st and 3rd person singular: *mōt / moot*; 2nd singular: *mōst*; plural: *mōten*. Preterite indicative, all persons: *mōste / muste* (the form with the short *u* appearing in the course of 1400 with present value). Present subjunctive, all persons: *mōte*.

Different forms have often been found within the same text. However, they cannot be considered just as free spelling variations, as the following extract from the *English Wycliffite Sermons* shows:[5]

(3) Soþ hit is þat alle þingus *mote*[1] nede come as God haþ ordeyned, and so eche dede of Crist *mut*[2] nede be doon as he dide hyt. And þus, Zif men schulde not sewe Crist her, fore he *muste*[3] neede suffre, noo cristene man schulde sewe Crist in noo þing þat he dyde, for alle þe þingus þat Crist dide *musten*[4] nedly comen as þei cam. And so suche heretykes *musten*[5] nede sewen anticrist and be dampned wiþ hym for defawte of here byleue. And Zif þei seyn þat þis is false, þat alle þingus *mute*[6] þus nedely come, Lord!
(WESERM: 43, I.416)

Truth it is that all things *must*[1] necessarily come as God has ordained, and so each of Christ's deeds *had to*[2] be done necessarily as he did it. And thus, if men should not follow Christ here, because he (and they following him) *would*[3] necessarily suffer, no Christian person would follow Christ in anything that he did, because all the things that Christ did *had to*[4] come necessarily as they did come. And so such heretics *must*[5] necessarily follow antichrist and be damned with him for the lack of their belief. And if they say that this is false, Lord, *let*[6] all things come as they do come.

Mote [1] and *mut* [2] are present forms, the former subjunctive, the latter indicative, expressing universal truths in a present/timeless context. However, in this case, *mut* [2] implies *had to,* i.e. a past tense with future reference. *Muste* [3] and *musten* [4], [5] are past forms. However, while the tentative [3] and the past [4] refer to future time, [5] shows present / timeless reference. The final *mute* [6] is a periphrastic subjunctive with an implied time reference to 'now and forever'.

Concerning variety of forms, the E3 section offers quite a different scenario. Apart from the standardised form *must* (224 out of 226), only *most* survives as a variant in 2 instances, both occurring idiosyncratically in the same private Letter:

(4) In consederation of it yo[u] *most* come and take bands of her and her housban if yo[u] can get thim to give yo[u] bands before it runes to fare. (JPINNEY: 39)

---

5 For a thorough interpretation of this passage see Traugott / Dasher (2002: 136).

(5) But I *most* tell yo^{u} it is so bad heare, yo^{u} cannot besensabell unles yo^{u} ware hare to see and heare. (JPINNEY: 39)

As to subject frequency, the presence of 1st, 3rd and clearly identifiable 2nd person plural subjects remains approximately the same in the two periods, while there is a significant decrease in 3rd person singular subjects (61% vs 37%). The greater percentage of 1st (4% vs. 25%) and 2nd (9% vs. 20%) singular subjects is certainly due to the presence in E3 of more speech-based texts. As to the trait +animacy, there is an increase in E3 of inanimate 3rd person singular subjects (M3 55% vs. E3 66%). This may signal a shift from more objective (expression of God's will, prediction of inevitable facts) to more subjective pragmatic uses (laying obligations, making conclusive judgements) of the modal under examination.[6]

No instances of negative contracted forms are present either in M3 or in E3.

1.1. MUST-forms with adverbial satellites

The original meaning of the ancestor of MUST was 'to find / have room'. As is well-known, the modal sense of granting permission developed from it already at a very early period (cf. Visser 1963-73: 1791). The further shift was fostered by the presence in its semantic environment of adverbs belonging to the semantic field of necessity, which worked as 'invited inferences' (Traugott 1990: 511, Traugott / Dasher 2002: 126-128) to stress both the obligational / deontic and necessity / epistemic meanings of the modal.

In M3 texts 41 instances out of 118 (35%) still occur in combination with 8 morphological variants of an adverb belonging to the semantic field of necessity (*nedes, nede, nedis, nedys, nedly, neede, nedely, nyede*).

---

6 According to Coates (1983: 37), "The strength of any given example of non-epistemic *must* seems to depend on the person of the subject and on the involvement of the speaker (subjectivity). Instances with second person subject tend to be performative and more subjective ('It is obligatory', 'It is imperative') than those with first person subjects, which, in turn, are more subjective than those with third person subjects."

The percentage of necessity adverb collocates shows a significant decrease in E3, where only 15 instances (M3 35% vs E3 7%) occur in combination with adverb satellites such as *needs* (9 times), *necessarily* (4), *of necessity* (2). The comparison between the same text types in the two sub-sections clarifies the relevance of the phenomenon: 17 occurrences out of 30 in the *Wycliffite Sermons* collocate with the adverb of necessity (57%); 13 out of 20 in Chaucer's *Boethius* (65%). In contrast, in E3 Sermons only 2 occurrences out of 12 collocate with *needs* (17%); in Preston's *Boethius* the adverb combines with the modal 7 times out of 29 (24 %). The epistemic adverb *certes* also occurs 4 times in harmonic combination with the modal. The following instance from Chaucer's *Boethius*, uttered by Philosophy herself, can be seen as one of the most modally coloured examples, since the modal form occurs together with *certes* and *nedes* and a verbal complement *be nedy*:

(6) for if so be that ther is a thyng that in ony partie be feblere of power, certes, as in that, it *moot* nedes be nedy of foreyne help. (BOETHCH: 429)

In E3 MUST collocates four times with epistemic adverbs such as *certainly, sure, doubtlesse, without doubt*. The following instance with *always* is further strengthened by the hedge *I am sure:*

(7) The manner of doing it, so unsought for and unexpected, must take, with any good mind, more than the thing itself, and I am sure the sense *must* always last with me. (SOMERS: IV, 329)

2. Distribution according to text type

Table 1 summarises the distribution of MUST in M3. There are no occurrences in 4 text types (Documents, Homilies, Letters and Bible). Minimal distribution is present in Scientific texts, History books and Travelogues. The highest frequency is recorded in the *English Wycliffite* Sermons and in the Philosophical texts by Chaucer; a relatively high frequency is also present in Chaucer's and Gower's Fiction.

Text Type	*No.*	*o/ooo*
SERMONS	30	*22*
PHILOSOPHY	25	*20*
FICTION	23	*16*
RULES	5	*9*
HANDBOOKS	12	6
RELIGIOUS TREATISES	17	5
SCIENCE	1	3
HISTORY	4	2
TRAVELOGUES	1	2
All texts	118	6

Table 1. Distribution of MUST-forms in M3. (Above-average frequency in italics).

In the E3 section, the modal under scrutiny is present in all text types. Table 2 shows that the highest frequency is present in Drama and Philosophy, followed by Fiction, Handbooks, Educational treatises and Letters. The distribution in Sermons is below average.

Text Type	*No.*	*o/ooo*
DRAMA	44	*35*
PHILOSOPHY	29	*33*
FICTION	31	*26*
HANDBOOKS	26	*23*
EDUCATIONAL TREATISES	22	*19*
LETTERS	28	*15*
SERMONS	12	10
SCIENCE	10	9
BIOGRAPHIES	6	5
TRIALS	5	4
DIARIES	5	4
HISTORY	5	4
TRAVELOGUES	2	4
LAW	1	1
All texts	226	13

Table 2. Distribution of MUST-forms in E3. (Above average frequency in italics).

Table 3 shows that, where a comparison between similar text types can be made, normalised figures increase in the E3 texts, except for Sermons. Handbooks and Letters have low frequencies (or no tokens) in M3 but above-average frequencies in E3. Since the highest frequencies occur in E3 Drama, Philosophical texts in dialogue form, Fiction and Handbooks in fictionalized form with dialogues or directed at the reader, we can clearly see that evolving MUST is mainly associated with speech-related texts.

Text Type	*M3*	*E3*
SERMONS	22	10
PHILOSOPHY	20	33
FICTION	16	26
HANDBOOKS	6	23
SCIENCE	3	9
HISTORY	2	4
TRAVELOGUES	2	4
LETTERS	0	15
RULES	9	-
RELIGIOUS TREATISES	5	-
HOMILIES	0	-
DOCUMENTS	0	-
BIBLE	0	-
DRAMA	-	35
EDUCATIONAL TREATISES	-	19
BIOGRAPHIES	-	5
DIARIES	-	4
TRIALS	-	4
LAW	-	1
All texts	6	13

Table 3. Normalized frequencies of MUST by text type.

3. Sentence structure

The presence of MUST in non-assertive contexts increases in the E3 period. This may be due to its wider subjective use in dialogical formats and Letters. No instances of MUST tokens in negative clauses are present in M3 while in E3 they represent 11% of the total occurrences (26 instances). They are mostly found in Fiction, Drama and Letters, but are also present in Science and Sermons, especially with subject *I*. In 20 cases the modal is followed by *not*:

(8) I *must* not forget to take notice of the Globular form into which each of these is most curiously formed (HOOKE: 13.5, 46)

(9) I *must* not trust my own senses in the case (TILLOTS: II, ii.445)

In 3 cases, the prohibition is determined twice by *by no means* and once by *upon noe occasion:*

(10) In these things therefore which are believed able to satisfy our Desires, we *must* by no means seek for Happiness. (BOETHPR: 127)

(11) His Majesty will continue you in the station of his Agent, but you *must* upon noe occasion make use of that character for transacting any business (SPENCER: IV, 315)

The others are interrogative-negative clauses. The number of interrogative clauses is similar (3 in M3, 5 in E3). In assertive contexts, the majority of instances in both periods is in declarative clauses.

In at least 6 M3 instances the MUST variants are periphrastic present subjunctive clearly expressing desire or wish:

(12) With wild thonder-dynt and firy levene / *moote* thy welke nekke be tobroke! (CTBATH: 108.C2)

The majority of instances of MUST in M3 occurs in main clauses (77%), almost half of them being syndetic co-ordinate clauses of the copulative, adversative, conclusive and disjunctive types. The widespread use of co-ordinating conjunctions in all text types, especially in Sermons, such as *and, but, for, then, therefore, thus, so, or ellis*, seems due to a preference in ME texts for paratactic devices to signal the beginning of a main clause. In E3 the percentage of occurrences in main clauses of the same types is unchanged. The subordinate clauses containing MUST are of a relatively wide range of types, with a slight preference in both sections for nominal and relative clauses.

4. Verb phrase structure

No examples of non-modal MUST, of MUST followed by another modal or of MUST with an understood verb of motion,[7] have been found in the texts under examination.

	M3	*E3*
bare infinitive	83%	80%
passive infinitive	14%	15%
perfect infinitive	-	2%
Ø	3%	3%
Total	100%	100%

Table 4. Verbal complementation after MUST.[8]

The overwhelming majority of occurrences are followed by a bare infinitive in both sub-corpora (M3 83 % vs. E3 80%). The percentage of passive infinitives is almost the same (M3 14% vs. E3 15%). The cases of MUST followed by a perfect infinitive[9] indicate the trend towards its modern epistemic use:

---

7 Visser (1963-73: 1791 n.1) gives two ME examples of this type. Both belong to Chaucer's works: c1384, House of F. 1049, 'For all *mot* out, other late or rathe'; c1386, C.T. B 281, 'Allas! Unto the Barbre nacioun I *mooste* anoon'.

8 One token in M3 – the second *musten* in example (3) – governs both a bare and a passive infinitive and so has been counted twice.

9 According to Traugott / Dasher (2002: 137): "By the fifteenth century examples of *must* begin to appear in Modal - *have* - V Past Participle

(13) Sure this Addition of Quality, *must* have so improv'd this Coxcomb, he can't but be very good Company for a quarter of an Hour (VANBR: I, 35)

Two of the three cases of ellipsis of the main verb in the M3 subcorpus occur in contexts where meter or rhyme seem to impose phonological constraints,[10] whereas the 7 cases of ellipsis in E3 belong to dialogues in Fiction and Drama:

(14) And thus was al the game schent; / She soffreth him as sche *mot* nede (GOWER: II, 72)

(15) Your Lips *must* seal the Promise. They *must*, they *must* (FARQUHAR: 59)

Only in one case is the MUST-form followed by the periphrastic structure *be* + *ing*, a structure that was still rare in ME:

(16) For alle þes foure newe ordris *moten* be lernyng al þer lif of þe rewle þat þei han foundon. (WESERM: 27, I. 588)

5. Time reference

Although past forms are frequently used in M3, no cases of past reference have been found. The modal under examination occurs in narrative reports with future reference especially in the E3 period:[11]

---

constructions. *Have-* Past Participle is the marker of past tense after a modal (as in MdE *She must have left*), and therefore examples of this construction unambiguously demonstrate that *most-* was no longer understood as marked for past tense. Most examples of *must have* in ME are in counterfactual conditionals [...]; in EModE they begin to be found in other contexts, especially when *must* is epistemic".

10 The third occurs in *De Institutione Inclusarum*. See example (20) below.

11 The use of deontic MUST as a past tense in indirect speech, though often *had to* is used instead, has survived in PDE: 'You *must* be in by ten tonight' his parents told him / His parents told him that he *must* / *had to* be in by ten that night. According to Jacobsson (1979: 304 ff. and 1994: 171), independent past-tense deontic *must* (i.e. past-tense *must* outside reported speech) still exists in examples such as: 'For them life had stopped, though they must go on living'.

(17) but withal I told him, I *must* go away the (Monday) following
(LISLE: IV, 123.C1)

(18) how the wench cried when she told her that she *must* come to her old mistress
(PEPYS: VIII, 315)

Future reference is also found in non-reported narrations, showing that past forms of modals were already used for non-past meanings in M3:[12]

(19) And therfore, he that first was so mighty that he sholde nat have dyed, bicam swich oon that he *moste* nedes dye, wheither he wolde or noon
(CTPARS: 296.C2)

The *he* in example (19) is Adam who 'at first was so mighty that he ought not to have died' and after the sin 'became such as one who had to/was inevitably fated to/would have to die, whether he wanted or not'.[13] The example illustrates that even if *moste* can be paraphrased by *had to*, it refers to the future of predictive inevitability and predestination.

Clear present time reference is observed in a limited number of instances in the M3 section. In addition, several examples can be considered as timeless in that the question of time reference simply does not arise: the situation described is perceived as outside time altogether. This is true for Philosophical and theological reasoning, for Religious instruction and 'gnomic utterances' describing tendencies, generalities and assumed regularities which are specifically culture-dependent (cf. Lyons 1977: 680ff). The same is true of instructions, which are perceived by the encoder as having, by definition,

12 This is confirmed by Traugott / Dasher (2002: 136): "The number of examples of past form *most-* for non-past meanings is small in the early part of the fourteenth century but increases from the earlier to the later fourteenth century, especially in Sermons and texts on Religious subjects. This is true of both deontic and epistemic *must*. It is favored, but [...] not obligatory in the Wycliffite Sermons, which must have had a significant influence on English."

13 In this example, as in others, the past form collocates with the adverb of necessity which fostered also the generalization of past *must* for non-past meanings (Cf. Traugott / Dasher 2002).

omnitemporal validity. The majority of dynamic and deontic[14] examples, however, show future time reference.

The number of instances with overt present time orientation increases in the E3 period so that present and future references altogether rise up to about 70%. This may be due to the consistent increase in the number of instances in dialogues from Drama, Fiction and Trials, as well as in Letters, Biographies, Diaries and Travel books. Timeless orientation remains fairly stable thanks to the consistent number of occurrences in Handbooks, Philosophical and Educational treatises.

6. Type of modality

There is no doubt that both idiomaticity and indeterminacy are some of the prominent features of the English modal verbs.[15] This is true for

14 Deontic modals are usually performative and have, by definition, no past tense forms. As to deontic *must*, "there is an intrinsic connection between the proposition and futurity" (Lyons 1977: 824).

15 Sometimes paraphrases do not seem to be able to account for idiomatic uses of modals. As Hermerén states: "It seems that the assurance of idiomaticity is often of greater importance than semantic clarity as far as the modals are concerned" (1978: 186). For example, it would be rather controversial to explain utterances issuing an invitation (*You must come and visit us sometime*) or making an offer (*You must have another piece of cake*) in a host/guest context in terms of pure obligation or necessity. Indeed, Palmer (1987: 125) refers to them as expression of social conventions and politeness: "Here the speaker is not laying an obligation in the sense that he is trying to force the addressee to act. Rather it appears at first that he is merely giving permission. But in the situation it is polite from the speaker to insist, because the addressee might be hesitant. To give explicit permission (with *can* or *may*) might, in fact, be quite rude. Although then this use of *must* is associated with social convention, it can still be treated as deontic necessity". As to the problem of indeterminacy and borderline cases, Coates (1983: 32), following Zadeh's theory (1965, 1972), adopts the fuzzy set model and argues that: "Root (non-epistemic) *must* can be related to a fuzzy set with examples assigned to a cline extending from strong to weak obligation (from cases which can be paraphrased 'it's imperative/obligatory' to cases where the paraphrase 'it is important' is more appropriate). Despite this range of

the past as well as for the present.[16] The MUST-forms present in the M3 and E3 sections convey preponderantly obligation and necessity meanings. However, in M3 they are not the only ones. Firstly, there are a limited, though significant, number of instances where the deontic OE sense 'be allowed' can still be attached to the modal under examination. Secondly, there are a number of instances where the MUST-form is a clear periphrastic subjunctive expressing wish or desire. Thirdly, there is at least one instance that can be considered as conveying epistemic possibility. Though few, these examples may suggest that, though it had gone far, the semantic shift was not fully completed in the period under examination.

	deontic		*epistemic*		*dynamic*		*Total*	
Text Type	*No.*	*o/ooo*	*No.*	*o/ooo*	*No.*	*o/ooo*	*No.*	*o/ooo*
SERMONS	15	11	9	7	6	4	30	22
PHILOSOPHY	12	10	13	10			25	20
FICTION	21	15	2	1			23	16
RULES	5	9					5	9
HANDBOOKS	12	6					12	6
RELIGIOUS TR.	12	3			5	1	17	5
SCIENCE	1	3					1	3
HISTORY	4	2					4	2
TRAVELOGUES	1	2					1	2
All Texts	83	5	24	1	11	1	118	6
%	70		20		9		100	

Table 5. Occurrences of MUST according to modality type in M3.

meaning, a basic meaning can be identified which is common throughout; roughly 'It is necessary for...".

16 Although in this chapter, as elsewhere, epistemic, deontic and dynamic categories are used, the problematic quality of such distinctions is stressed when the verb involved is MUST, as "there is no clear line between its uses for deontic and neutral dynamic necessity" (Palmer 1990: 58). Further on the same author adds that: "We have now arrived at a position where the issue is no more than a terminological one. What I have called deontic modality would now be subjective deontic, and what I have called dynamic would be objective deontic" (Palmer 1990: 107).

Table 5 summarizes the occurrences of the modal according to modality type in the M3 section. Deontic MUST (70%) conveys mostly obligational meanings; epistemic meanings (20%) correlate with Philosophical texts and Sermons; dynamic modality (9%) is related to modally coloured predictional contexts in Sermons and Religious texts. Table 6 shows that in the E3 section the values of deontic modality (65%) are approximately the same as in M3, that there is a general increase in epistemic uses (30%) and that dynamic necessity meanings (5%) correlate mostly to Educational texts.[17] Volition and possibility meanings are no longer present in E3.

	deontic		*epistemic*		*dynamic*		*Total*	
Text Type	*No.*	*o/ooo*	*No.*	*o/ooo*	*No.*	*o/ooo*	*No.*	*o/ooo*
DRAMA	37	29	7	5			44	35
PHILOSOPHY	4	5	25	28			29	33
FICTION	26	22	5	4			31	26
HANDBOOKS	20	18	6	5			26	23
EDUC. TREATISES	8	7	4	4	10	9	22	19
LETTERS	21	11	7	4			28	15
SERMONS	7	6	5	4			12	10
SCIENCE	4	4	6	5			10	9
BIOGRAPHIES	6	5		0			6	5
HISTORY	3	3	1	1	1	1	5	4
DIARIES	4	4		0	1	1	5	4
TRIALS	5	4		0			5	4
TRAVELOGUES	2	2		0			2	2
LAW			1	1			1	1
All Texts	147	9	67	4	12	1	226	13
%	65		30		5		100	

Table 6. Occurrences of MUST according to modality type in E3.

17 It is very likely that more examples, also from other text types, could have been subsumed under this label. It is mainly a question of interpretation and choice on the part of the writer (see note 16, this chapter).

6.1. Deontic meanings

Clearly deontic examples are to be sought either in the desiderative or in the instrumental function of the language to indicate wants and desires, on the one hand, and to issue directives of various types, on the other.

6.1.1. Volition

In the M3 sub-corpus there are 9 instances of modally coloured periphrastic subjunctives with a desiderative function (cf. Lyons 1977: 826). The expression of a wish, which often takes the form of exclamations with subject inversion of the type 'So *mote* subj. + infinitive', was fairly common in Late OE and was similar to the Dutch use of *moeten* in formulae of wishing (cf. Visser 1963-73: 1795).[18] There are 3 occurrences in Rules:

(20) and so *mote* we wit þe scharpe ȝerd of discipline putte awey alle superfluites [...] And so we by long perseuerance *mote* dure in oure goode purpos [...] riȝt so we *mote* þorouȝ vier of tribulacioun and water of scharp contricioun, er we come fully to the refreschyngge of chastete (AELR3: 35)

The others appear in Religious, Fictional and Historical texts:

(21) Of alle men yblessed *moot* he be, / The wise astrologien, Daun Ptholome, / That seith this proverbe in his Almageste (CTBATH: 109.C2)

(22) And ioseph sli greting þam gaf, / Godds peis *mot* yee all haf, (CURSOR: 220)

The following are the only two volitional examples which may be considered as overt threats:

(23) I dampned thee; thou *most* algate be deed (CTSUMM: 133.C1)
(I condemned you and therefore you must/will be put to death)

(24) And thou also *most* nedes lese thyn heed, / For thou art cause why thy felawe deyth. (CTSUMM: 133.C1)

---

18 According to Visser, the rival form MAY appeared in writing for the first time in the second half of the 13th century, but remained comparatively rare until the beginning of the ModE Period.

6.1.2. *Necessity*

Directives account for 81% of deontic uses in M3 and 100% in E3. Tables 7 and 8 show their pragmatic uses.

Text Type	*order*	*instruction / advice*
SERMONS	14	
FICTION	12	3
RELIGIOUS TR.	11	1
PHILOSOPHY	6	2
RULES	2	
HISTORY	2	
TRAVELOGUES	1	
HANDBOOKS		12
SCIENCE		1
All Texts	48	19
%	72%	28%

Table 7. Pragmatic uses of deontic necessity MUST in M3 (absolute numbers).

Text Type	*order*	*prohibition*	*instr. / advice*
DRAMA	34	2	1
FICTION	16	7	3
LETTERS	16	5	
BIOGRAPHIES	6		
TRIALS	5		
HANDBOOKS	4	1	15
SERMONS	4	3	
SCIENCE	4		
DIARIES	4		
PHILOSOPHY	3	1	
EDUCATIONAL TR.	3	1	4
HISTORY	3		
TRAVELOGUES	2		
All Texts	104	20	23
%	70%	14%	16%

Table 8. Pragmatic uses of deontic MUST in E3 (absolute numbers).

6.1.2.1. Order

In M3 texts orders (both direct and reported) are present especially in Sermons, Fiction and Religious texts:

(25) And for dred of deth he *mot* make hym redy to his God (CTMERCH: 2)

(26) alle þyse iapes þu *most* flen as contrarie to þy professioun. (AELR3: 33)

In E3 texts they are widespread in almost all text types:

(27) I say once again (and be sure you remember this last Article of our agreement) you *must* destroy, kill, and slay them all, if possible. (PENNY: 269)

(28) but you *must* do me one courtesie, it *must* be done instantly. (WALTON: 216)

(29) & Coll Kirby gave order to ye goaler y[t] noe flesh alife *must* come att me for I was not fitt to bee discourst with by men. (FOX: 83)

Under this heading have been subsumed not only explicit transparent orders, either direct or indirect, but also all the many obligations found in Religious instruction, moral and physical constraints, self-admonishments and the like. These represent the overall majority of deontic necessity meanings and occur with approximately the same frequency in both periods. Here follow some examples from M3:

(30) Ne wiste ȝe not þat I *muste* be in þe nedys of my Fadyr? (WSERM: 32, I. 356)

(31) My Sone, I have wel herd how thou / Hast seid, and that thou *most* amende (GOWER: I, 320)

(32) For all þat he seyth *moste* ben holden (MAND: 143)

The following are from E3:

(33) & they said hee *must* bee forct to breake it (FOX: 153)

(34) For often he *must* stand in need of Necessaries, he *must* be subject to great anxieties (BOETHPR: 126)

(35) Ay, Child, as the saying is, we *must* go cunningly to work, Proofs we *must* have (FARQUAR: 8-9)

Several cases of idiomatic uses with subject *I,* where the notion of compulsion is considerably obscured (cf. Visser 1963-73: 1807), have been found in E3 Drama and Scientific prose:

(36) I *must* confess I am not much its Friend (VANBR: I, 36)

(37) but the Title of this Paper promising some Experiments about the Production of Electricity, I *must* not omit to recite, how I have been sometimes able to produce or destroy this Quality in certain bodies, by means of alterations (BOYLE: 21)

Instances of this type are used holophrastically and they are "odd in that the speaker is actually performing what he is in the act of urging himself to do" (Coates 1983: 36).

The following two interrogative instances with subject *I* seem to imply 'Shall I / Do you want me to ...?'

(38) *Must* I tell what Religion I am of? (OATES: IV, 74)

(39) *Must* I dance too (PENNY: 118)

6.1.2.2. Prohibition

Prohibitions occur only in the E3 section.[19]

(40) you *must* not be so jealous now as to listen. (VANBR: I, 39)

(41) I hope he doe well, but they say I *must* not venter him in the coach so farr a great whill. (FHATTON: I, 148)

---

19 Even in ModE there is not a negative deontic MUST independent of NEED or HAVE TO. With deontic MAY, CAN, WILL, negation normally affects the modal predication. This is not the case with MUST, which is anomalous also in this respect (cf. Coates 1983: 46), *mustn't* being not a negation of necessity but rather the assertion of the necessity for something not to be done, i.e. the assertion of a negation. When used in epistemic meanings this modal does not allow the negation to be attached to it, *can't* being its negative. However, especially in AmE, epistemic statements such as 'His absence *must not* have been noticed' are increasingly accepted and used (Cf. Quirk *et al.* 1985: 225).

6.1.2.3. Instruction and advice

Instructions are mainly found in Handbooks, where they represent all 12 uses of M3 MUST:

(42) Then þou *most* use þe cure aforsaide (HORSES: 127)

(43) & in euery equant *mot* be a silk thred (EPLANETS: 26)

(44) over-gret a poynt of a compas (for bothe these thinges may causen errour as wel in knowing of the tide of the day, as of the verrey ascendent), thou *must* worken in this wise (ASTR: 671.C2)

Of the 26 uses of MUST in E3 Handbooks, 15 are deontic instructions:

(45) And your paste *must* be thus made: Take the flesh of a Rabbet (WALTON: 297)

(46) and then you *must* (as at all times you ought) be very quick in the doing of it. (LANGF: 38)

The others convey epistemic meanings or express orders.[20] Instructions also correlate with Fictional texts. The following examples are from Chaucer's *Prologue:*

(47) Therfor in stede of wepynge and preyeres / Men *moote* yeve silver to the povre freres. (CTPROL: 275.C1)

(48) Whoso shal telle a tale after a man, / He *moot* reherce as ny as evere he kan / Everich a word (CTPROL: 35.C1)

Here is an instance from E3:

(49) We *must* not take care only for sleeping places, but a place to get mony in. (PENNY: 117)

As argued by Visser (1963-73: 1806), in the 2nd person the meaning of MUST may easily develop into advice:

---

20 See, among the others, example (28) above.

(50) Thanne thus in getynge richesses ye *mosten* flee ydelnesse (CTMEL: 233.C2)

(51) Afterward, in getynge of youre richesses and in usynge of hem, yow *moste* have greet bisynesse and greet diligence that youre goode name be alwey kept and conserved. (CTMEL: 234.C2)

However, such examples are always tinged with some instructional purposes on the part of the encoder.

6.1.3. Possibility

In the M3 sub-corpus, there are 7 cases where the OE deontic sense 'be allowed', 'be permitted', can still be attached to the modal under examination. However, the idea of permissibility is almost everywhere tinged with some objective possibility (cf. Visser 1963-73: 1793):

(52) "Sun," he said, "þou *most* now ga to Paradis / þat i com fra" (CURSOR: 80)

(53) And also if I wolde werke by thy conseillyng, certes, my conseil moste som tyme be secree, til it were tyme that it *moste* be knowe, and this ne may noght be. (CTMEL: 220.C1)

(54) Now, sire, now wol I telle forth my tale. / As evere *moote* I drynken wyn or ale, / I shal seye sooth. (CTBATH: 107.C2)

The sense 'be allowed' may also be attached to the following examples from Chaucer's *Boethius* since the notion of *nihil obstat* is implied. Permission here is not granted by the will of a person, but by reasoning – indicated by *as it is* (55), *thanne* and the subordinate *if*-clause (56), *certes* and *also* (57), and *thanne* and *by sembable resoun* (58). In all these examples, the *that*-clauses contain the subjunctive *be*:

(55) "I mai nat" quod I, "denye it, but I *moot* granten, as it is, that this thyng be ryght celebrable by clernesse of renoun and noblesse" (BOETHCH: 429.C2)

(56) "Thanne *mote* we graunten," quod sche, "that this thing be ful of gladnesse, if the forseide thynges ben sothe" (BOETHCH: 429.C2)

(57) "And certes also *mote* we graunten that suffisaunce, power, noblesse, reverence, and gladnesse be oonly diverse by names, but hir substaunce hath no diversite" (BOETHCH: 429.C2)

(58) "Thanne *mustow* graunten," quod sche, "by semblable resoun that oon and good be o same thing". (BOETHCH: 435.C1)

6.2. Epistemic meanings

6.2.1. Possibility

There is only one example (occurring in Chaucer's Fiction) which could be interpreted as expressing epistemic possibility. This view is supported by Skeat's PDE translation (1906: 172) of the same: "Or else he *may* be telling what's untrue":

(59) Or ellis he *moot* telle his tale untrewe, / Or feyne thyng, or fynde wordes newe. (CTPROL: 35.C1)

6.2.2. Necessity

Unambiguous examples of epistemic MUST are quite frequent in Chaucer's *Boethius*. They follow the logic of the deductive reasoning of Philosophical discourse. This is clearly shown by the constant combination with *needs*, and the frequent presence of the adverb *then* and of coordinating conjunctions such as *so, for* and the like.

Here follow some instances with existential *it*, where the modal collocates always with the verb *be* and with the adverb satellite *needs* by which the encoder strengthens the assertion:[21]

(60) Thanne *moot* it nedis be that verray blisfulnesse is set in sovereyn God. (BOETHCH: 432.C1)

---

21 This point needs some discussion. The OED does not attest instances of epistemic MUST earlier than 1652. However, Visser (1963-73: 1810) argues that the notion 'inferred or presumed probability that borders on certainty' is to be taken in a wider sense than is done in OED. Starting from the following example 'That *must be* the Prince' (I conclude or infer from his behaviour (manner of speaking, etc.) that this is the Prince', he shows that "this *illative must* has been of frequent use from the last part of the fourteenth century" and points out that "a noteworthy fact is the preponderance of the colligation of *must* with the verb *to be*."

(61) the whiche destynal causes, whan thei passen out fro the bygynnynges of the unmoevable purveaunce, it *moot* nedes be that thei ne be nat mutable. (BOETHCH: 452.C1)

The following is the only example introduced by existential *there*:

(62) And herof cometh it that in every thing general, yif that men seen any thing that is imparfit, certes in thilke general ther *moot* ben som thing that is parfit. (BOETHCH: 431.C2)

Though less frequently, we also find instances of epistemic use with animate subjects:

(63) For yf that schrewednesse makith wrecches, than *mot* he nedes ben moost wrecchide that lengest is a schrewe. (BOETHCH: 447.C1)

In Chaucer's *Boethius* 11 out of 13 epistemic occurrences collocate with the adverb of necessity. This is not the case in Preston's *Boethius* where the adverb combines with the modal only 7 times out of the 25 times it is used with epistemic meaning. Here follow some parallel examples from Chaucer's and Preston's translations:

(64) or elles, yf ther be any thing to whiche alle thinges tenden and hyen to, that thing *muste* be the sovereyn good of alle goodes. (BOETHCH: 436.C2)

(65) or if there be any thing to which all things do tend, that *must* be the chief of all Goods. (BOETHPR: 147)

(66) "Certes," quod she, "thou seyst aryght; for if so be that that ther is a thyng that in ony partie be feblere of power, certes, as in that, it *moot* nedes be nedy of foreyne help." (BOETHCH: 429)

(67) Thou thinkest right indeed; for if there be any thing which, upon any occasion of Performance, doth shew a Weakness or want of Power, it *must*, as to that, necessarily need foreign Aid. (BOETHPR: 124)

Examples following the same 'must needs be' pattern are present in the *Wycliffite Sermons*:

(68) it *mot* nedis now be neer to þe ful helþe of þe chirche þan it was byfore tyme, whan þe chirche only byleuede (WESERM: 1, I.477)

(69) For eche man schulde serue God, byfore þat he seruede oþur þing, for his furste entent schulde be to worchype God whateuere he dide; and þis *mut* nede be in Crist, for he dide alle þing as he schulde. (WSERM: 32, I.356)

The use of epistemic MUST in generic sentences combined with *needs* played a key role in its semanticization.[22] Examples of this type are present in Sermons:

(70) he þat fayluþ to helpe oon, *mut* nedys fayle aȝenys hem alle. (WESERM: 11, I.522)

The following is the only instance found in Chaucer's Fiction:

(71) So buxom and so vertuous is she, / They *moste* nedes lyve in unitee. (CTMERCH: 155.C1)

Epistemic uses are present in almost all texts types in the E3 period:

(72) Strong! It *must* be so, or how should we be strong that drink it? (FARQUHAR: 2)

(73) Provisions will at least put them in a condition to undersell y[e] English, and so y[e] manufacture of England *must* necessarily ly upon their hands, and y[e] navigation thereof be much obstructed (COMMISS: I, 55)

(74) But now a very acute and scholastical man that would argue that God *must* needs have done whatever he fancies convenient for the World should be done, might by the very same way of Reasoning conclude the necessity of (TILLOTS: II, 445)

The traditional collocation with *needs* and the verb *be* is still common:

(75) MISS. Sir, I never disobey my Father in any thing, but eating of green Gooseberries.
Y. FASH. So good a Daughter *must* <u>needs</u> <u>be</u> an admirable Wife (VANBR: I, 62)

---

22 "If a speaker explicitly states that some event is necessarily obliged or compelled to occur in the future, especially if the source is God's authority, Law, spiritual awareness or logic, the inference is readily invited that the state of affairs represented in the proposition not only will be true in the future but is virtually present" (Traugott / Dasher 2002: 128).

(76) that you can bee in no danger of that kind, although in a matter so nice as this yr Excellency *must* needs bee ye best Judge. (OSBORNE: 22)

6.3. Dynamic meanings

Under this much debated label, at least as far as MUST is concerned,[23] have been here subsumed both M3 modally coloured predictions of a future that is perceived as fated or inevitable, and E3 objective, general necessity senses.

6.3.1. Prediction

Fixed or certain futurity allows the paraphrase 'X is fated or certain to...', 'X shall / will certainly or inevitably...'. Instances of this type are present in M3 Sermons and Religious texts:[24]

(77) for þat gras *mot* nedis rote and fade in colour and swetenesse. (WESERM: 27, I.591)

(78) This is to seyn that the moore that clooth is wasted, the moore *moot* it coste to the peple for the scarsenesse. (CTPARS: 300.C1)

(79) þan *mot* þe saul in grete dred abyde, / Until þat stryfe be broght to ende (PRICK: 80)

---

23 See note 16 above for Palmer's definition of dynamic MUST as "objective deontic"; Nuyts (2001: 182, n. 9) argues that: "The inferential meaning could as well have developed straight out of the dynamic meaning, the deontic meaning being a parallel development". Further on he adds: "And as Goossens (1999) shows, in Historical data one can trace a gradual metonymic development involving contextual reinterpretation of *must* from a general necessity sense (which he considers closely associated with the deontic sense, but which in my analysis would probably better qualify as dynamic meaning) via intermediary stages to the epistemic (i.e. inferential) meaning, it thereby being influenced by the deontic use" (Nuyts 2001: 183).

24 In Religious contexts some instances, which have been grouped in this section, could be interpreted as cases of ambiguity between deontic and epistemic necessity (Cf. Traugott / Dasher 2002: 128-129).

The following can be considered as an example of prophecy:

(80) for which thus seith David the prophete: "Wikked deeth *moote* come upon thilke lordshipes" (CTPARS: 301.C2)

6.3.2 Necessity

Locke's *Directions Concerning Education* contains 10 instances of the following type:

(81) They *must* not be crossed forsooth, they *must* be permitted to have their wills in all things (LOCKE: 50)

(82) The fondling *must* be taught to stricke and call names, *must* have what he cryes for, and doe what he pleases. (LOCKE: 50)

(83) They *must* be permitted the foolish and childish actions suitable to their ages without takeing notice of them. (LOCKE: 58)

On the one hand, the intrinsic deontic nature of MUST is absent since children are not obliged to do (or not to do) anything, yet these examples cannot be considered as pure instructions.[25] On the other hand, no conclusive judgement is implied as following from some evidence. Instead, the philosopher's argumentation proceeds as if his *directions* were objectively grounded. Since instances with 3rd person subjects tend to be more objective than those with 2nd and 1st person subjects and tend to cluster more at the weak end of the continuum (cf. Coates 1983: 37, 32), the paraphrase could be 'It is essential / necessary / important for children to…'. The following instance in a past context may be seen as an example of what Visser glosses as 'would of necessity' (1963-73: 1801):

(84) *Portugals* striving to possess themselves of *Muschat*, were put to such stress, that had not their *Armado* come to their relief, they *must* have desisted their Enterprize (FRYER I: 193) (they would have had to desist…)

25 Nordlinger / Traugott (1997) argue that deontic modals can have a wide scope. From this perspective, these instances could be classified as deontic.

7. Concluding remarks

This analysis of the occurrences of MUST gives clear indications about where this modal had come from and where it was heading to. The fact that no examples of non-modal MUST, of MUST in double modal combinations or of MUST without infinitive have been found gives further indications of its grammaticalized nature, while the comparison between the two periods sheds light on the multi-stranded evolution of the modal under examination. First of all, the demise of MUST-forms, other than *must*, between the two periods cannot be interpreted as pure morphological change since the variants recorded in M3 texts often encoded functional and semantic values (subjunctive, conditional, past, modally coloured futurity) as well as regional varieties, encoder's choices, etc. The significant decrease of necessity adverb collocates gives an important indication of lexicalization and sematicization. Borderline instances of use seem to decrease in E3 owing also to the shift from more objective to more subjective pragmatic uses of the modal (the examples which have been classified as dynamic necessity in the E3 period do not contradict this assertion, as they may be seen as more peripheral 'objective' uses). Table 9 shows some slight but interesting differences between the two periods: volitional and possibility meanings disappear in the second period as well as modally coloured predictional instances, while the values of epistemic MUST show a significant increase.

Modality		*M3*		*E3*	
deontic		70		65	
	volition		7		–
	necessity		57		65
	possibility		6		–
epistemic		20		30	
	necessity		19		30
	possibility		1		–
dynamic		9		5	
	prediction		9		–
	necessity		–		5
Total			100		100

Table 9. Modal meanings of MUST (percentage of total occurrences).

Figure 1 shows that non-epistemic and epistemic uses of MUST have begun an evolution which leads towards PDE where both meanings occur with approximately the same frequency.[26]

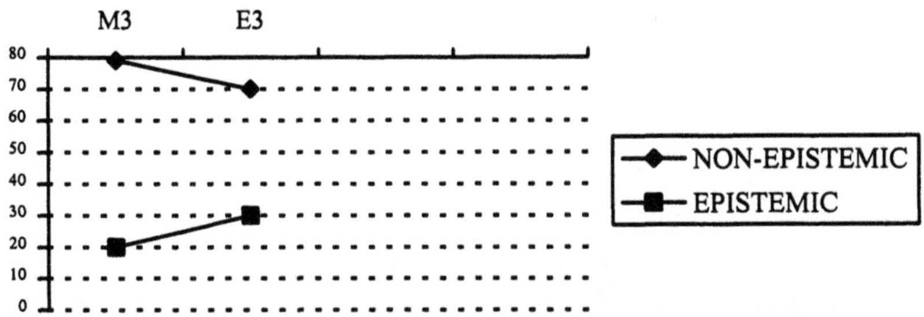

Figure 1. Trend of non-epistemic and epistemic MUST.

The few M3 examples of deontic possibility give us an idea of the evolution from permission to implied expectation which played such an essential role in the semantic and pragmatic development of MUST and that might be seen as 'surviving' in contemporary polite idiomatic utterances expressing invitations and offers.

26 The data of Coates' analysis, based on PDE corpora, reveal that "MUST is unusual in having two meanings [root and epistemic] which occur with similar frequency. All the other modals have one meaning which predominates quantitatively" (1983: 24).

VII. Shall

A comparison between the SHALL-forms in the M3 and E3 parts of the Helsinki Corpus shows a significant decrease in their occurrences, not only in absolute numbers (from 1,336 to 541) but also in normalised figures (from 73 to 32 per 10,000 words). These figures confirm the high frequency of SHALL-forms – particularly in the ME period – already pointed out in previous studies (cf., for instance, Warner 1993: 146).

1. Spelling variants

The number of spelling variants in the two subsections decreases considerably: from 34 forms in M3[1] to only 4 in E3.[2] The corpus analysed also contains the following contracted forms, present only in E3 (the number of occurrences for each variant is shown in brackets):

– *I'le* (14) / *'ile* (1) / *ile* (3) / *I'll* (54) / *he'll* (4) / *she'll* (3) / *they'l* (2) / *they'll* (3) / *thou'lt* (1) / *we'l* (2) / *we'll* (9) / *you'll* (18)

These forms, however, have not been included in our analysis, as they cannot be attributed to either SHALL or WILL with any degree of certainty. In E3 *shall* is the most frequent form, representing 529 occurrences out of 541 (98%); *shan't* and *shant* (present in small

1 The spelling variants of SHALL-forms found in M3 are the following: *sal, sale, sall, salle, scal, schal, schall, schalt, schalte, schillen, schole, scholen, schollen, schul, schulen, schull, schulle, schullen, schullon, schulon, shal, shall, shalle, shalt, shaltou, shaltow, sholle, shollen, shul, shulen, shull, shulle, shullen, shuln.*

2 The spelling variants of SHALL-forms found in E3 are the following: *shall, shalt, shan't, shant.*

numbers) seem to be associated with 1st person subjects in particular; *schalt* is always used with the subject *thou*. In M3 the various spelling and dialectal forms of the modal verb combine with various types of subjects. Indeed, only the quotations including *sal* show its combination with any kind of subject. *Sall* appears with all subject forms except *I*,[3] while *shal* appears with all subjects except *thou*. *Schal*, on the other hand, is used in all cases except with 2nd person pronouns; on the contrary, *schalt* is always used with the subject *thou*, apart from the following instance, which represents a spelling mistake:[4]

(1) And þerfore bewar. For sekirly what beestly herte þat presumiþ for to touche þe hiȝe mounte of þis werke, it *schalt* be betyn awey wiþ stones. (CLOUD: 87)

Other variants used exclusively with the subject *thou* are *schalte* and *shalt*, while *shaltou* and *shaltow* include the subject in the verbal form. *Schull* and *shull*, instead, always appear in combination with the subject *ye*. Some variants – such as *schul*, *schulen* and *shullen* – are found with any kind of plural subject, while *shul* – in addition to plural subjects – is also used with 3rd person singular subjects. *Schulle*, *schullen* and *shulle* have been found in quotations having 1st and 3rd person plural subjects; *schall* and *shall*, instead, only appear with 1st and 3rd person singular subjects. *Schole* and *schulon* have been found only in combination with 1st plural personal pronouns, while *salle, schillen, scholen*, *schollen*, *schullon*, *sholle*, *shollen*, *shulen* and *shuln* usually accompany a 3rd person plural subject. *Sale* appears once with a 2nd person singular subject and once with a 3rd person plural; the only quotation containing *scal* shows its use with a 3rd person singular subject, while that with *shalle* has the pronoun *I* as subject. In terms of frequency, the prototypical paradigm in M3 is therefore the following:

---

3 However, here – as in other cases – the number of occurrences is quite small, and therefore lack of first person singular cases could be the result of sampling.

4 I thank Merja Kytö for checking the hard copies in the Helsinki archive and for confirming that the edition used in the selection of the corpus (by Hodgson, EETS 218) has "it schal".

1st person singular	*sal / schal*
2nd person singular	*sal / schalt*
3rd person singular	*sal / schal*
1st person plural	*sal / schulen*
2nd person plural	*sal / schulen / shul*
3rd person plural	*sal / schulen / schul*

The forms presenting final morphemes characterising a specific subject (such as the *-t* termination for the 2nd person singular subject or the *-(e)n* suffix for plural subjects) show a significant decrease in the two periods taken into consideration: SHALL-forms terminating in *t* after a 2nd person singular subject are 200 out of 230 (87%) in M3, but only 6 out of 32 (19%) in E3; SHALL-forms ending in *(e)n* are 115 out of 468 (25%) in M3, and none out of 173 (0%) in E3.

The comparison between M3 and E3 also shows the appearance in the later period of the negative contracted forms *shan't* and *shant*. Their number, however, is still low (only 6 cases out of 541) and their occurrence is limited to Fictional dialogues (the former has only been found in Vanbrugh's comedy, while the latter is used exclusively in Samuel Pepys' *Penny Merriments*).

The analysis of the corpus sometimes shows cases of free variation in spelling, in which different orthographic forms are used within the same kind of text to accord with the same type of subject. This spelling variability has also been found in poetry: here, however, alternative one- and two-syllable variant forms may depend on metrical requirements:

(2) Sire, now have I shewed you how ye *shul* / do in getynge richesses, and how ye *shullen* / usen hem, (CTMEL: 234, C2)

2. Distribution according to text type

Table 1 shows that normalised SHALL-form figures per 10,000 words decrease in the second part of the corpus analysed.[5]

Text types	*M3*	*E3*
HANDBOOKS	78	29
HISTORY	56	6
FICTION	54	54
SERMONS	36	16
TRAVELOGUES	34	0
LETTERS	32	30
PHILOSOPHY	29	17
SCIENCE	3	9
RULES	124	-
BIBLE	119	-
RELIGIOUS TREATISES	107	-
HOMILIES	67	-
DOCUMENTS	57	-
LAW	-	187
DRAMA	-	48
EDUCATIONAL TREATISES	-	15
BIOGRAPHIES	-	4
TRIALS	-	2
DIARIES	-	2
All texts	*73*	*32*

Table 1. Normalised occurrences of SHALL-forms per text type (per 10,000 words).

As can be seen, in some text types (such as Fiction and Letters), the normalised data remain stable in the two periods; others (Handbooks, Philosophical works and Sermons) show a degree of decrease similar to the general one; in History books and Travelogues the decrease rate is much higher than average; Scientific texts, on the other hand, show the opposite trend, with a rise in the normalised numbers of SHALL-forms. Some text types only appear in one of the two parts of the corpus and therefore it is not possible to compare figures; in E3 Educational books, Trials, Diaries and Biographies show figures

5 The '– ' sign means that no texts are included in this category.

below average; above-average frequencies are found for M3 Rules, Biblical texts and Religious treatises and for E3 Legal texts and Drama.

In M3 only three text types show a frequency clearly above average (73 per 10,000 words): Rules, Religious treatises and Biblical texts. In the case of Rules, frequency is almost double the average and can be explained by the large number of occurrences expressing obligation which characterises this kind of text. As regards Religious treatises and Biblical texts, the particular preference for SHALL-forms can be explained by the frequent reference to future events (as in prophecies) and the expression of deontic meanings, mainly occurring in sentences in which God's will is reported. Five text types show a frequency of SHALL-forms clearly below average: Scientific texts, Philosophical works, Sermons, Travelogues and Letters; the great discrepancy found in these genres can be explained by the rare occurrence of prescriptive or intentional speech acts in a few of them, or by the prevalent reference to past rather than future events in others (cf. below for a more detailed analysis).

As regards E3, in Statutes, Fictional works and Drama the frequency of SHALL per 10,000 words is much higher than the average occurring in the rest of the corpus, while in Scientific texts, Educational treatises, Philosophical works, Sermons, Trials, History books, Travelogues, Diaries and (auto)Biographies the frequency is clearly lower.

The normalised data confirm the use of SHALL as a fundamental feature of Legal English, a feature which continues also in the following centuries and which is still salient in PDE legal texts (cf. Danet 1980: 477, Kurzon 1986: 21-23). The frequent adoption of SHALL in this text type may be explained by its double possibility of expressing both obligation and futurity, implicit in the very nature of regulative acts; in addition, the SHALL-forms found in the statutes included in the corpus also frequently express prohibition and permission, as well as being used for dynamic hypothesis and qualification.[6]

SHALL is common in speech-based prose, which explains its frequent appearance – mainly to denote prediction and intention – in

6 On the language of early statutes cf. Rissanen (2000b).

Fictional works and Drama. The very low normalised figures for SHALL-forms in Scientific texts, transcriptions of Trials, History books, Travelogues, Diaries and (auto)Biographies can be explained by the rare cases of future events and prescriptive speech acts contained in them.

3. Verb phrase structure

As Table 2 shows, the most frequent structure in both periods is SHALL + bare infinitive (1130, i.e. 85%, in M3 and 425, i.e. 79%, in E3), followed by SHALL + passive infinitive (184, i.e. 14%, in M3 and 102, i.e. 19%, in E3).

	M3		*E3*	
	No.	*%*	*No.*	*%*
bare infinitive	1130	85	425	79
passive infinitive	184	14	102	19
Ø	13	1	11	2
modal verb	6	0,4	0	0
BE + ING	2	0,1	2	0,4
HAVE + PP	1	0,1	1	0,2
Total	1336	100	541	100

Table 2. Verbal complementation after SHALL.

In M3 the SHALL + passive infinitive construction seems to be particularly frequent in Handbooks – a feature which was to become one of the characteristics of specialized texts; here is an example:

(3) in the middel *shal be nayled* a plate of metal rownd [...] for in this plate *shollen ben perced* alle the centris of this equatorie [...] vp on the same centre aryn but litel quantite fro the forthest forseid cercle in the lymbe in whiche space *shollen ben deuyde* mynutes of the lymbe (EPLANETS: 18)

In E3, instead, most instances (86, i.e. 84%) occur in Legal texts, where they represent over one third of all cases (35%). One quotation presents a combination of the two most popular phrase structures:

(4) to signify to you Our Pleasure that the last choice made by the Lord Mayor [...] *shall stand* and *be confirmed*, (CHARLES: I, 113)

No cases have been found in either part of the corpus of main lexical verb usage of SHALL – with the lexical meanings it had in OE (ie. 'be under an obligation', 'be bound to', 'owe') and commonly followed by a direct object – which had become rare in ME.[7] Almost all the cases of SHALL-forms not followed by any other verb consist of elliptical forms, usually avoiding the repetition of a verb already mentioned in the same or in a previous sentence, as the following example taken from M3 illustrates:

(5) and vnderstonde bi which lettres, amonges al other blessed spede and graciouse tithinges in hem conteyned, for which we thanke hyly, and euer *shulle*, the lord almighty, (LLETT: 72)
(and euer shulle thanke)

In E3 all instances of ellipsis occur in dialogues appearing in fictional works or comedies, with ellipted verb contained in the words of the previous speaker:

(6) JO. Ay pretty one, every body will strive to dance with the Bride.
KA. Ide rather dance with thee John, than with them all.
JO. So thou *shalt* my dear. (PENNY: 118)
(So thou shalt dance)

In some M3 instances the verb omitted is part of a set phrase typical of the particular genre; this is the case with petitions, in which the formulaic set of words *and shall by the grace of God* (= *and shall ... by the grace of God*) is often placed after the expression *the counseil*

7 This rare usage of SHALL is reported in Fischer (1992: 263): "And by that feith I *shal* Priam of Troie." (*Troilus* III: 791) (And by the faith I owe Priamus of Troy). Another example of the semantic value of SHALL as 'owe' can be found in Lightfoot (1979: 101): "The leeste ferthyng that y men *shal*." (c.1425 Hoccleve, *Min. Poems* XXIII: 695) (The least farthing that I owe to people).

which that the kyng hath assigned (or similar) as can be seen in the following two quotations:

(7) that ony replicacions wolde maken aȝeyns ony of the articles of my billes after the forme that sueth ȝif it like to the kyng: with swich conseil as he hath a(ss)igned to me and *shal by the grace of god*: for to declaren the entente of my billes for the kynges auantage and for fortherynge of his trewe lieges better than I can in this heye Court of rightwisnesse: (PET3: 199)

(8) that they wryten her replicacions aȝens the articles of myne billes by a day assigned by oure liege lord the kyng vp on forfeture of her ferme: wherby that I may haue a copie ther of to my conseill which that the kyng hath assigned me and *shal by the grace of god* to make trewe relacion vnto the kyng of her replicacions (PET3: 200)

In M3 we find one example (9) of the omission of a verb of motion after SHALL, which we know was frequent in OE and which could still – though rarely – be found in ME,[8] where the verbal complement is implied by the presence of a directional adverb or a prepositional phrase with *to*:

(9) I wot nevere what I am, / Ne whider I *schal*, ne whenne I cam,
(Ne whider I schal go) (GOWER: I, 317)

Its very limited number of occurrences suggests the gradual phasing out of this use in the period taken into consideration. The same is true for modal combinations; six cases (4 of SHALL + MAY and 2 of SHALL + CAN)[9] have been found in M3, while none have been found in E3. Here are the four instances of a SHALL-form followed by a MAY-form:

(10) The whiche thinges yif that any wyght loketh wel in his thought the strengthe of that oon and of that oothir, he *schal* lyghtly mowen seen that thise two thinges ben dyvers. (BOETHCH: 451, C1)

8 An example of this usage may be seen in the following quotation in Plank (1984: 325): "Thou *shalt* with me to helle to-night." (c 1386 Chaucer, *C.T.*).

9 The examples of modal combinations quoted in Visser (1963-73: 2404) also consist mainly of forms of SHALL MAY and SHALL CAN.

(11) and more-ouer wel I wote, bi verrey proef, þat of þoo þat ben to come I *schal* on no wise, for habundaunce of freelte & slownes of sperite, mowe kepe one of an hondred; so þat I am verrely conclude in þeese resons. (CLOUD: 21)

(12) And Y schal make thi seed as the dust of erthe; if ony man may noumbre the dust of erthe, also he *schal* mowe noumbre thi seed. (WYCOLD: XIII, 1G)

(13) I sey not þat þou *schalt* mowe euer contynow þer-in iliche fresche; for þat may not be. (CLOUD: 80)

Below are the two cases in which the SHALL-form is followed by a CAN-form:

(14) Do þis werk euermore wiþ-outyn cesyng & wiþ-outyn discrecion, and þou *schalt* wel kun beginne & ceese in alle þin oþer werkes wiþ a grete discrecion. (CLOUD: 81)

(15) And forþi þat þou *schalt* kun betir wite how þei schul be conceyued goostly, þees wordes þat ben spoken bodely, þerfore I þink to declare (CLOUD: 129)

The prevalent futural usage of the SHALL-forms in these modal combinations has led De la Cruz (1994) to hypothesize a possible medieval influence of French on the English language, based on calques of future forms of *pouvoir* and *vouloir*. Nagle, instead, explains the appearance of these combinations with the more widespread early use of SHALL as a marker indicating futurity and the less advanced progress of MAY and CAN in their loss of lexical-verb features:

> *Shall* even in the late OE had begun to undergo auxiliarization and by ME was advanced in the process. *May* and *can* on the other hand, were late in becoming full auxiliaries, in the sixteenth and seventeenth centuries respectively. Therefore, *shall* was a natural candidate to precede the two others, which could be both auxiliaries and main verbs throughout ME.
> (Nagle 1993: 367)

The instances we have found – presenting combinations of SHALL with MAY and CAN and no other modal – seem to confirm Nagle's hypothesis. Although the E3 part of the corpus does not contain any instances of modal combinations, in legal texts SHALL is often coordinated with MAY, so as to reinforce the deontic value of the speech act expressed;[10] two instances of this construction are as follows:

(16) and the said Penalties and Forteitures *shall* and may be recovered in the same manner and by the same Meanes (STAT7: VIII, 456)

(17) any one or more of them *shall* and may sũmon before him or them such Parties as hee or they shall think fitt (STAT7 VII: 77)

Both parts of the corpus contain two cases in which SHALL is followed by BE + *ing*-form, a structure which was still rare in ME (cf. Visser 1963-73: 2413, Strang 1970: 208 and Denison 1993: 407). In the instances found here, however, the *ing*-form seems to have prevalently an adjectival function. Indeed, in the first of the following M3 quotations the *ing*-form precedes SHALL and could serve as an appositional phrase to the noun it follows, while in the second the *ing*-form might have an adjectival function:

(18) and ech fleisch schal no more be slayn of the watris of the greet flood, neither the greet flood *distriynge* al erthe *schal be* more. (WYCOLD: IX, 1G)
(neither the greet flood schal be distriynge al erthe more / neither the greet flood, distriynge al erthe [= destroying all the Earth / which destroys all the Earth], schal be more)

(19) Breþren, we *schulen be wytinge* þat our is now us to ryse from sleepe (WSERM1: I, 475)

10 The equivalence of the deontic value of MAY to that of SHALL has been pointed out in previous literature; cf., for example the OED: "In the interpretation of statutes, it has often been ruled that *may* is to be understood as equivalent to *shall* or *must*" (MAY B.4.b). To support this interpretation, the following quotations are given:
1728 SKINNER *K. B. Rep.* 370 For *may* in the Case of a publick Officer is tantamount to *shall.*
1782 ATKYNS *Chancery Rep.* iii 166 The words *shall* and *may* in general acts of parliament, or in private constitutions, are to be construed imperatively, they *must* remove them.
1873 BLACKBURN in *Law Rep.* 8 *Q. B.* 482 There is no doubt that 'may', in some instances, especially where the enactment relates to the exercise of judicial functions, has been construed to give a power to do the act, leaving no discretion as to the exercise of the power.

As regards E3, the adjectival use of the *ing*-form can still be seen in the first of the following quotations, while the second shows a more marked verbal use:

(20) The King has directed me to attend him tomorrow about the matters of yr Excellencie's last letter and I *shall not bee wanting* to acquainte you with his Ma[ties] pleasure so soon as I know itt (OSBORNE: 22)

(21) all Servants and others who *shall be* wittingly or willingly *aiding or assisting* in the makeing of the said Spiritts or Low Wines contrary to this Act (who shall aid or assist / who shall be found in the state of aiding or assisting) (STAT7: VIII, 457)

In both the M3 and E3 parts there is also one case of SHALL + HAVE and a past participle; only in the M3 quotation, however, can this be interpreted as a perfect infinitive, while the E3 quotation may be interpreted as an instance of the 'HAVE something done' construction:

(22) thanne shaltow se (þ[t]) yif thow haue trewely compased thy cercles / þ[t] the poynt of thy respindle *shal haue towched* the closere of the signes in direct of the hed of cancer in thyn equatorie (EPLANETS: 24)

(23) Then we *shall have wattered* our whole fleet for one month, and victualld compleat for 2 months, (RHADDSR: 15)

4. Time reference

The SHALL-forms found in both parts of the corpus generally have future time reference (1242, i.e. 93%, in M3 and 501, i.e. 93%, in E3, cf. Table 3) and convey such dynamic values as prediction and prophecy or deontic meanings like order, prohibition and intention.

None of these forms has a past time reference,[11] although some are used to report future events in a past context. Although in PDE this

11 Also in Kytö (1991) all the instances of SHALL have present or future reference.

function is mainly carried out by SHOULD, in ME SHALL-forms could remain unchanged when reported in the past:

(24) Whan that Demetrius was come, / Anon his fader hath him nome, / And bad unto his brother Perse / That he his tale *schal* reherse / Of thilke tresoun which he tolde. (GOWER: I, 175)

The use of *schulen* with this function is not to be interpreted as an instance of SHOULD, as this form is a variant of SHALL; this can clearly be seen in the following two quotations, the second of which reports the future expressed in the first after introducing it with a verb in the past tense:[12]

(25) Lo! Y go, and ȝe *schulen* seke me, and ȝe *schulen* die in ȝoure synne; (WYCNEW: VIII, 20)

(26) Therfor Y seide to ȝou, that ȝe *schulen* die in ȝoure synnes; (WYCNEW: VIII, 20)

	M3		*E3*	
	No.	*%*	*No.*	*%*
future	1242	93	501	93
timeless	72	5	32	6
present	22	2	8	1
Total	1336	100	541	100

Table 3. SHALL time reference.

The second largest time reference group in M3 is timeless reference[13] (72 cases, i.e. 5%). Some of these verbal forms occur in the context of instructions:

(27) thise last seid .9. diuisiouns in the midnyht lyne *shollen* seruen for Equacioun of the 8ᵉ spere. (EPLANETS: 22)

12 Of course, the use of *shall* in reported speech is also normal in PDE in free indirect speech and when the event under discussion has not occurred yet.

13 Mindt uses the term 'timeless reference' to refer to the case in which "The speaker can [...] refer to a state which can be described as a general rule and which has no temporal relation with the speaker's time orientation" (Mindt 1995: 50).

In addition, divine prohibitions and sentences referring to moral obligation may be considered permanently valid and have therefore a timeless aspect:

(28) For þis maundement of God þat bidduþ (þou *schalt* not be a lechour); þe secounde maundement þat byдduþ þat (þow *schalt* not sle þi broþur); þe þridde maundement þat bidduþ þat (þou *schalt* not stele his goodis);
(WSERM: III, 522)

Other cases of timelessness occur in the description of habitual actions and permanent characteristics:

(29) ȝif he be ranke of blod he wol gnappe himsilf & rubbe him a-ȝens þe walle þat he stondeþ bi. his kaym *schal* stynke. & hos pisse *schal* be rede & þicke.
(HORSES: 89)

(30) & men clepen hem Apples of Paradys & þei ben right swete & of gode sauour. And þogh ȝee kutte hem in neuer so many gobettes or parties ouerthwart or endlonges euermore ȝee *schull* fynden in the myddes the figure of the holy cros of oure lord Ihesu. (MAND: 31)

Only 22 (2%) of the SHALL-forms found in the M3 part of the corpus have a clear present time reference; they appear mainly in set formulas introducing an exposition or concept:

(31) Goostly freende in God, þou *schalt* wel vnderstonde þat I fynde, in my boistous beholdyng, foure degrees and fourmes of Cristen mens leuyng; and ben þeese: (CLOUD: 13)

As regards E3, future reference is again dominant, with only a few other non-past uses (principally present reference: 8 cases, i.e. 1%) mainly included in phrases referring to the exposition itself:

(32) but yet I *shall* remember you of what I told you before, that he is a very subtil Fish, and hard to be caught. (WALTON: 296)

32 of the SHALL-forms found in the E3 part of the corpus have timeless reference: these may occur in the description of habitual actions and permanent characteristics, or in sentences referring to moral obligation and permanent rules of behaviour, or in the context

of instructions and general advice, as shown in the following examples:

(33) It has often griev'd the Heart of me, to see how some inhumane Wretches murther their kind Fortunes; those that by sacrificing all to one Appetite, *shall* starve all the rest. You *shall* have some that live only in their Palates, and in their sense of tasting *shall* drown the other Four: Others are only Epicures in Appearances, such who *shall* starve their Nights to make a Figure a Days, and famish their own to feed the Eyes of others: (FARQUHAR: 6)

(34) And it is the rather to be believed, because you *shall* scarce or never take a (Male-Carp) without a (Melt), or a (Female) without a (Roe) or (spawn), and for the most part very much; (WALTON: 293)

5. Types of modality

In both parts of the corpus only deontic and dynamic uses of SHALL have been found.[14] The analysis of the M3 part of the Helsinki Corpus has indicated quite a wide range of semantic values and pragmatic uses of the SHALL-forms. As Table 4 shows, deontic (44%) and dynamic (56%) meanings occur with approximately the same frequency overall. In addition, certain types of modality seem to correlate strongly with specific text types. This is the case with deontic necessity, which – as expected – characterises Rules, but is also widespread in official Documents, which include not only statutes and proclamations, but also a wide section drawn from *Returns*, which contains the rules of a fraternity. Normalised figures for deontic necessity are high in Handbooks too, due to the frequency of instructions in them. Religious treatises, Homilies and Biblical texts – in which prophecies frequently occur – are characterised by prediction; Biblical texts also include a high number of expressions of volition, generally relating to divine utterances.

14 The main semantic values of SHALL continue to be deontic and dynamic in PDE. On the subject cf., among others, Coates (1983), Haegeman (1981), Hermerén (1978), Palmer (1990) and Perkins (1983).

	Deontic			*Dynamic*					
	volit.	*necess.*	*Tot.*	*poss.*	*pred.*	*necess.*	*habit*	*Tot.*	*Tot.*
RULES		78	78		46			46	124
BIBLE	41	23	64	1	53			54	118
RELIGIOUS TR	6	14	20		87	0.5		87	107
HANDBOOKS	3	53	56	1	19	1	1	22	78
HOMILIES	10	8	18		49			49	67
DOCUMENTS	6	43	49		8			8	57
HISTORY	18	15	33		23			23	56
FICTION	9	6	15		37		1	38	53
SERMONS		8	8		28			28	36
TRAVELOGUES	7	7	14		16		4	20	34
LETTERS	8		8		26			26	34
PHILOSOPHY	1	14	15		14			14	29
SCIENCE					3			3	3
All texts	11	21	32	0.2	39	0.1	0.3	40	72
Abs. Numbers	198	396	594	4	729	3	6	742	1336
ambig. cases	12	12	24	0	31	1	2	34	58
% ambig. cases	6%	3%	4%	0%	4%	33%	33%	5%	4%

Table 4. Occurrences of SHALL by modality type in M3 (normalised frequencies; in order of overall text type frequency).

In some cases the prevalence of a certain speech act depends to a large extent on the text selected for the corpus; this is true, for example, of the high number of occurrences of prediction found in Religious treatises, which may be explained by the presence of a large extract from *The Pricke of Conscience*, which provides a detailed description of what will happen on Doomsday.

In the E3 subsection, the SHALL-forms analysed are also associated with quite a wide range of semantic values and pragmatic uses. Table 5 shows the figures for the various types of modality found; as can be seen, the quantitative difference between deontic and dynamic meanings is minimal (265 vs 276 instances).

	Deontic				*Dynamic*				
	volit.	*necess.*	*poss.*	*Tot.*	*pred.*	*necess.*	*habit*	*Tot.*	*Tot.*
LAW		94	5	99	88			88	187
FICTION	13	13		26	28			28	54
DRAMA	13	6	1	20	24	1	3	28	48
LETTERS	10	3		13	17			17	30
HANDBOOKS	11	5		16	11	1	1	13	29
PHILOSOPHY	2	1		3	14			14	17
SERMONS	4	1		5	10	1		11	16
EDUC. TR	6	1		7	8			8	15
SCIENCE	8			8	1			1	9
HISTORY	5			5	1			1	6
BIOGRAPHIES	2			2	2			2	4
DIARIES	1			1	1			1	2
TRIALS	1			1	1			1	2
All texts	6	10	1	16	16	0.2	0.3	16	32
Abs. Numbers	97	160	8	265	268	3	5	276	541
ambig. cases	7	5	0	12	20	1	1	22	34
% ambig. cases	7%	3%	0%	5%	7%	33%	20%	8%	6%

Table 5. Occurrences of SHALL by modality type in E3 (normalised frequencies; in order of overall text type frequency).

As we have already seen for M3, Table 5 also shows interesting variations of text type and modality type. This is the case with deontic necessity and prediction, which characterise Statutes; in addition, this text type – although containing a very high number of instances – presents a limited range of modal functions. The typical structure of a statute usually consists of some prescriptive speech act (either an order or a prohibition) to be performed (in a future time) by a specified category of people in a particular context (hence the frequent recourse to qualification) should a specific event take place (hypothesis).[15] Here is an example of this structure:

15 For a more detailed analysis of the use of SHALL (and WILL) in EModE statutes cf. Gotti (2001).

(35) And if any Prisoner who *shall* take the Benefitt of this Act [QUALIFICATION] and *shall* in pursuance of the same take the Oaths for any the Purposes hereby or by any the before mentioned Act' appointed [QUALIFICATION] *shall* forsweare himselfe or herselfe [HYPOTHESIS] then *shall* such person being thereof lawfully convicted beyond and over and above the Penalties which may by Law now in Force bee inflicted upon Persons convicted of Perjury [QUALIFICATION] suffer Imprisonment for the space of seven yeares [ORDER] (STAT7: VII, 76)

The other genres, instead, are characterised by a much wider range of modal categories. This is the case, in particular, with Handbooks, Sermons and Comedies, which present instances of several deontic and dynamic uses. A variety of modal functions has also been found in Educational treatises, Philosophical works, History books, Fictional works and Letters.

5.1. Deontic meanings

5.1.1. Volition

The semantic value of volition is expressed by the SHALL-forms found in the corpus in a variety of pragmatic uses, both in the M3 and the E3 subsections, as can be seen in Tables 6 and 7.

The two subsections do not contain any instance of offer to do something – roughly equivalent to the expression 'do you want me to ...?' –, which occurs in PDE in questions like the following:

(36) *Shall* I ring you when I get back?
(Do you you want me to ring you?)[16]

16 In PDE the same pragmatic value may be found also with non-first person subjects:
Shall Mary do the dishes for you?
(Do you want Mary to do the dishes for you?)

	intention	*threat*	*promise*	*Total*
BIBLE	37	20	29	86
HISTORY	23	8	13	44
RELIGIOUS TR	13	2	8	23
FICTION	11		2	13
DOCUMENTS	5		4	9
HANDBOOKS	7			7
HOMILIES	3		4	7
LETTERS	2		2	4
TRAVELOGUES	4			4
PHILOSOPHY			1	1
RULES				-
SCIENCE				-
SERMONS				-
All texts	105	30	63	198
ambig cases	8	0	4	12
% ambig cases	8%	0%	6%	6%

Table 6. Pragmatic uses of SHALL expressing volition in M3 (absolute numbers).

	intention	*threat*	*promise*	*Total*
LETTERS	13		5	18
DRAMA	5	1	11	17
FICTION	9	1	6	16
HANDBOOKS	5		7	12
SCIENCE	9			9
EDUC TR	6		1	7
HISTORY	1	4	1	6
SERMONS	5			5
PHILOSOPHY	3			3
BIOGRAPHIES	2			2
TRIALS	1			1
DIARIES	1			1
LAW				-
All texts	61	6	30	97
ambig cases	6	0	1	7
% ambig cases	10%	0%	3%	7%

Table 7. Pragmatic uses of SHALL expressing volition in E3 (absolute numbers).

5.1.1.1. Intention

Intentional usages of SHALL-forms are quite widespread in the corpus and commonly correlate with first-person pronouns:

(37) þan þe eorle seide, "Ich have y-doo þat y schulde; here after y *schal* doo what me nedeþ: myn owne lord fongeþ me nouȝt but for myne; þerfore y *schal* goo to hym þat is more redy to geve þan to fonge." (TREVISA: VIII, 111)

In M3 these forms are particularly common in Biblical texts in utterances expressing the intentions of the speaker; this is particularly evident in the extract taken from *Genesis*, which reports God's intentions concerning the newly-created world and its first inhabitants:

(38) Lo! Y *schal* brynge watris of diluuye (ether greet flood) on erthe, and Y *schal* sle ech fleisch in which is the spirit of lijf vndir heuene, and alle thingis that ben in erthe, schulen be wastid. And Y *schal* sette my couenaunt of pees with thee; (WYCOLD: VI, 1G)

In E3 speech acts of intention are most frequent in Letters, Fictional works, Handbooks and Educational treatises:

(39) But I *shan't* put you to the trouble of farther Excuses, if you please this Business shall rest here. (VANBR: I, 34)

(40) Now, my Lord, we *shall* go to our Evidence to prove, that all this is absolutely false: (OATES: IV, 72. C2)

In Handbooks, Educational treatises, Biographies and Sermons, speech acts expressing intention are often used to introduce an exposition or a concept:

(41) And yet I *shall* tell you, that the crumbs of white bread and honey made into a paste is a good bait for a (Carp), and you know it is more easily made. (WALTON: 298)

(42) To the foregoing Experiments, whose success is wont to be uniform enough, I *shall* adde the Recital of a surprising (Phaenomenon), which, though not constant, may help to make it probable, that Electrical Attractions (BOYLE: 26)

In these types of texts the speech acts containing SHALL-forms have an argumentative purpose, as they aim to guide the reader's decoding activity or clarify the author's discourse strategies, as the following instances show:

(43) But I *shall* confine my discourse to the Dead. (BURNETROC: 144)

(44) there is just measure of Subjection and Obedience due from the wife to the husband (as I *shall* after explain) (JETAYLOR: 23)

In some cases, SHALL-forms are used with second-person pronouns to inquire about the interlocutor's intentions:

(45) He is ful redy, and doþ bot abideþ þee. Bot what *schalt* þou do, and how *schalt* þou put? (CLOUD: 16)

(46) But for Y seie treuthe, ȝe bileuen not to me. Who of ȝou *schal* repreue me of synne? If Y sey treuthe, whi bileuen ȝe not to me? (WYCNEW: VIII, 40)

Intention may also be detected in sentences containing a third person subject, as can be seen in the following quotation:

(47) The old man dotes on her: she must not set neare a doore when she was hot with dancinge and tell her he *shall* give her somethinge; (HOXINDEN: 333)

5.1.1.2. Threat

In the M3 subsection of the corpus analysed, threats have only been found in biblical texts, history books and religious treatises. Their forms are usually combined with a first-person subject and are addressed to a second-person interlocutor:

(48) þou has him and his in despite, / þat wit his grace i *sal* þe quite. / þi bodi *sal* i giue to gifte, / To ete wit foghuls of þe lift, (CURSOR: 436)

The second-person interlocutor may at times be placed in the subject position; in this case the threatening force of the speech act relies on the fact that the action will be performed or caused by the speaker. Here are two examples of this usage:

(49) Ete thou of ech tre of paradis; forsothe ete thou not of the tre of kunnyng of good and of yuel; for in what euere dai thou shalt ete thereof, thou *schalt* die bi deeth. (WYCOLD: II, 1G)

(50) At on worde, Sir Andrew, y telle þe, þat or þis ȝer be gon, þat ȝe *shal* be take and holde for a traitoure, and more þan ȝe holde vs nowe; and in worse deth ȝe *shul* die, þan euer ded Knyght of Engeland; and vnderstonde wel þat neuer ȝe dede þing þat sorer ȝow *shal* repent. (BRUT: 218)

Threats sometimes concern a third-person referent; this is commonly placed in the subject position, but the threatening agent is normally mentioned elsewhere in the sentence:

(51) Y schal sle ech fleisch in which is the spirit of lijf vndir heuene, and alle thingis that ben in erthe *schulen* be wastid. (WYCOLD: VI, 1G)

In the E3 subsection, threats have only been found in History books, Fictional works and Drama, and usually have a second or third person interlocutor placed in the subject position, as in the following instances:

(52) since ye refuse to accept of peace with your brethren, ye *shall* have War from your enemies; and since ye will not with us preach the word of life, to whom ye ought, from their hands ye *shall* receive death. (MILTON: X, 149)

(53) therefore they first, saith he, *shall* feel our Swords; for they who pray against us, fight heaviest against us by their prayers, and are our dangerous enemies. (MILTON: X, 149)

5.1.1.3. Promise

Promises convey a committed undertaking to carry out a certain action of benefit to another. This commitment is often made manifest by means of specific adverbs or marked phrases, as can be seen in the following quotations:

(54) "Certes," quod sche, "that *schal* I undo the be verray resoun, yif that tho thinges that I have concluded a litel herebyforn duellen only in hir first grauntynge." (BOETHCH: 434, C2)

(55) forsothe Y *schal* make thee prince on a greet folk, and strongere than is this. (WYCOLD: XIV, 1N)

(56) ye may be sure we *shall* not recompense you with any molestation, but *shall* provide rather how we may friendliest entertain ye; (MILTON: X, 144)

Promises having a second person subject are often used in dialogues and correspondence, as the following instances show:

(57) for y loue ȝow as miche as me oweþ to loue my fader; and forto bryng ȝow more in certeine how loue goþ, I shal ȝow telle, for-as-miche as ȝe bene worþe, as muche *shal* ȝe bene louede. (BRUT: 104)

(58) TOM. but if any should offer any such thing to you, you must be sure to let me know what they say or do to you.
IONE. You *shall* be sure to know all Sir. (PENNY: 268)

At times the subject is a third-person pronoun, yet the locutor remains responsible for the action promised:

(59) late me wetyn whiche it is & þi conceyte þer-apon; and at my simple kunnyng it *schal* be amendid ȝif I kan. (CLOUD: 130)

(60) No, no, Wench, God forbid that I should be against thy Relations comming to see thee. No, no I say, he *shall* be welcome; (PENNY: 269)

Solemn undertakings and pledges, such as those included in official documents, may also be classified in this category; here are a few examples:

(61) "Sir, þe soth i wil þe tell, / þi doghter for to spus, rachell." / "þan sal þou serue me seuen yeir, / Ar þou sal haue mi doghter dere." / "Blithili, sir, sua *sal* it be." (CURSOR: 329)

(62) And yef eny man fynt hym y-greued in eny poynt forsaid, come and pleyne hym to the Mair and aldermen and he *shal* haue right and resoun. (LPROCL: 33)

At times the pragmatic value of promise is made clearer by the use of harmonic verbs such as *grant*, *swear* or *engage* in a superordinate clause, explicitly referring to an act of promising:

(63) ȝif ȝe wyl wepe for ȝoure synne, / And shryue ȝow clene, and þerof blynne, / And graunte me þat ȝe *shul* faste, / And yn preyers wel to laste, (HS: 63)

(64) Bot þou sal <u>suere</u> me a nath, / þat þou *sal* neuer forth fra to night / In þi forbirth do claim na right. (CURSOR: 302)

(65) on condition they be sent constantly to the Schoole, and that their Parents do <u>engage</u> they *shall* keep good order, and be cleanly and neat in their apparel; (HOOLE: 228)

5.1.2. Necessity

The semantic value of deontic necessity is expressed in various pragmatic forms, as can be seen in Tables 8 and 9. In M3 there is a prevalence of orders and instructions, while in E3 the great majority consist of orders and prohibitions (89% of all cases).

	order	*prohib.*	*instruct.*	*advice*	*Total*
HANDBOOKS			99	2	101
DOCUMENTS	62	4		1	67
RELIGIOUS TR	14	4	12	23	53
BIBLE	41	3	2	3	49
RULES	32	5		5	42
HISTORY	27		2	8	37
PHILOSOPHY		1	1	15	17
SERMONS	3	5	1	2	11
FICTION	3	1	1	4	9
HOMILIES	2	1	1	2	6
TRAVELOGUES			3	1	4
LETTERS					-
SCIENCE					-
All texts	184	24	122	66	396
ambig cases	3	0	5	4	12
% ambig cases	2%	0%	4%	6%	3%

Table 8. Occurrences of SHALL with pragmatic uses expressing necessity in M3 (absolute numbers).

	order	*prohib.*	*instruct.*	*propos.*	*advice*	*Total*
LAW	96	28				124
FICTION	9	2		3	1	15
DRAMA		1		6		7
HANDBOOKS	1		2	2	1	6
LETTERS	5					5
EDUC TR					1	1
PHILOSOPHY					1	1
SERMONS					1	1
BIOGRAPHIES						-
DIARIES						-
HISTORY						-
SCIENCE						-
TRIALS						-
All texts	111	31	2	11	5	160
ambig cases	3	0	0	1	1	5
% ambig cases	3%	0%	0%	9%	20%	3%

Table 9. Occurrences of SHALL with pragmatic uses expressing necessity in E3 (absolute numbers).

5.1.2.1. Order

The largest number of deontic occurrences can be classified as orders. In M3, these are specially frequent in Documents and Biblical texts. As already mentioned, the former text type includes the detailed rules of fraternities, while the latter often reports prescriptive statements expressed by God or a religious leader. Most of these orders are addressed directly to a second-person interlocutor and occur either in quoted speech or in dialogues:

(66) In alle þees *schalt* þou kepe discrecion, þat þei be nouþer to mochel ne to lityl. Bot in þis werk *schalt* þou holde no mesure; for I wolde þat þou schuldest neuer seese of þis werk þe whiles þou leuyst. (CLOUD: 80)

(67) TOM. Why then in brief these they are. First, you *shall* kiss my hand and swear that you will acknowledge me to be your Lord and Master.
IONE. I will Sir.

> TOM. Secondly, when I come home drunk a nights, you *shall* be diligent to make me unready and get me to bed, and if I chance to befoul my self, you are to make me clean without chiding me. (PENNY: 268)

SHALL-forms are also used to give orders in an indirect way, as can be seen in the following quotation:

(68) And so thou schalt make it. The lengthe of the schip *schal* be of thre hundrid cubitis, the brede *schal* be of fifti cubitis, and the hiȝnesse therof *schal* be of thretti cubitis. Thou schalt make a wyndow in the schip, and thou schalt ende the hiȝnesse thereof in a cubite; (WYCOLD: VI, 1G)

Orders concerning third persons are often given through a second-person interlocutor:

(69) and of werk beestis in her kynde, and of ech crepynge beeste of erthe, by her kynde; tweyne and tweyne of alle *schulen* entre with thee, that thei moun lyue. (WYCOLD: VI, 20G)

If no second-person interlocutor is addressed in the sentence, the specific ordering function of these speech acts is often made clear by the use of SHALL in nominal clauses after superordinate verbs such as *ordain*, *bid, award, will* or after nouns such as *commandment*:

(70) And first is ordeined þat alle þe bretheren & sostren of þis fraternite *schul* vche Twelfday þe Midwynter be all to-gedere at þe masse in þe forseid chirche of seint Thomas, & heren deuoutelich þilke masse, & offren þer-at in þe worscehpe of (RET: 41)

(71) And herfore byddeþ Crist þat men *schullen* suffre boþe þese t[w]o growe til þe tyme of repyng, (WSERM: 361, 375)

(72) þa Mair and Aldermen, willyng þat suche shul be war be hym in tyme comyn, han awarded, after þe custome of this Cite, þat he, as a fals lyere and disceyuer of þe comune peple, *shal* stonde here vpon pillorye thre market dayes, eche day an hour, wiþ a Weston aboute hys necke in tokene of a Lyere. (JUDG: 95)

(73) þe Kyng wille þat þow bene honged & drawe, and þin heuede smyten of, and þi bowelles taken out of þi body, and þi bowelles brent, and þi body quarterede, and þin heuede smyten of, and sent vnto London; and þere hit *shal* be sette oppon London Brigge; and þi iiij quarters *shal* be sent to iiij tounes of Engeland, þat alle oþere mowe be-ware and chastisede by þe. (BRUT: 228)

(74) and, ȝif þer be ony oþur maundement, in þis word it is instorud, þow *schalt* loue þi neyȝebore as þiself (WSERM: 11, I.522)

In lists of orders, this syntactic context is sometimes omitted, but it can be easily inferred. An instance of the omission of the expression *is ordeined* can be seen in the following quotation:

(75) Also þat no broþer *schal* be resceyued but on þe dayes of our assembles. [...] Also þat four gode & trewe men *schul* kepe þe catel longynge to þe companye, & trewely ȝiue vp here acounte þe day of seint Fabian & sebastian, byfore all þe breþeren, or elles sixe of þe wiseste of þe same bretheren; & eche ȝeer þo foure *schul* be chaunged, but it so befalle þat þey be þe more profitable to þe companye. (RET: 53)

The cases described in this section also concern obligation deriving from legal or moral constraints, which is particularly frequent in Rules, Religious treatises and History books. Some examples of moral obligation can be seen in the following quotations:

(76) in worschippe of God and of holy seyntes, þat man haveþ in mynde efte by suche ymages, God allone *schal* be princepalliche worschipped, and after hym creatures *schal* be i-worschipped in worschippe of hym. (TREVISA: VI, 211)

The following quotation also refers to obligation deriving from moral principles or legal logic, according to which the traitor should be hanged; a dynamic interpretation of prediction is excluded by the reference to the king's forgiveness:

(77) & Thomas, as a traitoure ȝe *shull* be hongede by resoun, but þe Kyng haþ forȝeue ȝow þat gewys for þe loue of Quene Isabell. (BRUT: 222)

In the E3 subsection order is the most common pragmatic function performed by the deontic aspect of the modal analysed; with its 111 occurrences it corresponds to two thirds of all SHALL-forms found in the corpus. In particular, these appear in Statutes (86%), where they represent the most frequent type of modal meaning; for SHALL this is not surprising, as the main function of statutes is to provide prescriptive statements. Here is an example:

(78) And it is further enacted by the Authority aforesaid That [...] such Justice or Justices *shall* by Sũmons cause to come and call before him or them any Sheriff Goaler or Keeper of Prison of such Goal or Prison of and from which such Prisoner or Prisoners hee shee or they is or are and *shall* administer and give to such Sheriff Goaler or Keeper of Prison an Oath to this Effect following viz[t]. (STAT7: VII, 75)

The prescriptive speech act performed by means of SHALL is at times made more explicit by the use of adverbial phrases like *according to the order of X* or *by order of X*:

(79) and the Money thereby raised *shall* be imployed and accounted for according to the Order & Direction of the said Justices for and toward' the purchasing of the Land to enlarge the said Highways and for the making the said Ditches and Fences and the said Assessment *shall* by order of the said Justices be levied by the Overseers of the High-ways by Distresse and Sale of the Good' of Persons so assessed not paying the same within Ten Days after Demand (STAT7: VII, 210)

To increase the performative value of the legal text, the verbal form containing SHALL is often accompanied by the adjective *lawful*, as can be seen in the following example:

(80) Provided alwaies and be it enacted by the Authority aforesaid That in case His Majesty at any time or times before the said Tenth Day of February One thousand six hundred ninety nine shall find the Price of Corn to decrease in the Publick Marketts and for that reason (in His Royall Discretion) shall judge it to be most for the Benefitt and Advantage of his Kingdom to permitt the Exportation of Corn that then it *shall* be lawfull to and for His Majesty by His Royall Proclamation or Proclamations to be issued by and with the Advice of His Privy Councill from time to time to permitt and suffer all and every (STAT7: VIII, 456)

The deontic value of SHALL is also increased when the main modal is coordinated with MAY, another deontic modal auxiliary (as shown in quotations 16 and 17). As in the previous instance, the adjective *lawful* may be added to intensify the force of the speech act:

(81) Provided neverthelesss and it is hereby declared That it *shall* and may be lawfull to and for any Distiller to keepe and make use of any Pipe Stopcock or other Conveyance above Ground which are Publick (STAT7: VIII, 457)

(82) And that it *shall* and may bee lawfull to and for such Creditor or Creditors of such Prisoner soe discharged as aforesaid his her or their Executors Administrators or Assignes to take out any new Execution against the Land' (STAT7: VII, 76)

In our legal texts SHALL only occurs in third person verbal forms, as the obligations to which the documents refer usually concern agents who are presented in a general and impersonal way; hence the subject is often *he or she*, *any person or persons*, *any Justice or Justices of the Peace*, *hee shee or they* etc. Also in official correspondence – where the tone is formal and prescriptive acts are often performed – the subject is frequently a third person singular or plural noun or pronoun:

(83) For which these Our Letters *shall* bee your Warrant. (CHARLES: I, 25)

5.1.2.2. Prohibition

Prohibitive commands with SHALL NOT (which can be seen as an order not to do something) are quite widespread, particularly in the M3 subsection, where they are especially frequent in Sermons, Rules, Documents, Religious treatises and Biblical texts. Prohibitions are often addressed directly to the interlocutor, and thus the subject is a second-person pronoun:

(84) þe fourþe maundement þat bidduþ þat (þow *schalt* not seye false witnesse); þe fyueþe maundement also (þow *schalt* not coueyte þi neyȝeborus good; (WSERM: 11, I.522)

(85) Why then thus it is; you shall give me leave to make void all those promises I made you before marriage, and next that you *shall* not lye with me, nor desire to lye with me at any time but when I please. (PENNY: 272)

In Documents and Rules, however, prohibitions are often expressed indirectly and the use of a third-person subject is typical:

(86) Also is ordeined þat, if any debate be bytwene any of þe brotherede, þa[t] non of hem *schal* folwe aȝen oþer in none maner, til þe wardeines & þe bretheren han asayed wheþer þey (RET: 43)

In E3 prohibitions are particularly common in Statutes (90%), where they provide rules to prevent a certain type of behaviour:

(87) that such Malt shall be landed in the said Islands of Jersey and Guernsey or one of them the Danger of the Seas only excepted for the Use of the Inhabitants there and *shall* not be landed or sold in any other Parts whatsoever (STAT7: VIII, 455)

In some cases, however, the negative command is conveyed by sentences with a negative subject, as we can see in the following examples:

(88) Provided alsoe That noe Person *shall* bee discharged out of Prison or have any Benefitt or Advantage by force or virtue of this Act who shall bee really and (bona fide) indebted in more than the Sũm of One hundred (STAT7: VII, 76)

(89) Provided always That noe Man being under Forty Yeares of Age *shall* dureing the present Warr with France bee discharged from his Imprisonment or have any Benefitt or Advantage by means or virtue of this Act or any thing therein contained unlesse such Man or Person (STAT7: VII, 77)

In the event of two prohibitions, the second is often preceded by *nor*:

(90) and that no Distiller from and after the said Eight and twentieth Day of February *shall* have or keepe any Private Pipe Stopcock or other Private Conveyance by which any Wash or other Liquors fitt for Distillation may be conveyed from one Back or other Vessell to another or from any such Back or other Vessell to his or her Still or Stills or into any other Place nor *shall* have or keepe any Hole in any such Back or Washbatch by which any Wash or any other Liquors (STAT7: VIII, 457)

5.1.2.3. Instruction

Deontic SHALL expressing instruction is also very frequent. Its forms usually depend on a second-person subject:[17]

---

17 In analysing a corpus of medical English texts from the late 14th century to the middle of the 16th century Taavitsainen (2000) has found several examples of SHALL-forms used in instructions with a second-person pronoun subject, which she explains thus: "Instructive texts refer to the addressee directly and focus the attention on him/her. Second person pronouns are an essentual feature of this text type, which gives directions for future action" (Werlich 1983:124).

(91) Fro this litel cros [...] up to the ende of the lyne meridionall, under the ryng, *shalt* thou fynden the bordure divided with 90 degrees; and by that same proporcioun is every quarter of thin Astrolabe divided. (ASTR: 664, C2)

(92) Than hast thou a label that is shapen like a reule, save that it is streit and hath no plates on either ende with holes. But with the smale point of the forseide label *shalt* thou calcule thin equaciouns in the bordure of thin Astralabie, as by thin almury. (ASTR: 669, C2)

In some cases, instructions are given in an indirect way:

(93) And aftur take a drie stikke of wyþi or of hasel & þwyte þer-on longe sponus & þynne in-to þat on ende of þat styke. & þat oþer ende of þe styke *schal* be scharpe. (HORSES: 119)

(94) tak thanne a cercle of metal þ^{t} be .2. enche of brede / & þ^{t} the hole dyametre (w^{t} in this cercle *shal*) contene the forseide .68. enches / or .5 fote (& .8. enches) / & subtili lat this cercle be nayled vp on the circumference of this bord or ellis mak this cercle of glewed perchemyn. (EPLANETS: 18)

In specialized texts, instructions are often given in the passive voice; here are a few examples drawn from *The Equatorie of the Planetis*:

(95) in the lymbe in whiche space *shollen ben deuyde* mynutes of the lymbe / mak thanne a narwere cercle som what ferther distaunt fro the laste seid cercle / in whiche *shal be deuyded* the degres of the same lymbe mak yit a narwere cercle som what ferthere distaunt fro this laste cercle in which *shal ben writen* the nombres of degres / mak yit a narwere cercle som what ferther distaunt fro this laste seid cercle in which *shollen ben writen* the names of 12 signes & þ^{t} this laste seid cercle wole I calle the closere of the signes / now hastow .5. cercles in thy lymbe / & alle ben descriued vp on centre aryn / and euerich of the .4. quarters in thi lymbe *shal be deuided* in 90 degres þ^{t} is to sein .3. signes & eueri degre *shal be deuided* in 60 mi^{a} / & shortly thi lymbe is deuided in maner of the lymbe in the bakside of an astrelabie (EPLANETS: 18-20)

The deontic value of these speech acts is confirmed by their alternation with verbs in the imperative or accompanied by MUST-forms with the same pragmatic value:

(96) grynde hem al to-geder & þen þou *schalte* schaue þe heere a-boute þe holes. & ley þis plaster þer-to. Or ellus take arnement. & brenne in þe fyer. (HORSES: 95)

(97) But if it be so þat þe corn be genderid. þen þou moste schaue it aboute þe corn oþer þe swellynge. & þen *schalt* þou garce it with many smale pikes meneliche depe. þat þe brused blod may out ren. (HORSES: 119)

The instructional purpose is at times reinforced by harmonic lexemes such as the verb *to teach* or the noun *directions:*

(98) anoynte him with an oynement þat j schal þe teche. þou *schalt* tak þe rote of þe rede docke & þe rede docke & þe rote of hemlok. & seþe hem wel in vyneger or eysel or wyn. (HORSES: 101)

(99) I shall therefore give you three or four more short observations of the (Carp), and then fall upon some directions how you *shall* fish for him. (WALTON: 294)

SHALL-forms are also used for argumentative purposes in a superordinate clause of the type 'you shall know that' to introduce an exposition or a concept and thus guide the reader's decoding activity. This is most frequent in Religious treatises and Travelogues. The interlocutor is often addressed directly as the recipient of the new point to be explained, as can be seen in the following quotations:

(100) First ȝee *schull* wel knowe þat the naturell bawme is full cleer & of cytryne colour & strongly smellynge. (MAND: 33)

(101) And þou *schalt* vnderstonde þat þou schalt not only in þis werk forȝete alle oþer creatures þen þi-self, or þeire dedes or þine, bot also (CLOUD: 82)

(102) þerfore *schalt* þou chaungabely mene þees two wordes – SYNNE and GOD; wiþ þis general knowyng: þat and þou haddest God, þen schuldest þou lacke synne, and miȝtest þou lacke synne, þen (CLOUD: 79)

A parenthetic variant of the formula is also found:

(103) Blind þai er, þat *sall* ȝe ken, / And also leders of blind men, / For with þaire laws þai lese and bind / Omang þe Jews, and both er blind. (NHOM II: 73)

5.1.2.4. Proposal

Proposals have only been found in the E3 subsection, and commonly occur in Handbooks, Fiction and Drama, always in the context of a dialogue. In some cases the suggestion concerns the interlocutor's behaviour and thus requires a 2nd-person pronoun, as in the following examples:

(104) let me invite you along with us; I'll bear you[r] charges this night, and you *shall* bear mine to morrow; for my intention is to accompany you a day or two in Fishing. (WALTON: 212)

(105) Why then if we are to take it by turns, it's the same thing; I'll obey you now, and when we are Married, you *shall* obey me. (VANBR: I, 62)

(106) AIM. You're very exact, I find, in the Age of your Ale.
BON. As punctual, Sir, as I am in the Age of my Children: I'll shew you such Ale – Here, Tapster, broach Number 1706. As the saying is; – Sir, you *shall* taste my (Anno Domini); (FARQUHAR: 2)

Proposals may also concern the settling of issues or the behaviour of people other than the interlocutors; in this case the SHALL-form is preceded by a third person pronoun or a noun, as in the following instances:

(107) Then if it please thee to begin, thy hand-maid *shall* bear a part, but be sure it be such pure Language as is used among our Friends when assembled at Bull-and-Mouth. (PENNY: 149)

(108) But I shan't put you to the trouble of farther Excuses, if you please this Business *shall* rest here. (VANBR: I, 34)

(109) And it *shall* be to morrow Morning still, if you'll consent? (VANBR: I, 62)

5.1.2.5. Advice / Request for advice

Instances of advice have been found in various text types. The addressee of the advice is commonly placed in the subject position, usually denoted by a 2nd-person pronoun:

(110) Wiþ þis worde þou *schalt* bete on þis cloude and þis derknes abouen þee. Wiþ þis worde þou *schalt* smite doun al maner þouȝt vnder þe cloude of forȝeting. (CLOUD: 28)

(111) And though the grete men and the myghty men geten richesses moore lightly than thou, yet *shaltou* nat been ydel ne slow to do thy profit, for thou *shalt* in alle wise flee ydelnesse. (CTMEL: 233, C2)

Even when *thou-* or *you*-forms are not used, the 2nd person appears in the subject as a possessive adjective or pronoun:

(112) but that they myghte been opened by pitee and debonairetee' (that is to seyn, to yeven part to hem that han greet nede), 'ne thy goodes *shullen* nat been so opene to been every mannes goodes.' (CTMEL: 234, C1)

Where no addressee is specified, the advice is given to people in general:

(113) Manie such aduerbis, coniuncciouns, and preposiciouns ben set ofte oon for another, and at fre chois of autouris sumtyme; and now tho *shulen* be taken as it acordith best to the sentence. (WYCPROL: I, 60)

(114) And as amongst men and women humility is the way to be preferr'd; so it is in Husbands, they *shall* prevail by cession, by sweetness and counsel, and charity and compliance. (JETAYLOR: 23)

At times the value of the speech act is clarified or reinforced by the use of a harmonic expression in a superordinate clause, such as the verb *to counsel*, as used in the following quotation:

(115) But lyue we wel, and God fayluþ not to counselen vs how we *schullen* do. (WSERM: 36, I. 376)

As with advice, cases of requests for advice are also present in various text types. Most instances occur in dialogues or quoted speech and commonly represent direct requests:

(116) Therfor thei seiden to hym, What *schulen* we do, that we worche the werkis of God? (WYCNEW: VI, 20)

(117) O Master Master, by and by, nay, 'tis my Dames voice, whether *shall* I depart? where *shall* I run to hide myself from Sarah? (PENNY: 149)

(118) (saith she) see how well and irrefragably thou canst prove what I have said, to wit, that god is wholly replenished with the sovereign Good. How *shall* I do that? (replied I). (BOETHPR: 135)

In other occurrences these speech acts are reported by the author to simulate a dialogue between himself and the reader. This structure is typical, for example, of *The Cloud of Unknowing*, which alternates requests formulated in direct questions, such as in the first of the following quotations, with other requests for advice in the form of indirect questions, as in the second:

(119) Bot sorroufuly þou seist now: 'How *schal* I do? And siþ þis is soþ þat þou seist, how *schal* I ȝeue acompte of iche [time] diuersly; (CLOUD: 20)

(120) And forþermore, ȝif þou aske me what discrecion þou *schalt* haue in þis werk, þan I answere þee and sey: 'Ryȝt none!' (CLOUD: 79)

However, indirect requests for advice also appear:

(121) Shal y, hym my douȝtyr take? / Sey þou me þe certeyn of alle / Wheþer y *shal*, o y ne *shalle*. (HS: 9)

In some sentences the subject is 1st person plural and the request concerns the interlocutor's advice or opinion on the action to be taken jointly, as in the following instances:

(122) Oh me, all the Horses are got over the River, what *shall* we do now? *Shall* we follow them over the water? (WALTON: 211)

(123) Well, well honest Jone, I know thy meaning, come give me thy hand, let us to Church and be married with speed but now I think on't, what Church *shall* we go to Ione? (PENNY: 269)

The two patterns (the first including a 1st person singular subject, and the second a 1st person plural subject) are very similar in use and are often adopted within the same context, as can be seen in this series of questions that a bride-to-be asks her fiancé:

(124) This will be brave indeed John, but what *shall* we do with our Ale? [...]
What *shall* we do for Clothes? [...]
Who *shall* we bid to our Wedding? [...]
What Musick *shall* we have? [...]
I laugh to think how the young men will turn the Lasses about in dancing, and how they will buss them, methinks I see them already, but good Jack how *shall* I do to behave my self at that time amongst so many; I shall be so ashamed I shant know what to do. [...]
What Favours *shall* we give? (PENNY: 117-8)

5.1.3. Possibility

Another deontic use of SHALL expresses possibility; the instances found in the corpus only occur in E3, in the context of Statutes and Comedies. In the former text type, when permission is granted to judges, the SHALL-form is usually accompanied by the expression *have power*, as can be seen in the following quotations:

(125) That the Justices of the Peace [...] *shall* have power to enlarge or widen any Highways in their respective Counties Ridin' Divisions Liberties or Places (STAT7: VII, 210)

(126) and the said Justices of the Peace for any County City Riding Division Liberty or other Place or the major part of them being Five att the least *shall* have power to order one or more Assessment or Assessment' to be made levied or collected upon all and every the Inhabitant' Owners or Occupiers of Land' Houses Tenement' or Hereditament' in their respective Parishes or Places (STAT7: VII, 210)

Instead, when permission is granted to common citizens, harmonic words such as *at liberty* or *free* are generally employed:

(127) the Party injured *shall* be at liberty to bring his Action for the Damages by him sustained (STAT7: VIII, 457)

(128) to which all Persons concerned (upon reasonable Request) *shall* have free accesse without Fee or Charge Any thing herein contained to the contrary notwithstanding (STAT7: VIII, 459)

In comedies deontic possibility occurs whenever some sort of authorization is implied in the locutor's words:

(129) O my dear (Nurse), forgive me this once, and I'll never misuse you again; no, if I do, you *shall* give me three thumps on the Back, and a great pinch by the Cheek. (VANBR: I, 60)

(130) Well, I'm such a tender-hearted Fool, I find I can refuse nothing; so you *shall* e'en follow your own Inventions. (VANBR: I, 64)

5.2. *Dynamic meanings*

5.2.1. Possibility

Four of the occurrences of SHALL-forms found in the M3 subsection of the corpus express dynamic possibility, since they can all be paraphrased by 'it is possible for + SUBJECT + INFINITIVE'. Instances of this semantic value – which is not normally realized in PDE by SHALL – resemble some of the cases presented by Visser as having "the sense 'will be able'" (Visser 1963-73: 1593). These instances have been recorded in Handbooks and Biblical texts; three of them have an inanimate subject:

(131) þese cures as I vnderstonde *schal* hele an hors for þe farcioun ful wel. (HORSES: 97)

(132) as that sentence (unkynde ȝonge trees *shulen* not ȝeue depe rootis), owith to be thus, (plauntingis of auoutrie *shulen* not ȝeue depe rootis). (WYCPROL: I, 59)

In one quotation the SHALL-form is followed by *be able*, thus presenting the structure that has become popular in PDE to express ability in the future; here, however, the adjective *able* has the meaning of 'suited, appropriate, fit':

(133) And alle men *schulen* be able for to be tauȝt of God. Each man that herde of the fadir, and hath lerned, cometh to me. (WYCNEW: VI, 40)

No occurrences of dynamic possibility have been found in E3.

5.2.2. Prediction

Prediction is the most common pragmatic function associated with SHALL-forms both in M3 and in E3 (cf. Tables 4 and 5); in M3 it corresponds to over one half (55%) of the cases taken into consideration, while in E3 to nearly one half (49%). In both periods prediction is expressed in different pragmatic forms, as can be seen in Tables 10 and 11.

	neutr. predict.	*prophecy*	*assurance*	*Total*
BIBLE	90	5	15	110
DOCUMENTS	12			12
FICTION	33	10	9	52
HANDBOOKS	34		2	36
HISTORY	53	2	2	57
HOMILIES	25	5	6	36
LETTERS	13			13
PHILOSOPHY	15	3		18
RELIGIOUS TR	273	34	14	321
RULES	17	7	1	25
SCIENCE	1			1
SERMONS	20	14	4	38
TRAVELOGUES	10			10
All texts	596	80	53	729
Ambiguous cases	26 (4%)	0	5 (9%)	31 (4%)

Table 10. Occurrences of SHALL with pragmatic uses expressing prediction in M3.

	neutr. predict.	*prophecy*	*assurance*	*Total*
BIOGRAPHIES	3			3
DIARIES	1			1
DRAMA	27		3	30
EDUC TR	9			9
FICTION	32		2	34
HANDBOOKS	11		2	13
HISTORY	1			1
LAW	116			116
LETTERS	31	1	1	33
PHILOSOPHY	11		1	12
SCIENCE	1			1
SERMONS	10	3		13
TRIALS	2			2
All texts	255	4	9	268
Ambiguous cases	20 (8%)	0	2 (22%)	22 (8%)

Table 11. Occurrences of SHALL with pragmatic uses expressing prediction in E3.

5.2.2.1. Neutral prediction

Neutral prediction (or 'pure future', as this category is often referred to in the literature) occurs in all the text types included in the corpus. There are examples of usage with all persons, and in all kinds of sentences: affirmative, negative and interrogative. The prediction is often in an object clause after a main clause verb like *I hope, I'm afraid, I expect*:

(134) In this part I hope I *shall* finde easy beleive and noe body can have a pretence to doubt (LOCKE: 49)

(135) I'm afraid we *shall* lose that Character, Madam, whenever you happen to change your Condition. (VANBR: I, 5)

(136) You shall be hang'd first, but if ever you expect that I *shall* be friends with you, there must be two things granted. (PENNY: 271)

In Philosophical books and Sermons this predictive usage of SHALL often expresses a result or consequence:

(137) Thou hast now then the Form and causes of that adulterate Felicity: now turn again the Eyes of thy Consideration upon the contrary Prospect, and thou *shalt* soon comprehend that true and genuine happiness which I so long have promised thee. (BOETHPR: 127)

(138) it is as if a King should beat his Viceroy and use him like a Dog; from whom most of that Reverence and Majesty must needs depart, which he first put upon him, and the subjects *shall* pay him less duty, how much his Prince hath treated him with less civility; and the government of the whole family *shall* be disordered, if blows be laid upon that shoulder which together with the other ought to bear nothing but the cares and the issues of a prudent government. (JETAYLOR: 25)

With this meaning they can be found in a variety of genres, although more frequently in Handbooks. This can be explained by the particular function this modal verb performs in writings on Science, where it often expresses something that follows from an action or set of conditions. The result clause is usually introduced by *(and) then, and, (and) so* or *(so) that*. Here are a few examples of this usage:

(139) And if you abate the quantite of the houre inequale by day out of 30, than *shal* the remenaunt that levith parforme the houre inequale by night. (ASTR: 672, C2)

(140) tak than thy blake thred & ley it so þ[t] it kerue the centre of the Epicicle / & streche forth vp vn to vpperest part of the same epicicle / and than *shal* this blake thred shewe bothe the verrey (motus (locum)) of the epicicle in the grete lymbe / & ek the verrey aux of the planete in the epicicle (EPLANETS: 26)

(141) & it peliþ awei þe heere up bi þe rotes so þat þe hors wille rubbe him-self þat þe necke & þe dok of his tailes *schal* be al bare & þat wol come of superfluyte of blod. or of oþer wicked humourr. (HORSES: 48)

SHALL-forms may also express result in non-scientific texts, as can be seen in the following quotations:

(142) quod he, "if we gone toward þe north, men wil seyn þat we gon toward þe Scottes: and so we *shul* be holde traitoures, for cause of distaunce þat is bituene Kyng Edward and Robert þe Brus, (BRUT: 217)

(143) I shall observe my own the more, but you must not look towards me, for then I *shall* laugh and that will shame me quite. (PENNY: 118)

5.2.2.2. Prophecy

Cases of prediction based on an appeal to authority – and which have thus acquired a stronger predictive force – have been found more frequently in Religious genres, but are also present in others, such as Fiction, Rules and Letters. The source most frequently quoted is the Bible, particularly Christ's words in the Gospels:

(144) For, as þis gospel telliþ, þese taares *schul* be gedrid furst, but at þe day of doom Cristis lymes *schulle* furst be counfortid. (WSERM: 36, I. 375)

(145) Als Crist to his desciples dere / In þe godspell sais on þis manere, / "All ȝowre care *sall* turned be / Vnto aylastand gamin and gle." (NHOM: II, 206)

Other predictions are taken from the Old Testament to quote words uttered by God and the prophets:

(146) as God seith by the prophete Ezechiel, "Ye *shal* remembre yow of youre weyes, and they *shuln* displese yow." (CTPARS: 290, C1)

(147) and eft Dauith seith, "the Lord *schal* telle in the scripturis of puplis, and of these princis that weren in it," that is, in holi chirche, (WYCPROL: I, 56)

At times the source of the prophetic quotations is explicitly specified:

(148) St. Jude in his Epistle gives much the same character of them that St. Peter here does, ver. 18, 19. (There *shall* come in the last days mockers, walking after their own ungodly lusts, sensual, [...]) (TILLOTS: II, ii. 419)

The explicit mention of the biblical source is justified by the fact that the interpretation of the prophetic quotations is often the very object of the sermons themselves, as can be seen in the following examples:

(149) First, we will consider the nature of the sin here mentioned, which is scoffing at Religion, (There *shall* come scoffers): These it seems were a sort of people that derided our Saviour's prediction (TILLOTS: II, ii. 418)

(150) and reasons of his coming to judgement, infidelity, and prophane scoffing at Religion. (When the Son of man comes, *shall* he find faith on the earth?) And St Jude out of an ancient prophecy of Enoch (TILLOTS: II, ii. 430)

The following are quotations from other sources:

(151) And yet seith this Pamphilles moreover that 'they that been thralle and bonde of lynage *shullen* been maad worthy and noble by the richesses.' [...] And this Pamphilles seith also, 'If thow be right happy – that is to seyn, if thou be right riche – thou *shalt* fynde a greet nombre of felawes and freendes. And if thy fortune change that thou wexe povre, farewel freendshipe and felaweshipe, for thou *shalt* be alloone withouten any compaignye, but if it be the compaignye of povre folk.' (CTMEL: 232, C2)

(152) Als a versifiour says in a verse þarby, / þe whilk es made in metre þus schortly: / "With þe sight of God þai *sal* be fed, / And with brightnes of light þai *sal* be cled, / And þair werk *sal* be ay lovyng," (PRICK: 252)

5.2.3. Assurance

Various cases of SHALL-forms expressing assurance have been found in the two subsections of the Helsinki Corpus; they are not concentrated in any specific text type. In these cases predictions are made stronger by the locutor by means of an emphasizer or booster

(Holmes 1984) meant to increase the illocutionary force of the speech act. Two types of emphasizers have been found in the corpus: the first corresponds to locutor-oriented boosters, whose function is to highlight the truthfulness and reliability of the utterer. Here are a few examples:

(153) And he seide to hem, Treuli, treuli, Y seie to ȝou, ȝe *schulen* se heuene opened, and the aungels of god stiynge vp and comynge doun on mannys sone. (WYCNEW: I, 40)

(154) Therfor if the sone make ȝou fre, verili ȝe *schulen* be fre (WYCNEW: VIII, 20)

(155) Wha cums to me he sal be saue / And hunger sal he neuer haue, / And who in me will trewly trist / Hertly *sal* he neuer haue thrist. (NHOM: II, 76)

(156) and I *shall* wait upon thee too that same day, as it is my duty. (PENNY: 118)

(157) Prevail with him – or he *shall* never prevail with me, I can tell him that. (VANBR: I, 64)

The second type of instances of assurance, instead, relies on content-oriented boosters, meant to increase the illocutionary force of the speech act by underlining the certainty of the proposition asserted and thus emphasizing its validity. The following are examples of this usage:

(158) For certes there availleth noon essoyne ne excusacioun. And nat oonly that oure defautes *shullen* be jugged, but eek that alle oure werkes *shullen* openly be knowe. (CTPARS: 291, C1)

(159) He is to greet a nygard that wolde werne / A man to lighte a candle at his lanterne; / He *shal* have never the lasse light, pardee. (CTBATH: 109, C2)

(160) and then we *shall* have good handsel indeed, (PENNY: 120)

In some cases, emphasis is laid on the certainty of the interlocutor's acceptance of the validity of the proposition, as can be seen in the following quotations:

(161) You shall not doubt it long, for you *shall* see me do it presently: (WALTON: 215)

(162) Be sure that nothing *shall* be squandered away can be prevented. (HOXINDEN: 276)

(163) They *shall* be dispoil'd of it sooner than perhaps thou wouldst have them, (BOETHPR: 178)

A proposition may also be stressed by means of a change in the conventional word order:

(164) I'll give my Wench a Wedding-Dinner, tho' I go to Grass with the King of Assyria for't, and such a Dinner it *shall* be, as is not to be Cook'd in the Poaching of an Egg. (VANBR: I, 61)

(165) Now on my Knees, my Dear, let me ask your pardon for my Indiscretion, my own I never *shall* obtain. (VANBR: I, 40)

5.2.4. Necessity

Dynamic necessity concerns those cases of obligation in which the accomplishment of one action is to be considered as an essential requisite for the successful achievement of another. Here are two instances of this type of modality found in the corpus:

(166) þou schuldest haue maad a bodily schewyng vnto hym, ouþer in contenaunce, or in voyce, or in worde, or in som oþer rude bodely streynyng, as it is when þou *schalt* schewe a þing þat is hid in þin hert to a bodely man; (CLOUD: 90)

(167) ARCH. If the Sun rides fast, and disappoints not Mortals of to Morrow's dawn, this Night shall crown my Joys.
MRS. SULL. My Sex's Pride assist me.
ARCH. My Sex's Strength help me.
MRS. SULL. You *shall* kill me first. (FARQUHAR: 60)

5.2.5. Habit

Our corpus also contains SHALL-forms used to express habitual actions. PDE usage of SHALL does not include this meaning, nowadays commonly covered by WILL. In ME, however, both modal verbs were used for this function; this is shown in the following quotation, in which the two auxiliaries alternate:

(168) ȝif he be ranke of blod he wol gnappe himsilf & rubbe him a-ȝens þe walle þat he stondeþ bi. his kaym *schal* stynke. & his pisse *schal* be rede & þicke. his eyȝenwebbe blod-schote & wateri with-alle. And ouer al his bodi þer wol rise litel smale bleynes þe whiche þou schalt aspie bi felyng of þyn honde. For þei buþ I-hud vndur þe heere. And he *schal* leue his mete more þan he was I-wonede. (HORSES: 89)

The use of SHALL-forms to express habitual actions and permanent characteristics continued in EModE, as five instances have been found in the E3 part of the corpus. Four of these, however, occur in one specific text and may indicate the author's preference for this usage:

(169) It has often griev'd the Heart of me, to see how some inhumane Wretches murther their kind Fortunes; those that by sacrificing all to one Appetite, *shall* starve all the rest. You *shall* have some that live only in their Palates, and in their sense of tasting *shall* drown the other Four: Others are only Epicures in Appearances, such who *shall* starve their Nights (FARQUHAR: 6)

6. Concluding remarks

A comparison of the percentage share of the various types of modal meaning for SHALL shows interesting differences in the two periods, as Table 12 shows. From M3 to E3 the slightly larger percentage share of dynamic uses is reduced until dynamic and deontic uses are virtually of the same frequency (from 55: 45% in M3 to 51: 49% in E3). This is due to an increase in the use of SHALL for the expression of volition, compensated by a decrease in the conveyance of predictive meanings.

However, as can be seen in Table 13,[18] this change is not uniform, as the increase in deontic meanings occurs in most text types (such as Scientific works, Sermons, Historical books, Fiction and

18 The first figure in each column refers to M3, the second to E3.

Letters) but not in all. As regards the various categories of modality usage, apart from that of volition (whose percentages rise in all text types), the others do not show uniform trends. It is interesting to notice, however, that in general the increase in deontic meanings does not occur in the traditional semantic categories of order, prohibition, instruction, advice, threat and promise, but more in those of intentionality and proposal.

Modality types	*M3*		*E3*	
Volition	15		18	
Necessity	30		29	
Possibility	–		2	
Total deontic		45		49
Possibility	0.3		–	
Prediction	54		50	
Necessity	0.2		0.6	
Habit	0.4		0.9	
Total dynamic		55		51
Total		100		100

Table 12. Percentages distribution of SHALL-forms by modality type.

The data found in the corpus thus enable us to draw two main conclusions: on the one hand, the picture offered by the M3 subsection seems to confirm the general trend in the grammaticalisation process, exemplified by the following scale (Goossens 1987: 118):

Facultative > Deontic > Epistemic[19] > Futurity

The process of grammaticalization of SHALL thus seems to have been completed in the first period examined here. On the other hand, the data found in the second period show that in the intervening two centuries there had been a decline in the use of SHALL for the expression of futurity, mainly due to the strong competition of WILL in the performance of this same function (cf. Chapter 9). As studies on corpora from later historical periods have shown (cf., for example,

19 Goossens adopts the distinction of modal categories into root and epistemic, the latter including our dynamic values.

Coates 1983: 186), this process of reduction in the use of SHALL for the expression of futurity continued in the following centuries.

	Deontic modality								*Dynamic modality*									
	volit		*nec*		*possib*		*Tot*		*possib*		*predic*		*nec*		*habit*		*Tot*	
	M3	*E3*	*M3*	*E3*	*M3*	*E3*	*M3*	*E3*	*M3*	*E3*	*M3*	*E3*	*M3*	*E3*	*M3*	*E3*	*M3*	*E3*
DOCUMENTS	10	–	76	–	0	–	86	–	0	–	14	–	0	–	0	–	14	–
LAW	–	0	–	50	–	2	–	52	–	0	–	47	–	0	–	0	–	47
HANDBOOKS	5	37	67	18	0	0	72	55	1	0	24	39	1	3	2	3	28	45
SCIENCE	0	90	0	0	0	0	0	90	0	0	100	10	0	0	0	0	100	10
EDUC. TR.	–	41	–	6	–	0	–	47	–	0	–	53	–	0	–	0	–	53
PHILOSOPHY	3	19	47	6	0	0	50	25	0	0	50	75	0	0	0	0	50	75
HOMILIES	14	–	12	–	0	–	26	–	0	–	74	–	0	–	0	–	74	–
SERMONS	0	25	22	5	0	0	22	30	0	0	78	65	0	5	0	0	78	70
RULES	0	–	63	–	0	–	63	–	0	–	37	–	0	–	0	–	37	–
TRIALS	–	33	–	0	–	0	–	33	–	0	–	67	–	0	–	0	–	67
RELIG. TR.	6	–	13	–	0	–	19	–	0	–	81	–	0	–	0	–	81	–
HISTORY	32	86	27	0	0	0	59	86	0	0	14	0	0	0	0	0	14	0
TRAVELOGUES	21	–	21	–	0	–	42	–	0	–	53	–	0	–	5	–	58	–
DIARIES	–	50	–	0	–	0	–	50	–	0	–	50	–	0	–	0	–	50
BIOGRAPHIES	–	40	–	0	–	0	–	40	–	0	–	60	–	0	–	0	–	60
FICTION	17	25	12	23	0	0	29	48	0	0	68	52	0	0	3	0	71	52
DRAMA	–	28	–	12	–	3	–	43	–	0	–	49	–	2	–	7	–	58
LETTERS	24	32	0	9	0	0	24	41	0	0	77	59	0	0	0	0	77	59
BIBLE	35	–	20	–	0	–	55	–	1	–	44	–	0	–	0	–	45	–
All texts	15	18	30	29	–	2	45	49	0.3	–	54	50	0.2	0.6	0.4	0.9	55	51

Table 13. Percentages of SHALL-forms according to text and modality types.

VIII. Should

The M3 part of the Helsinki Corpus contains 504 SHOULD-forms; these, however, also include two instances in which SHOULD reflects non-modal usage:

(1) as hire infortune *scholde*, Sche granteth him al that he wolde.
(as her fate imposed…) (GOWER: I, 322)[1]

(2) and as Jewis, […] signefien clerkis, that *schulden* knouleche to God,
(that owe knowledge to God)
(WYCPROL: I, 56)

Non-modal usage is not recorded in the E3 part, in which 320 SHOULD-forms appear. The decrease in the number of occurrences does not only concern absolute figures, but also normalized frequencies per 10,000 words: from 27 in M3 to 18 in E3.

1. Spelling variants

In the M3 section *suld* (which, together with *sulde*, occurs only in Northern texts) is the only spelling variant found with all subjects; *schulde*, however, is the most frequent. Forms in *-st* (*schost, scholdest, schuldest, schuldist, schuldust* and *shuldest*) are only found with 2nd person singular subjects, while forms in *-en* correlate with plural subjects (especially 3rd person plural).

1 As a matter of fact, this instance could be interpreted as a case in which the verb BE is ellipted after the modal, which would thus express a deontic value. However, the idea of imposition conveyed by an almost personified fate is perhaps more forceful (and, possibly, therefore more appropriate) in this context.

In the E3 part a dramatic increase in orthographic and morphological regularization is apparent; *should* accounts for 84% of all instances. A relatively high number of occurrences in which *-l-* is omitted (37, i.e. 11.5%) may be taken to signal a phonological rendering of the modal. As for morphologically marked forms in *-st*, a few instances were recorded in informal or speech-based texts (private Letters, Drama and Philosophical dialogues).

2. Distribution according to text type

Normalized data per 10,000 words summarized in Table 1 show the distribution of SHOULD-forms by text type. As we can see, in the M3 section there is a fairly high correlation between SHOULD use and texts in which moral instruction is given: in particular, Sermons have a number of occurrences that is nearly three times as high as average. Relatively high figures also appear in Historical texts and Fictional works, in which orders given by people in authority are frequently reported; similarly, authoritative advice is at the basis of the significant correlation between SHOULD-forms and text types in Homilies and Philosophical works; this function may also explain an equally high number in Documentary texts. On the other hand, a remarkably low correlation is observed in Handbooks and Travelogues: prescriptive speech acts are virtually lacking in the latter, while in the former they tend to be expressed less tentatively than through a SHOULD-form.

A high degree of correlation continues in E3 between the occurrence of SHOULD-forms and text types in which behaviour is recommended, advice is given and suggestions are put forward: Educational treatises, Philosophical and Fictional dialogues, but also non-private Letters, in which orders can be reported. In contrast, we find significantly low numbers in texts in which few tentative forms are required: Travelogues, Diaries and Historical narration. The lowest figure is found for Legal documents, in which SHOULD-forms are only used to express reported orders or requests.

Text Type	*M3*	*E3*
SERMONS	75	22
HISTORY	36	9
FICTION	29	29
PHILOSOPHY	29	43
SCIENCE	22	13
LETTERS	9	21
TRAVELOGUES	3	4
HANDBOOKS	2	10
DOCUMENTS	28	-[2]
HOMILIES	28	-
RELIGIOUS TREATISES	24	-
RULES	22	-
BIBLE	21	-
EDUCATIONAL TREATISES	-	53
BIOGRAPHIES	-	19
DRAMA	-	18
TRIALS	-	12
DIARIES	-	8
LAW	-	2
All texts	27	18

Table 1. Normalized occurrences of SHOULD-forms per text type.

On average, the number of SHOULD-forms decreases in the second part of the corpus analysed, except in Letters, Travelogues, Philosophical treatises and Handbooks. On the other hand, there seems to have been quite a dramatic fall in Sermons, Science and Historical texts. In Fiction, instead, values are stable in both subcorpora. It will be interesting to compare these patterns of increase and decrease in relation to changes in modal meaning (cf. § 6) and, possibly, to similar or divergent patterns concerning WOULD, in order to see whether usage had become more or less specialized.

2 This signals that no samples were included in the subcorpus and therefore no comparison can be made in relation to rates of increase or decrease.

3. Sentence structure

Table 2 summarizes the distribution of occurrences of SHOULD-forms in different clause types. As we can see, most are found in subordinate clauses, with a slight increase in the percentage of tokens in subordinate clauses in E3. The absolute and normalized numbers of tokens (not shown on the table) decrease for all subclauses, except for noun clauses, indirect questions and conditional clauses. As regards the latter, which in E3 represent a significantly greater percentage of SHOULD-use than in M3, it will be interesting to compare the pattern of development in usage of WOULD in the same type of clause.

Clause type		*M3*	*E3*
Main		29	22
Subordinate clauses		71	78
	Noun	32	41
	Final	14	7
	Relative	13	11
	Cause	4	1
	Indirect questions	3	5
	Conditional	2	12
	Concessive	2	0
	Time	1	1

Table 2. Percentage of SHOULD-forms occurring in different clause types.

Main clauses in both M3 and E3 include genuine or rhetorical questions, the latter often introduced by *how* or *why*:

(3) How *schulde* blynde fooles aftyr amende þis rewle þat Crist haþ ȝyuen? (WSERM: I, 357)

(4) "Qui *suld* man," said he, "be sua radd þat es in rightwis batail stadd, [...]" (CURSOR: 436)

(5) Strong! It must be so, or how *should* we be strong that drink it? (FARQUHAR: 2)

Exclamations introduced by *that* have been classed as noun clauses, though they might have been classed as main clauses due to their crystallized form:

(6) Allas þat euer soche a gentil blode *shulde* ben don to deþ with-outen cause and resoun! (BRUT: 223)

(7) Jesu God! that we *should* live to see any such Creatures among Mankind, (LISLE: IV, 122.C1)

Final clauses may express both purpose and expected result. When the latter has a negative connotation, it is introduced by *lest, for fear that* or *ere*; lower likelihood of the event (or greater hope of its unlikelihood) may be signalled by the adverb *peradventure*, while in E3 we also find *in case*. The following quotations show a few examples of the different possibilities in M3 and E3:

(8) Meny Iewes come to þis solempnite leste þe welþe þat þei hadde under þe olde kyng *schulde* be wiþdrawe in þe newe kynges tyme. (TREVISA: VIII, 83)

(9) He had lever thole here þis payne, [...], Ar he þe syght of his face *suld* tyne, (PRICK: 256)

(10) He would not let me have it for fear I *should* play the ill husband (PENNY: 116)

(11) Upon some he lays grievous heavy Crosses, lest they *should* grow luxurious by too long a Course of Felicity (BOETHPR: 198)

In both M3 and E3 noun clauses form the largest class of subclause with SHOULD, probably because these forms frequently convey reported speech acts concerning future actions or states (such as promises, requests, or predictions):[3]

---

3 In these cases SHOULD may have a bleached, generically subjunctive meaning – cf., among others, Mossé (1952/1968: 108-109), Traugott (1972: 150-151), Harris (1987: 183), Anderson (1991: 22; and 2001), Warner (1993: 148-149) and Bybee (1995). However, the modal can often be interpreted as retaining some of its semantic value in relation to harmonic elements in the context. On this point Coates argues: "Where SHOULD functions as a pure quasi-subjunctive, it is semantically empty. But in many contexts, where the preceding adjective or verb is not incompatible with the sense of weak

(12) William bisshop of Hely demede þat monkes *schulde* be putte awey from Coventre (TREVISA: VIII, 93)

(13) They tooke an oath of there people y^t they *shoulde* neither buy or sell or eate or drinke with freindes (FOX: 153)

Word order is typically SVO, except in conditional clauses, which in E3 may be introduced by the inversion between the subject and the verb:[4]

(14) I should have been the most ungrateful Person living, *should* I have been disloyal (LISLE: IV, 122.C2)

(15) we began to turn our back upon the Gulf, and steer a more Northern Course, from whence to reflect what Sustenance this barren Earth could produce, that, *should* our Stores fail, we might want (FRYER: II, 181)

4. Verb phrase structure

The most widespread construction has the modal followed by an active infinitive, which may be expressed or ellipted: the two possibilities together account for 80% of the total in M3 and 73% in E3.[5] Passive infinitives occur in a range of text types; in E3 they are relatively frequent in Educational treatises and Philosophical texts,

---

obligation expressed by Root SHOULD, we have merger [...]. That is, it is not clear which of the two uses the speaker / writer intended, as both are possible [...] [and] the two meanings are not mutually exclusive" (1983: 68) – cf. also van Kemenade (1992: 304). We have therefore decided to follow Coates' approach and distinguish between a bleached periphrastic subjunctive use and other uses that can be placed in our semantic categories. On modals in speech acts and statements cf. also Boyd / Thorne (1969).

4 This use of SHOULD as a "marker of unreal condition" in PDE is also described by Hermerén (1978: 143). On the use of SHOULD in the apodosis of conditional clauses cf. also Leirbukt (1997: 56).

5 However, in E3 the bare infinitive is only ellipted in one rhetorical question: "Neither can wretched Men agree amongst themselves. And why *should* they?" (BOETHPR: 199)

with 20 and 10 occurrences respectively, thus accounting for nearly 42% of all instances.

An interesting decrease is observed in the use of perfect passives, which fall from 10 tokens in M3 to just 1 token in E3. Instances of perfect infinitives also decrease, though less dramatically (from 19 tokens in M3 to 14 in E3); these normally occur where the counterfactuality of the proposition is signalled, as is typical of past conditionals:

(16) and Sir Hugh Dauill þe next day after was taken and put into prisoun, & *shulde* haue ben done to þe deþ if he hade nouȝ spousede þe Kynges nece, þat was þe Erl Gilbertus sustre of Gloucestre. (BRUT: 220)

Modal combinations including SHOULD and another modal form are restricted to M3; indeed, they have all been found in the same text, *The Cloud of Unknowing*, and they are all followed by *mow*:

(17) it may not be after þe cours of kynde ne of comoun grace, þat I *schuld* <u>mowe</u> kepe or elles make aseeþ to any mo tymes þan to þoo þat ben for to come. (CLOUD: 21)

(18) For I may not trowe þat a soule contynowyng in þis werk niȝt and day wiþ-outyn discrecion *schuld* <u>mowe</u> erre in any of þees outward doinges; and elles me þink þat he schuld alweis erre. (CLOUD: 81)

(19) For ne were it þat a soule were sumwhat fed with a maner of counforte of his riȝt worching, elles *schuld* he not <u>mow</u> bere þe pyne þat he haþ of þe wetyng and felyng of his beyng. (CLOUD: 84)

No instances of the modal followed by progressive forms (either active or passive) have been found to occur in the corpus, either in the M3 or E3 sections.

5. Time reference

As far as SHOULD is concerned, time reference is of little classificatory interest, as no tokens were observed to be associated with past time reference. Concerning uses of this modal in reported utterances (which, from the point of view of the reporter, are set in the past by definition), these can be described as expressing present, future or timeless reference in relation to the temporal collocation of the finite verb in the superordinate clause:[6]

(20) the Lord God brouȝte tho to Adam, that he *schulde* se what he *schulde* clepe tho (WYCOLD: II, 1G)

(21) and þrew þe body [...] wiþ oute þe citee, and fleyȝ awey as a þeef *schulde*.
(and ran away like a thief normally would)
(TREVISA: VIII, 91)

6. Type of modality

SHOULD-forms have been found to express a very similar range of semantic values and pragmatic uses to those conveyed by SHALL (cf. Ch. 7); these values and uses, however, normally occur in contexts in which they are displaced onto a level of hypotheticality, counterfactuality or tentativeness.

In several cases at least two semantic values may overlap: as a result, the attribution to one category or the other has been based on the prevalent function in the context of the text analysed. In the following quotation, for instance, *schulden* may express both prescription (thus having a deontic value) and dynamic prediction in

6 These labels, however, are best used to refer to tense, rather than time. Consequently, in narrative contexts, where events are reported, it might be clearer to describe the time reference of the modalized clause as *preceding*, *simultaneous* (i.e., coincidental with the time reference expressed by other predications in the same context), *subsequent*, or *neutral* (= timeless).

the form of a hypothetical consequence, but the former value has been judged to be more prominent than the latter in the light of the emphasis placed in the context on the active role of the interlocutor as a subject:

(22) Jhesus seith to hem, If God were ȝoure fadir, sotheli ȝe *schulden* loue me;
(WYCNEW: VIII, 40)

In order to provide an indication of the importance of SHOULD-forms with such overlapping meanings, a separate category collects occurrences in which bleached (as in the case of periphrastic subjunctives – cf. n. 3) or underdetermined meanings are found. Most occurrences, however, were disambiguated in the way already described. Table 3 shows a summary of all occurrences (in absolute numbers and in percentage) with their different values in M3 and E3.

		M3		*E3*	
Modal cat.	*Meaning*	*No.*	*%*	*No.*	*%*
deontic	volition	24	4	44	14
	necessity	251	50	113	35
	possibility	1	0	3	1
	total	276	55	160	50
dynamic	ability	3	0	2	1
	possibility	23	4	20	6
	prediction	135	26	93	29
	necessity	23	4	5	2
	habit	2	0	0	0
	total	186	37	120	38
epistemic	possibility	0	0	0	0
	inference	3	0.5	3	0.5
	necessity	0	0	0	0
	total	3	1	3	1
bleached and underdet. mngs		37	7	37	11
TOTAL		502	100	320	100

Table 3. Distribution of SHOULD-forms in relation to modal meaning.

Table 4 summarizes the distribution of these same values in each text type of our subcorpus. As shown previously, in the M3 subcorpus the highest frequency of occurrences is observed in Sermons; this is predictably associated with deontic modality (52% of all occurrences), as it is typical of this genre to provide rules of conduct and moral advice. Epistemic values are still very rare, and only seem to occur in the more narrative contexts; cases of merging meaning mostly involve the possibility of deontic / dynamic undecidability.

	M3					*E3*				
	de	*dy*	*ep*	*mix*	*Tot*	*de*	*dy*	*ep*	*mix*	*Tot*
PHILOSOPHY	16	6	1	4	29	7	23	2	9	43
FICTION	14	13	0	2	29	14	12	0	1	29
SERMONS	53	17	0	3	75	12	5	0	4	22
LETTERS	5	3	0	0	9	8	8	0	4	21
SCIENCE	0	22	0	0	22	1	10	0	0	13
HANDBOOKS	2	0	0	0	2	4	5	0	0	10
HISTORY	20	14	0	1	36	6	2	0	0	9
TRAVELOGUES	0	3	0	0	3	0	1	0	1	4
DOCUMENTS	20	7	0	0	28	-	-	-	-	-
HOMILIES	16	9	0	2	28	-	-	-	-	-
REL. TREATISES	8	13	0	1	24	-	-	-	-	-
RULES	16	3	0	1	22	-	-	-	-	-
BIBLE	10	7	0	3	21	-	-	-	-	-
ED. TREATISES	-	-	-	-	-	47	3	0	0	53
BIOGRAPHIES	-	-	-	-	-	8	9	0	1	19
DRAMA	-	-	-	-	-	5	9	0	3	18
TRIALS	-	-	-	-	-	7	3	0	1	12
DIARIES	-	-	-	-	-	2	5	0	0	8
LAW	-	-	-	-	-	2	0	0	0	2
All texts	14	10	0	2	27	9	7	0	2	18

Table 4. Distribution of SHOULD-forms with different modal meanings in different text types (normalized figures per 10,000 words).

In M3 deontic modality appears to correlate significantly with Historical texts and Documents, in which orders, commands and authoritative decisions are frequently reported; similarly, the number of occurrences per 10,000 words shows a fair degree of correlation between deontic modality and such text types as Homilies, Rules and Philosophical works, the frequently explicit aim of which is to provide moral and ethical guidance. Dynamic modality, on the other hand, does not appear to correlate specifically with any text type, except for Scientific texts, in which the predicted results or the purpose of some action is described; reported predictions are also observed in Religious texts (both Biblical and exegetic, such as Sermons, Homilies and Religious treatises) and in Fictional works or such texts as Documents and Historical works.

In E3, too, deontic modality is the largest category, although dynamic modality, especially with a predictive value, also features quite prominently. Instances of epistemic modality, however, are still rather infrequent and generally restricted to Philosophical texts; similarly, the number of occurrences in which the merging of epistemic and non-epistemic meanings can be identified appears fairly stable. As regards deontic modality, Educational treatises are (perhaps predictably) the text type in which the largest number of occurrences was recorded, as it is in this genre that encoders address recipients in order to put forward their views on recommended behaviour. Fictional dialogues are also rich in instances of advice and suggestions – a trait that appears to be shared by Sermons. SHOULD-forms may also be used to report orders, and it is with this value that they seem to occur more frequently in non-private Letters.

The highest frequency of dynamic SHOULD is found in Philosophy, with above-average frequencies in Biographies, Fiction, Drama, non-private Letters and Scientific texts (where experiments are narrated and expected results are predicted).

6.1. Deontic meanings

6.1.1. Volition

Volitional semantic values have been observed to occur more frequently in narrative contexts, whether Historical (as in M3, where they account for 58% of all occurrences) or Fictional (as in E3, where they account for nearly 31%). Both in M3 and E3 about two thirds of these occurrences convey a pragmatic value of intention, whereas the remaining tokens have a more loaded meaning of promise or threat, depending on whether the envisaged action is regarded as beneficial or detrimental to the interlocutor. The range of text types in which these loaded meanings occur, however, is rather limited.

As previously mentioned, SHOULD-forms generally occur with 3rd-person subjects in reported speech, as in the following instances:

(23) and he blesside the seuenthe dai, and halewide it; for in that dai God ceesside of al his werk which he made of nouȝt, that he *schulde* make.
(WYCOLD: II, 1G)

(24) And a litil kyng was, whos sone was sijk at Cafarnaum. Whanne this hadde herd, that Jhesu *schulde* come fro Judee in to Galilee, he wente to hym, and preiede hym, that he schulde come doun, and heele his sone;
(WYCNEW: IV, 40)[7]

In the one case in this category in which SHOULD occurs with a 2nd-person subject, intention is enquired after:

(25) Here I se þou sittes and restes And askes water als man þat thristes, And sais þou has water of þine awin; What *suld* þou do with oþer draun?
(NHOM: II, 78)

In other cases, the intentionality of the reported predication is emphasized by such harmonic expressions as *by common assent*, as we can see in this instance:

(26) And by commune assent þai *shulde* alle gone to þe castel of Dunstanburghe, the whiche perteynede to þe Erldome of Lancastre, and þat þai *shulde* abide þere til þe Kyng hade forȝeue ham his male-talent. (BRUT: 217)

In Religious texts volition may refer to an intensely desired universal wish for salvation; this is the case of the following occurrence in *Cloud*, in which the SHOULD-form has an indefinite (i.e., universal) subject:

---

7 This is an interesting case in which SHOULD also functions as a distancing device on the part of the locutor in relation to the reliability of the information provided – i.e., it corresponds to the *dicitur* function described by Visser (1963-73: 1659). On this point cf. also Traugott (1972: 150-151) and Anderson (1991: 25).

(27) þou wost wel þis, þat God is a spirit; and who-so *schuld* be onid vnto hym, it behouiþ to be in soþfastnes and deepnes of spirit, ful fer fro any feynid bodely þing. (CLOUD: 88)

6.1.1.1. Promise

In hypothetical contexts promises may be represented by SHOULD-forms with 1st-person subjects, such as we see in the following quotation:

(28) þe man þat him wald fight a-gain, And moght ouer-cum him wit his main, I *suld* him riche in all his lijf, And giue mi doghter him to wijf. (CURSOR: 432)

When promises are reported, they also occur with 3rd-person subjects:

(29) The Earl of Rochester, and the last of these, entred into a formal Engagement, [...] that if either of them died, he *should* appear, and give the other notice of the future State, if there was any (BURNETROC: 16-17)

The subject of the modal can be the beneficiary and the verbal complement a passive infinitive, emphasizing the encoder's power to make the predication come true:

(30) she þat louede him best *shulde* best bene mariede. (BRUT: 16)

(31) And þe kyng ȝalde hym self uppon covenant þat he *schulde* nouȝt be putte in bondes of iren. Kynge Richard grauntede, but he put hym in bondes of silver (TREVISA: VIII, 109)

6.1.1.2. Threat

As with promises, threats can be set in a hypothetical context, in which case they occur with a 1st-person subject:

(32) "Quare es now," said he, "saul þe king? Moght i euer wit me wit him ming Suld he neuer aftur ber cron, I *suld* him sla, bi sir mahun! [...]" (CURSOR: 430)[8]

---

8 In a recent comparison of Northern and Southern manuscripts of *Cursor Mundi* Molencki (2001: 17) has observed that in the same context the Trinity

Threats may also refer to 3rd-person subjects,[9] though these cases are more frequent when threats are reported. In several of these instances the threat is introduced by the verb *to swear*, which emphasizes the encoders' forceful attitude in relation to their speech act:

(33) he aros vp anone in wraþ, and drow his suorde, & swore by Almygty God and by his holy names, but if þat he wolde go wiþ ham, he *shulde* be dede, and þat he wolde slee him þere (BRUT: 217)

(34) With mekill noyse and with grete rout Fro þaire cete þai kest him out. Obout him speres and sparthes þai bare; þat he *suld* dy ful fast þai sware. (NHOM: II, 69)

(35) He swore, that happy man whom she was going to name *shou'd* die (BEHN: 159)

6.1.2. Necessity

In both M3 and E3 deontic necessity – i.e., obligation – represents the largest general category of modal meaning in our system: 50% of M3 tokens and 35% of E3 tokens. The smaller share of SHOULD uses is accounted for by the growth of volitional uses (see Table 3). As we will see in § 6.1.2.4. below, deontic necessity most frequently has the pragmatic value of an instruction (moral or practical), as we see typically in Religious and Educational treatises.

6.1.2.1. Order

In both subcorpora orders account for the second highest number of occurrences of reported obligation; these appear to be most frequent in Historical texts and Legal documents, in which commands issued by authoritative leaders are reported.

---

9 College (Cambridge) MS has a WOULD-form ("Shulde he neuer bere no crowne I *wolde* hin sle bi seynt mahowne"), which he describes as "bleached". As a matter of fact, an instance of this can be observed in quotation (32), which includes a SHOULD-form with a 3rd person subject: "*Suld* he neuer aftur ber cron" (CURSOR: 430)

Both encoders and recipients are generally represented by 3rd-person subjects, as shown in the following quotation:

(36) Brenne [...] sent to his broþer Belyn, þat he *shulde* ȝelde aȝeyne his lande to his wif and to his folc, & his castelles also, or elles he wolde destroye his lande. (BRUT: 25)

The following quotation refers to an event that had been ordained by the laws of allegiance or by an honourable agreement, thus representing a kind of self-imposed moral order for the subject:

(37) and þow, as traitoure vnto þi lord þe Kyng, laddest his peple of þis contrey, þat *shulde* haue holpe him at þe bataile of Bihiland; (BRUT: 227)

In religious works occurrences of reported orders are most frequent in the Bible, especially in the extracts from Genesis, in which God's deliberations about the function of each element in the newly-created world are reported,[10] or when Adam and Eve's fate is decided after the Fall:

(38) And God made twei grete liȝtis, the gretter liȝt that it *schulde* be bifore to the dai, and the lesse liȝt that it *schulde* be bifore to the niȝt; and God made sterris; and settide tho in the firmament of heuene, that tho *schulden* schyne on erthe, and that tho *schulden* be bifore to the dai and nyȝt, and *schulden* departe liȝt and derknesse. (WYCOLD: I, 1G)

(39) And the Lord God sente hym out of paradijs of likyng, that he *schulde* worche the erthe, of which he was takun. (WYCOLD: III, 20G)

In Sermons, Homilies, Religious treatises and Rules, instead, reported orders are less frequent, as these texts provide guidance through instruction and advice, both of which will be discussed in a specific paragraph. As in the other genres, however, the original illocutionary force of the reported speech act may be made explicit by the co-occurrence of harmonic superordinate verbs like *ordain, bid, command*, etc., or nouns having a similar semantic value (cf. Visser 1963-73: 1655). The following quotations provide a few instances of

10 In these instances the modal is included in a final clause.

this – the first one introduces the command with reference to a non-verbal sign:

(40) Up roos tho oon of thise olde wise, and with his hand made contenaunce that men *sholde* holden hem stille and yeven hym audience. (CTMEL: 219.C1)

(41) And so, as Crist hymself hadde ordeyned, Baptist *schulde* dye byfore, and so go to purgatorye, and be taken owt by Crist. (WSERM: I, 414)

In other cases, explicit reference in the superordinate clause is made to obligation dictated by reason, human law or religious rules:

(42) And, Thomas, resoun wolde also þat ȝe *shulde* ben hongede; but þe Kyng haþ forȝeue þat gewys for cause and loue of ȝour lynage. (BRUT: 222)

(43) And among Iewes was þis Religioun kept þat men *schulde* goo by hemself and wymmen by hemself, for þei kepten hem fro lecherye in sych pilgrimage; (WSERM: I, 355)

In E3 the largest number of SHOULD-forms with an openly prescriptive meaning was recorded in Sermons; in other text types this use conveys what the encoder reports to have been ordained either by religious or secular authority:

(44) Holy Scripture instances not the duty in this particular; but it contains in it that the Husband *should* nourish and cherish her, that he *should* refresh her sorrows and intice her fears into confidence (JETAYLOR: 28)

(45) Mr Secretary Coventry came in and from his Ma[tie] told us that it was his Ma[ties] pleasure wee *should* immediately adjourne till 4 of ye clock in ye afternoon, when it was his pleasure we *should* attend him in ye bankquetting House (AUNGIER: 26)

6.1.2.2. Prohibition

SHOULD-forms expressing reported prohibition occur in a wide range of text types, though again they seem to be more frequent in genres in which reference is made to the authoritative will of political or religious leaders, legal constraints, moral obligation and divine prescription. Concerning this, the prohibition *par excellence* refers to the Biblical text in which God's command not to eat a certain fruit is reported; this, in turn, does not only occur in the samples from the Old Testament, but is also quoted in the Parson's Tale:

(46) Which serpent seide to the wornman, Why comaundide God to ȝou, that ȝe *schulden* not ete of ech tre of paradis? (WYCOLD: III, 1G)

(47) the serpent, [...] seyde to the wornman, "Why comaunded God to yow ye *sholde* nat eten of every tree in Paradys?" (CTPARS: 298.6.C2)

In E3 the only instance in which SHOULD is used to report a prohibition is set in a Religious context:

(48) Christ said yee *shoulde* not swear att all (FOX: 82)

The concept of prohibition may be conveyed through co-occurrence of the harmonic superordinate verb *forbid*; in many cases, however, we find terms like *statute*, *proclamation*, *ordain*, *command* or *cry* (used in its legal sense):

(49) and he ordeynede a statute þat, hade a man done neuer so miche harme, and he might come into þe temple, þere *shulde* no man him misdo, but gone þerin sauf and in pees, and aftre gone into what contre þat he wolde, withouten eny harme; (BRUT: 24)

(50) for thanne were such proclamacions made that no man ne woman *sholde* approche owre life lorde for sechyng of grace (PET3: 195)

(51) hit was late ordeynid & proclamyd, [...] þat no coupere, [...] *shold* wiþin þis Citee rase ne gumme, or in eny other wyse medle with vndewe makyng, medlyng, or contrefetyng of Romeney, (JUDG: 100)

In these quotations we also observe that the negative value of the proposition is not conveyed by the verb phrase, but through a universalized subject in which the noun is preceded by *no*. A similar structure appears in the following instance, in which authority comes from a *sui generis* source (recognizably, Chaucer's ineffable Wife of Bath); though possibly not a formal prohibition as in the other cases, the fact that the subject's typical reaction is described allows us to highlight its deontic value:

(52) In al the parisshe wif ne was ther noon That to the offrynge bifore hire *sholde* goon; And if ther dide, certeyn so wrooth was she That she was out of alle charitee. (CTPROL: 30.C2)

6.1.2.3. Request

In three M3 instances[11] SHOULD-forms express reported suggestions and proposals; they are preceded by quotative verbs or equivalent nouns[12] and occur with third-person subjects:

(53) Whanne this hadde herd, that Jhesu schulde come fro Judee in to Galilee, he wente to hym, and preiede hym, that he *schulde* come doun, and heele his sone; for he bigan to die. (WYCNEW: IV, 40)

(54) as moche as rumour and spekyngge is amonges some men of the Citee that vitaillers foreins, bringyngge fissh to the Citee of london to selle, *shulde* be restrained and ylet of hire comyngge to the citee wyth hire forsaid fissh to selle it freliche, (LPROCL: 32)

(55) þan bigan þai cal and cri, þat godd o þam *suld* ha merci; (CURSOR: 424)

6.1.2.4. Instruction and advice

Although these two meanings could be described separately (in relation to their different contexts of usage and varying presupposition in relation to acceptance on the part of the recipient), we have placed them in the same sub-section because SHOULD occurs in both cases as a distal form and, consequently, as a politeness marker which often presents veiled instruction under the form of tentative advice. This becomes especially clear in the E3 samples, in which a change in thought-styles becomes apparent in the language particularly of Scientific and Educational discourse.[13] In many cases it is therefore

11 No similar occurrences have been observed in the E3 subcorpus.

12 The bleached or unbleached meaning of modals after harmonic superordinate verbs as here (or as after *bid, command*, etc.) is a question yet to be clearly resolved. We feel, however, that 'He prayed that he come down' and 'He prayed that he *should* come down' are not semantically identical and that SHOULD adds a certain degree of deontic meaning.

13 The changes that were taking place in EModE scientific writing (both from the conceptual and the stylistic points of view) have been extensively

difficult to decide the extent to which the encoder actually wishes to give instructions to the recipient, leaving no margin to the latter's discretion and does this from a politely tentative perspective, or is actually expressing personal advice as to a recommended course of action. In these cases context can help decode one or the other pragmatic value (medieval religious texts, for example, can be deemed to be fairly confident in their suggestions as to ideal conduct, and therefore provide instruction); this, however, is seldom related to any intrinsic value of the modal form under discussion, but derives from such elements that convey encoder's stance or from present-day commentators' knowledge of the texts' epistemological traits.

As a matter of fact, the highest number of occurrences classed as obligation in M3 are in a context of instruction (122 out of a total of 249, i.e. 49%). Of these, the majority were recorded in Sermons (62, i.e. 51%); relatively frequent occurrences were also observed in Religious treatises and Philosophical texts, genres which aim to outline principles for their readers to follow. Fictional texts, in turn, evoke the type of guidance that interlocutors exchange in spoken interactions; this is occasionally shown by the occurrence of SHOULD-forms with 2nd-person pronouns in direct speech, or in noun clauses introduced by a quotative verb:

(56) Thou *sholdest* seye, "Wyf, go wher thee liste; Taak youre disport; I wol nat leve no talys. I knowe yow for a trewe wyf, dame Alys." (CTBATH: 109.C1)

(57) And yet seye I ferthermoore, that ye *sholde* alwey doon youre bisynesse to gete yow richesses, (CTMEL: 234.C2)

The formulaic character of instructive dicta may be emphasized by syntactic parallelisms, alliteration, use of proverb fragments, adoption of indefinite subject and timeless temporal dimension (as in 'you should never…'):

---

described by Taavitsainen (1994 and 2001) and Gotti (1996). In particular, Gotti (1996: 86-90) outlines the especially valuable role of politeness (i.e., face-saving moves) in argumentative contexts. Following this, it is possible to argue that various hedged forms in instructional contexts have a crucial interpersonal function, presenting as advice what prove in fact to be instances of (politely hedged) instruction.

(58) You *shou'd* never bestow your pity upon those who take pains for your Contempt (VANBR: I, 35)

(59) and seyden that right so as, whil that iren is hoot, men *sholden* smyte, right so men *sholde* wreken hir wronges whil that they been fresshe and newe; (CTMEL: 219.C1)

Instruction may also be presented through reference to the teachings of the Bible or classical works; indeed, when authority is quoted, the occurrence of the harmonic verb *teach* is not infrequent. Instances are provided in the following quotations:

(60) Poul techeþ here Romayns, and so alle cristene men, how þei *schulden* kepe charite þat God ȝyueþ; (WSERM: I, 521)

(61) "But for as moche," quod sche, "as it liketh to my disciple Plato, in his book of (\In Thymeo\) , that in ryght litel thynges men *schulde* byseche the help of God, what juggestow that be now to done, so that we may desserve to fynde the seete of thilk sovereyn good?" (BOETHCH: 431.C1)

(62) Gesner saies, *Carps* have no tongue like other Fish, but a piece of flesh-like-Fish in their mouth like to a tongue, and *should* be called a palate (WALTON: 295)

The high number of occurrences with 3rd person subjects is related to the use of passive forms whenever general instruction is provided:

(63) Moyses, er he miȝt come to se þis arke, & for to wite how it *schuld* be maad, wiþ grete longe trauayle he clombe up to þe top of þe mounteyne (CLOUD: 126)

(64) Iames techeþ in þis epistle how þe Religion of Crist *schulde* be clene kept of men wiþowten ordre of mannys fyndyng. (WSERM: I, 588)

Predictably, this usage of SHOULD also occurs in Handbooks: the following quotation provides an instance in which the way to carry out an experiment is described:

(65) þ^{t} other ende of thy thred *shold* lye .20 g^{a}. of virgo [...] yif þ^{t} on ende of thy thred laye agayn successioun of signes .10. g^{a} fro the hed of libra than *sholde* þ^{t} other ende lye in the .10. g^{a} fro the hed of aries (EPLANETS: 40)

However, no occurrences were recorded in Scientific texts, as these seldom provide guidance for action, but describe and predict phenomena.

When SHOULD-forms express advice or requests for advice, the encoder's attitude conveys a less markedly deontic force and indeed the interlocutor's opinion may be requested on a 3rd person's behaviour, as shown in the following quotation:

(66) how yow þenke þat oure brothir of Baiere *shulde* gouerne him anenst þe same Duc Iohan (HENRY5C/L: 106)

In two cases these forms occur in interrogative sentences with a 1st-person singular subject; they are both in Fictional texts, and they both convey the encoder's request for advice, though the context then makes clear that it is a purely rhetorical strategy:

(67) But sith I hadde hem hoolly in myn hond, And sith they hadde me yeven al hir lond, What *sholde* I taken keep hem for to plese, But it were for my profit and myn ese (CTBATH: 108.C1)

(68) 'Now wheither have I a siker hand or noon?' Quod he; 'Is al my myght and mynde agon? Hath wyn bireved me myn eyen sight?' What *sholde* I telle th'answere of the knyght? His sone was slayn; ther is namoore to seye. (CTSUMM: 133.C2)

When actual requests for advice are reported, alternatives may be presented:

(69) þe sarysyne to hys god ȝede, And askede cunseyl of swyche a dede, ȝyf he were of þe munke payde, Or, þe ȝyfte *shulde* be delayde.' (HS: 8)

As we can see, the concept of advice is here reinforced by the harmonic superordinate noun *cunseyl*. Especially in E3 texts, this may become a subtle rhetorical device, by means of which encoders distance themselves from the predication; however, the argumentation then proceeds along lines which leave recipients with relatively little possibility to discard the encoder's views if success is to be obtained (cf. n. 13):

(70) If therefore I might be heard I would advise that [...] children *should* be used to submit their desires and goe without their longings even from their very cradles [...] [Children] *should* be taught to know that [...] when ever they desire any thing not fit for them to have or doe, they *should* not be permitted it because they were litle and desird it. Nay what they once craved, [...] they *should* be sure for that very reason to be denyd. (LOCKE: 52-53)

(71) The Schoole-house *should* be a large and stately building [...]. It *should* have a large piece of ground adjoyning to it (HOOLE: 222-223).

Instances of advice were also recorded in contexts in which the encoder directly addresses a single specific recipient suggesting actions or the appropriate interpretation of words:

(72) The only method which I can propose now for supplying this, is, that when your Majesty does think fit to send this paper to the Lords Justices, they *should* be directed to require M^r. Attorney and M^r. Solicitors opinion, (SOMERS: IV, 326)

6.1.3. Possibility

In one M3 case SHOULD appears to express permission; this occurs in the context of a rhetorical question in which the preacher asks who is entitled to reverse God's will:

(73) And þus telluþ þe gospel þat God wole þat tare growe tyl þe day of doom among good corn; but who *schulde* reuerse God and don aȝeynes his wille? (WSERM: I, 376)

In E3, instances of SHOULD-forms expressing permission are slightly more numerous (3), but their meaning is relatively bleached and the modal could in fact be described as belonging to a periphrastic subjunctive, as shown in the following quotation:

(74) Wee cannot but take notice to you how unfitt Wee thinke it That any such Lycences *should* be granted, And therefore Wee doe not onely well approve yor refusall [...], But further Wee will (CHARLES: I, 24)

6.2. Dynamic meanings

6.2.1. Ability

In our subcorpus a few occurrences of SHOULD expressing dynamic ability were recorded (cf. Table 3) in contexts in which absolute qualities of the subject – whether animate or inanimate – are expressed, hence the ability to make or not to make a certain (hypothetical) event come true:

(75) þere ys no solas vndyr heuene Of al þat a man may neuene, þat *shuld* a man so moche glew As a gode womman þat loueþ trew. (HS: 69)
(that could please a man so much as)

(76) How a large Iron-bullet, let fall red or glowing hot upon a heap of Small-coal, *should* set fire to those that are next to it first (HOOKE: 13.5, 46)
(how a large iron bullet [...] is able to set fire)

(77) 'Tis a miracle to see, that she who can give such eternal desires, *should* her self be all ice and all unconcern. (BEHN: 188)

In (77) we see that the modal occurs in a noun clause after a main clause in which the predication is described as a miracle – i.e., the encoders' stance in relation to the proposition and indeed their evaluation of the same is highlighted. The modal may therefore function as a further distancing device, owing to which the (apparent) inexplicability of the state or of the event is emphasized.[14]

6.2.2. Possibility

Occurrences of SHOULD-forms expressing dynamic possibility are not very numerous (cf. Table 3), and they also tend to concentrate in Religious texts. In most cases the subject is a 1st- or 2nd-person pronoun – that is, the possibility or impossibility for the encoder or the interlocutor to do something is explicitly discussed:

---

14 The link between evaluative clauses and modality is outlined by Behre (1955: 177) and Palmer (1986: 154).

(78) How *scholdest* thou deserve grace, Whan thou thiself darst axe non
(how could it be possible for you to deserve grace, if you dare not ask for it)
(GOWER: I, 318)

(79) 'Syre, God forbede' - þat þow lyue þus in þi membris, for wytt and worschipe þat þow *schuldest* haue. (WSERM: I, 339)
(no matter how much wit and worship you might have)

In some cases, however, reference is made to objects, though in passive clauses:

(80) Also þat ȝere bygan grete derþe of þinges þat *schulde* be soolde, so þat þe sale of þynges was of double price to þat it was i-wont. (TREVISA: VIII, 347)
(of things that could be put on sale)

The (im)possibility of an event is highlighted in the following quotations by the co-occurrence of the harmonic adjective *(im)possible* in a superordinate evaluative clause:

(81) and it semiþ inpossible to myn vnderstonding þat any soule þat is disposid to þis werk *schuld* rede it, or speke it, or elles here it red or spoken, bot ȝif þat same soule *schuld* fele for þat tyme a verrey acordaunce (CLOUD: 129)

(82) It was impossible they *should* be stole away (WALTON: 294)

In another case this idea is reinforced through an explicit comment on the proposition:

(83) For how *schulde* a soule, þe whiche in his kynde haþ no maner þing of bodelines, be streinid upriȝt bodely? Nay, it may not be. (CLOUD: 114)

As we saw in the case of ability, the modal may also occur after a superordinate evaluative clause. In the following example regret is expressed that the king was 'deceived and misgoverned' by false courtiers; though SHOULD might at first sight appear to be pleonastic, it conveys a further evaluative connotation[15] which almost implies a resistance to the fatefulness of the situation, as in the

15 Cf. n. 14. However, Westney (1995) links these 'non-modal uses' [sic] to epistemic uses in relation to the concepts of 'logicality' and 'expectation'.

paraphrase 'And it was a pity that it was possible for a noble king to be deceived':

(84) And grete pitee hit was also, þat soche a noble Kyng *shulde* ben desceyuede and mysgouernede þrouȝ false Spensers, (BRUT: 223)

(85) It is a shame y[t] soe many errors *shoulde* bee seene & founde in ye face of ye country (FOX: 84) (that it is possible for so many errors to be seen and found)

6.2.3. Prediction

In both subcorpora most cases of SHOULD-forms expressing prediction convey an idea of general prospect. In a few instances SHOULD-forms occur after superordinate clauses like 'God forbid that', thus in a context which brings them very close to instances of periphrastic subjunctive:

(86) God forbid that I *should* be against thy Relations comming to see thee. (PENNY: 269)

(87) Being asked if he knew anything against him, he answered he did not, adding, God forbid he *should* say any thing more than he knew, he would not do that for all the world (BURNETCHA: 1, II, 160)

Increasingly delexicalised SHOULD-forms also appear in Letters in such phrases as 'I should be honoured / pleased / glad to do sth':

(88) I *should* take itt for an happy occasion to give yr Excellency a confirmation of my readinesse to pay you all manner of service and respect. (OSBORNE: 22)

(89) If my Father had soe great influence upon Sir Tho Tiddyman's son as to wish him to my Cosin Margaret I *should* take it as a perticuler obligatione doen to my self (EOXINDEN: 321)

(90) My deare Lord, I *should* be very glad you would bring some chocolate along with you (FHATTON: I, 148)

In general, SHOULD-forms may be used to report a prediction; when this is explicitly counterfactual, a perfect infinitive follows the modal:

(91) And herfore repreuede Crist ypocrisye of ordres, for he wiste wel þat þey *schulden* after do more harm in þe world. (WSERM: I, 314)

(92) nad it be for drede of our lord the kyng, I wot wel eueri man *sholde* haue be in others top (USK: 28)

Conditionality is also an important factor in the semantic attribution of SHOULD; indeed, a fairly high number of occurrences predict future events in a hypothetical way, occasionally selecting the same modal for the apodosis and the protasis:

(93) & if þer *schold* be don mynyscoun of þe cardiaca, þere *scholde* be mad mor febelynge (PHLEB: 45)

(94) I *should* have been the most ungrateful Person living, *should* I have been disloyal, (LISLE: IV, 122.C2)

Several M3 occurrences express a predictable result or refer to the purpose of an action; in these cases an additional deontic meaning of volition may also be detected, since this usage of SHOULD may be introduced by superordinate nouns like *entent*; however, contextual information highlights the predictive value of the modal:

(95) For he kyde he & hys felawe wolde kepe the dores that day, to that entent that ther *sholde* non haue kome jn but only that wolde haue chose John Norhampton to be mair; (USK: 27)

As for the distribution of these forms, we observe that predictive-hypothetical meanings occur with all subjects in a very wide range of text types; however, in M3 no occurrences were recorded in Handbooks and in Travelogues, possibly due to the expected objectivity of these genres, which leaves little or no place for unverified conjecture; in E3, instead, similar instances were recorded in all text types, except Statutes, as in this genre conditions seldom get expressed by means of hedged forms. When expectation of future events is under discussion, harmonic superordinate verbs like *expect* may co-occur:

(96) Haveing made them ill children we foolishly expect they *should* be good men (LOCKE: 51)

The hypothetical result may be presented as an alternative to a different scenario, in which case the modal is introduced by *else*:

(97) "Thanne ben thei none membres," quod sche, "for elles it *schulde* seme that blisfulnesse were conjoyned al of o membre allone; [...]" (BOETHCH: 433.C2)

We also find SHOULD in subordinate clauses introduced by *lest* (possibly reinforced by such harmonic items as *peradventure, for fear, dread*), expressing feared outcomes to be guarded against by the action in the superordinate clause:

(98) And þis I do for feerde lest þou *schuldest* conseyue bodily þat þat is mente goostly. (CLOUD: 121)

(99) soothly, of the fruyt of the tree that is in the myddel of Paradys, God forbad us for to ete, ne nat touchen it, lest per aventure we *sholde* dyen. (CTPARS: 298.6.C2)

The use of SHOULD in concessive and conditional clauses normally signals the remoteness of the hypothesis – again, this kind of usage could be described as periphrastic subjunctive:

(100) þogh we *suld* never helle se, Ne for syn *suld* never punyst be, In purgatory ne in helle, Ne in þis werld whar we duelle, Yhit suld we luf God [...] Right swa þe face of God alle-myghty, Sal be shewed in heven appertely, Tille alle þe men þat þider sal wende, þogh som *suld* duelle at þe ferrest ende. (PRICK: 248)

(101) The Town wou'd be robb'd of one of its chief Diversions, if it *shou'd* become a Crime to laugh at a Fool (VANBR: I, 35)

6.2.3.1. Prophecy

Statements may take on prophetic overtones when harmonic nouns and verbs co-occur which strengthen the predictive force of the predication; unexpectedly, only one M3 instance has been recorded in a Biblical text, i.e. the New Testament, while the others are in Fictional or Historical works:

(102) but whanne he was bischop of that ȝeer, he prophesiede, that Jhesu was to die for the folc, and not oneli for the folc, but that he *schulde* gadere in to oon the sones of God that weren scaterid. (WYCNEW: XI, 40)

(103) The hound was tokne and prophecie That lich an hound he *scholde* die, (GOWER: I, 180)

(104) and to him saide, þat 'or þat ȝere wer Don, he *shulde* ben take and holde a traitour': and so hit was, as þe holy man saide. (BRUT: 227)

In E3 the only instance of a (reported) prophecy occurs in a Religious treatise:

(105) But the Scripture hath foretold us that this sort of men *should* arise in the Gospel-age (TILLOTS: II, ii. 430)

6.2.4. Necessity

In some cases SHOULD-forms introduce predications which are presented as inescapable, either because they derive from divine prescription, or because they refer to fateful events:

(106) Maistir, what synnede this man, or hise eldris, that he *schulde* be borun blynd? (WYCNEW: IX, 1)

(107) Thus fell the thing which falle *scholde*, (GOWER: II, 223)

In one case SHOULD occurs in an exclamation of sorrow at the *mala tempora* experienced by the encoder:

(108) Jesu God! that we *should* live to see any such Creatures among Mankind, nay, and among us too, (LISLE: IV, 122.C1)

In M3 the necessity of the predication may be emphasized by the co-occurrence of nominal or adverbial *need*, as in (109) and (110):

(109) it was not nede to hym, that ony man *schulde* bere witnessyng, for he wiste, what was in man. (WYCNEW: II, 20)

(110) Hem þowte þat Crist *schulde* nede sey oþur 'ȝe' or 'nay'; (WSERM: I, 313)

In E3, instead, the harmonic adjective *necessary* or the harmonic noun *necessity* have been observed:

(111) How absolutely necessary it is, that he *should* constitute his Vicegerents here, (EVELYN: 901)

(112) If there were not a necessity that it *shou'd* be disposed of before the next great Sessions, (SOMERS: IV, 329)

When these do not occur, the reference to external circumstances in the immediate context allows us to distinguish such cases from deontic ones:

(113) When men live as if there were no God it becomes expedient for them that there *should* be none: (TILLOTS: II, ii. 420)
(that, necessarily, there is none)

(114) *Shou'd* I grow jealous, because you had Eyes? (VANBR: I, 34)
(Would it be necessary for me to grow jealous)

6.2.5. Habit

In earlier times SHOULD-forms could be employed to describe typical behaviour. However, this use was fast declining, as no instances were recorded in the E3 section and the only instances observed in the M3 section occur in the same source in the context of similes:[16]

(115) and þrew þe body by nyȝte wiþ oute þe citee, and fleyȝ awey as a þeef *schulde*. (TREVISA: VIII, 91)
(and ran away like a thief normally would)

(116) But for he couþe not selle and undo his clooþ as a womman *schulde*, he was i-take (TREVISA: VIII, 105) (as a woman would)

16 Such usage is described by Visser, who observes that "There is a strikingly large number of instances of 'habitual' *should* in the *Book of Margery Kempe*" (1963-73: 1635).

6.3. Epistemic meanings

6.3.1. Inference

In very few M3 and E3 cases a SHOULD-form has been found to express a reasonable conclusion deriving from previous predications; in one instance the subjectivity of the remark is emphasized by a content-oriented booster such as *certes*:

(117) for certes somthing possessyng in itself parfyt good *schulde* be more worthy than God, and it *scholde* semen that thilke thing were first and eldere than God. (BOETHCH: 432.C1)
(if something possessed perfect good, people would infer that it is more worthy than God and that it seems to precede God).

(118) But as from Mens being endowed with the Vertue of Justice, they are denominated Just; and from that of Prudence they are pronounced Wise, so *should* they who are possessed of Divinity by parity of reason be esteemed Gods. [...] He then who considers this cannot deny that Good and Happiness are of one and the same Substance.
Bo. I see no Cause why any Man *should* dissent from your Opinion.
(BOETHPR: 137; 139)

7. Concluding remarks

In the time span taken into consideration the frequency and meaning of SHOULD appears to change in a different manner in different text types. Although in general its frequency appears to decrease in favour of WOULD, as will be shown in Ch. 10, if we restrict our discussion to text types included in both the M3 and the E3 sections of our subcorpus we observe a more marked decrease in the frequency of use of this modal form for the expression of dynamic meanings in Sermons, Scientific and Historical texts. In contrast, the same meanings appear to be conveyed more frequently by SHOULD in Philosophical texts, Handbooks and Letters. As regards the use of SHOULD for the conveyance of deontic meanings, this becomes less frequent in Sermons, Philosophical and Historical texts of the E3 period, but it increases in Handbooks, Letters and Scientific texts, thus signalling that greater attention to politeness, conveyed by distal forms, was becoming a trait of modern discourse.

Within these broader categories, however, the analysis of individual instances has shown that in some cases more than one meaning may be expressed by the same modal; as a result, the context and the pragmatic value that may thus be identified in the predication prove of considerable value for the disambiguation of the occurrences. This kind of semantic ambiguity is also an important index of the progressive grammaticalization of the verbal form, as shown on the morpho-syntactic level by the disappearance of non-modal uses and modal + modal occurrences in the E3 section. The extent to which these traits are shared by the other modal forms investigated in our study will be discussed in Ch. 11.

IX. Will

A comparison between the occurrences of WILL-forms in the M3 and E3 parts of the Helsinki Corpus shows an increase not only in absolute numbers (407 in M3 vs 571 in E3) but also in normalised figures (22 vs 33 per 10,000 words).[1] Both subsections present cases of WILL-forms used as main verbs;[2] however, there is decrease of these in the periods taken into consideration, both in absolute and relative numbers (from 40 to 5, i.e. from 10% of all WILL-forms to 1%), and WILL becomes essentially an auxiliary. The semantic meaning of main-verb WILL usually corresponds to that of volition. Here are a few examples of this usage:

(1) "Sir," he said, "blithlik and son, if godd *will*, sal þi will be don."
(CURSOR: 214)

(2) þe pacient be stronge þat þe materie of þe sekenesse ymoved be more liȝtli brouȝt out, þof al þat olde men seme to *wille* or wesche. (PHLEB: 45)

With this function, the verb is frequently followed by a direct object, as can be seen in the following examples:

(3) For his crispe heer, shynynge as gold so fyn, / And for he squiereth me bothe up and doun, / Yet hastow caught a fals suspecioun. / I *wol* hym noght, thogh thou were deed tomorwe! (CTBATH: 109, C1)

(4) And also we *wilen* þis: þat alle þese poyntes ben wel & trewely holden among al our breþeren, (RET: 57)

1 These figures confirm the high frequency of WILL-forms – particularly in the EModE period – already pointed out in previous studies (cf., for instance, Warner 1993: 146).

2 The WILL-forms found in the M3 part of the Helsinki Corpus derive from both irregular and regular OE WILL; as there are evident syntactic blends between these two verbs in ME, their variants have not been kept separate in this analysis.

The direct object can also be a *that* clause:

(5) And whiles þai tarie yn oure land / we *wol* þat þere be shewed vnto hem / al þe fee fauor and chere / þat may be doon yn goodly wyse. (HENRY5C/L: 106)

The conjunction *that* is sometimes omitted:

(6) And *wol* ye wete / yat we haue Receiued youre lettres (HENRY5C/L: 120)

To express the meaning of volition, WILL is sometimes followed by a *to*-infinitive:

(7) For yif so be that it be wrecchidnesse to *wilne* to doon yvel, thanne is it more wrecchidnesse to mowe don yvel, (BOETHCH: 446, C2)

In other cases WILL indicates preference:

(8) "This ys," quod I, "a fair thing and a precious, clepe it as thou *wilt*, be it corolarie, or porisme, or mede of coroune, or declarynges." (BOETHCH: 433, C1)

Other instances of WILL as a main verb are found in the opening expressions used in testaments; here is an example:

(9) Also y *wille* and ordeyne þat alle the godes weche y haue be-quethe Katerine, þat it be in kepyng of my too executours, here for to take as sche had ned. (TEST: 209)

Non-modal WILL-forms in the E3 section of the Helsinki Corpus have a volitional meaning and are found in phraseological units such as *what you will*:

(10) For, let men pretend *what they will*, there is no ease and comfort of mind to be had from atheistical principles. (TILLOTS: II, ii. 420)

1. Spelling variants

The comparison between the two parts of the corpus shows a marked decrease in the number of spelling variants, from 26 in M3[3] to 9 in E3.[4] Negative forms deriving from the combination of negation + verb (e.g. *nel*, *nil*, *nile*, *nulleth*, *nyle*) appear only in the earlier period, while contracted forms (e.g. *'twill*, *twill*, *t'will*, *won't*) occur only in the later period. In addition the forms that end with a 2nd person singular subject suffix are frequent in M3 (25 out of 30, i.e. 83.3%) but become rare in E3 (12 out of 56, i.e. 21.4%).

The most common forms in M3 are *wol* (which appears in almost one third (31%) of the quotations analysed), *wil* (18%), *wole* (12%), *will* (10%) and *wyl* (9%). Of the most widespread forms, *wil* and *will* appear in combination with any kind of subject, while others – such as *wol*, *wole* and *wyl* – combine with all kinds of subject except *thou*. *Wolen* and *wile* are found with plural subjects. *Nel* combines with 1st and 3rd person singular subjects,[5] while *wille* is also used with 1st person plural pronouns. *Nyle* combines with both kinds of 2nd person pronoun, while *nile* appears only with *ye*. *Wilt*, *wilte*, *wylt* and *wolt*, on the other hand, are always accompanied by the subject *thou*, which also appears in the enclitic forms *wiltow* and *wyltow*. The occurrences of *wul* and *nil* are accompanied by a 3rd person singular subject; the only quotations of *nulleth*, *wilen*, *woll*, *wyle* and *wyllyn* have a 3rd person plural subject, while those of *wele* and *wiln* have the subject *we*. In terms of frequency, the prototypical paradigm is the following:[6]

---

3 The spelling variants found in M3 are the following: *nel*, *nil*, *nile*, *nulleth*, *nyle*, *wele*, *wil*, *wile*, *wilen*, *will*, *wille*, *wiln*, *wilt*, *wilte*, *wiltow*, *wol*, *wole*, *wollen*, *woll*, *wolt*, *wul*, *wyl*, *wyle*, *wyllyn*, *wylt*, *wyltow*.

4 The spelling variants found in E3 are the following: *'twill*, *twill*, *t'will*, *vill*, *wil*, *wilbe*, *will*, *wilt*, *won't*.

5 However, here – as in other cases – the number of occurrences is quite small, and therefore the limited choice of possible subject forms could be the result of sampling.

6 It should be remembered that the alternation between *wil-* and *wol-*forms also conforms to dialect differentiations.

1st person singular	*wol*
2nd person singular	*wilt / wolt*
3rd person singular	*wol*
1st person plural	*wil*
2nd person plural	*wil / wole(n)*
3rd person plural	*wol / wil*

Of the forms found in E3 only *will* combines with any kind of subject; *'twill*, *twill* and *t'will* – consisting of the pronoun *it* and the auxiliary *will* – only appear with a 3rd person singular subject, as do the forms *wil* and *wilbe*; *vill* only occurs with the subject *I*, while *wilt* always follows *thou*; *won't* has been found with 1st and 2nd person singular subjects and with 3rd person plural ones. Moreover, *will* occurs in any kind of text, while *wilbe*, *twill* and *t'will* have only been found in Letters (both private and official); *vill* is a form used exclusively by Farquhar, while *won't* is typical of dialogues in Drama; *wilt*, *'twill* and *wil*, instead, appear in different text types. The E3 part of the corpus also contains the following contracted forms (the number of occurrences for each variant is shown in brackets):[7]

I'le (14) / *'ile* (1) / *ile* (3) / *i'll* (54) / *he'll* (4) / *she'll* (3) / *they'l* (2) / *they'll* (3) / *thou'lt* (1) / *we'l* (2) / *we'll* (9) / *you'll* (18)

These forms, however, have not been included in our analysis, as they cannot be attributed to either SHALL or WILL with any degree of certainty. The corpus shows several examples of spelling variation, where different orthographic variants are used with the same subject and in close textual proximity. This variation, however, mainly occurs in M3, while in E3 the WILL-forms – and *will* in particular – become more standardised. Here is an example taken from M3:

(11) ffor we be fre tenentȝ and fre lond holderes annexed to the worthy coroune of oure most souereyn lord. the kyng and that we *wele* proue and declare by oure euydence wreten in the kynges eschekker at Westminstre: wherfore we *wole* answere as fre men oughte to done and proue that the suyte of the commission byfore seide (PET3: 202)

7 Also in Kytö (1991: 289) contracted forms have been found only in EModE.

2. Distribution according to text type

The normalised data for WILL-forms in Table 1 show an increase from M3 to E3.

Text types	*M3*	*E3*
FICTION	30	70
HANDBOOKS	28	83
TRAVELOGUES	26	2
PHILOSOPHY	18	22
LETTERS	13	62
HISTORY	11	2
SERMONS	3	36
SCIENCE	3	27
HOMILIES	34	-[8]
RELIGIOUS TREATISES	28	-
RULES	26	-
DOCUMENTS	15	-
BIBLE	13	-
EDUCATIONAL TREATISES	-	49
DRAMA	-	39
TRIALS	-	23
DIARIES	-	16
BIOGRAPHIES	-	9
LAW	-	5
All texts	20	33

Table 1. Normalised occurrences of WILL-forms per text type.

This increase occurs in most text types – only History books and Travelogues show a decrease. The increase in the use of WILL-forms is particularly high in Handbooks (200%), Scientific works (800%), Sermons (800%), Fiction (126%) and Letters (350%), while in Philosophy the increase corresponds roughly to the average. As regards the text types which appear in only one part of the corpus analysed, Homilies, Religious treatises, Rules and Educational books are above average, while Documents, Biblical texts, Legal texts, Trial proceedings, Diaries and (auto)Biographies are below average.

8 The '–' sign means that no texts are included in this category.

Higher than the average normalised figures are found in M3 for all texts in Homilies, Fictional works, Handbooks, Religious treatises, Rules and Travelogues; as will be seen below, these text types present numerous cases of prediction, intention and habit. In contrast, lower than average frequencies are found for Philosophical texts, Letters, Documents, Biblical works, History books, Sermons and Scientific treatises. The lack of WILL-forms in History books is not surprising, as they mainly deal with the narration and interpretation of past events, which therefore do not commonly require speech acts pertaining to futurity or intentionality; the low number of occurrences of WILL in Biblical texts may be due to the preference for SHALL-forms for the expression of prediction, intention, promise and command.[9]

As regards E3, numbers close to the average are only found in Scientific treatises, Sermons and Drama. Higher than the average numbers of WILL-forms are found in Handbooks, Educational books, Fictional works and Letters. This is due to frequency of prediction and volition present in Fiction and Letters, while Handbooks and Educational treatises are characterised by the numerically significant presence of semantic values denoting habit, hypothesis and consequence. Lower than average frequencies are found in Statutes, Philosophical works, Trial proceedings, History books, Travelogues, Diaries and (auto)Biographies. The lack of WILL-forms in Legal texts is due to the preference for SHALL to express volition, obligation and prediction (cf. Ch. 7), while the less frequent presence of WILL in Trial proceedings, History books, Diaries and (auto)Biographies is not surprising, as they mainly deal with the narration and interpretation of past events, which therefore do not commonly require speech acts pertaining to futurity or intentionality.

9 In Wycliffe's translation of the Bible, WILL commonly renders the Latin verb *volo*, while SHALL is used to translate a wider range of forms and meanings.

3. Verb phrase structure

As Table 2 shows, the most popular verb phrase structure in both periods is WILL + bare infinitive (345 instances, i.e. 94%, in M3 and 508, i.e. 90%, in E3). The table also reveals an interesting increase in the use of the passive infinitive (from 1% to 6%).

	M3		*E3*	
	No.	*%*	*No.*	*%*
bare infinitive	345	94%	508	90%
Ø	18	5%	17	3%
passive infinitive	4	1%	36	6%
BE + ING	0	0%	2	0.4%
perfect infinitive	0	0%	1	0.2%
HAVE + NP + PP	0	0%	1	0.2%
HAVE + NP + bare infinitive	0	0%	1	0.2%
Total	367	100%	566	100%

Table 2. Verbal complementation after WILL.

In M3 there are 18 occurrences of the modal appearing alone; in one case the verbal complementation is not present in the context but can be inferred as *be*, a type of omission possible at the time (cf. Jespersen 1949: 238 and Plank 1984: 310-1, 335):

(12) God manaceþ swyche, for swyche enchesun, / And ryȝt hyt *wyl*, and gode resun; (HS: 320) (And hyt wyl [be] ryȝt)

The other 17 occurrences are cases of ellipsis of the verbal complement in a preceding coordinate clause; in all instances the implied verb can be traced in the immediate context, as can be seen in the following quotation:

(13) And he may helpe hem yn þat kas, / And *wyl* nat, for vnkyndhede, /
(And wyl nat [helpe hem])
But late hem perysshe þer for nede, (HS: 160)

In the E3 part of the corpus analysed there are 17 cases of WILL-forms not followed by any other verb. In two cases – both occurring in dialogues appearing in Drama – the verb has to be inferred from the context:

(14) Ay, and I'll make him commend the Sauce too, or I'll bring his Gown to a Cassock, I *will* so. (VANBR: I, 64)
(I will do so.)

(15) I am for venturing one of the Hundreds if you *will* upon this Knight-Errantry; (FARQUHAR: 6) (if you will go upon this Knight-Errantry)

Twelve other cases found in E3 consist of elliptical forms, commonly used to avoid the repetition of a verb mentioned in the same or in a previous sentence. Here are a few examples:

(16) against all which any honest man may make a just quarrel, but I *will* not, (WALTON: 214) (but I will not make a quarrel)

(17) and the Lime kills often Stock and all, as *will* salt Clay, (LANGF: 121)
(as salt Clay will kill Stock and all)

The 3 other cases, instead, are part of tag questions (a structure which is present only in the later part of the corpus analysed and not in M3, thus confirming the process of grammaticalization of WILL); all these instances occur in dialogues in the same Fictional work:

(18) I know he will give me something when I marry, and so will thy Mistriss, *will* she not? (PENNY: 116)

(19) this young man I say, will often come to see me, you shall not be jealous of him *will* ye? (PENNY: 269)

(20) I hope thou wilt not make me a Cuckold, sweetheart, *wilt* thou? (PENNY: 272)

In E3 the second most popular phrase structure is WILL + passive infinitive (36, i.e. 6%). Although this structure appears in all text types, it presents a higher frequency in Handbooks, Scientific treatises and Educational works (39% of all occurrences in such text types).[10] Here are a few examples taken from these three kinds of texts:

10 This pattern has continued to be typical of specialized registers (cf. Barber 1962 and Huddleston 1971).

(21) And lastly, if it should miscarry (as it seldom doth) it *will* be perceived by Midsummer, and the stock may be enoculated again the same year. (LANGF: 37)

(22) and therefore the violence of the concussion *will* be exerted on that piece of steel which is cut off by the Flint. (HOOKE: 13, 5, 45)

(23) I thinke it is best the smart should come more immediately from another hand though by the parents order, who should see it donne, whereby the parents authority *will* be preservd and the childs aversion for the pain it suffers be rather turned on the person that immediately inflicts it. (LOCKE: 59)

In M3 this verb phrase structure was rarer, being found only in 4 cases, in constructions such as the following:

(24) He answerde to hem, Y seide to ȝou now, and ȝe herden; what wolen ȝe eftsoone here? whether ȝe *wolen* be maad hise discyplis? (WYCNEW: IX, 20)

(25) For wel woot every astrologien that smallist fraccions ne *wol* not be shewid in so small an instrument as in subtile tables calculed for a cause. (ASTR: 663)

Only in E3 are WILL-forms + BE and an *ing*-form present, a further sign of the use of WILL to build up more complex auxiliary phrases. Here below are the two cases found; as can be seen, in the first the participle shows a clear instance of verbal use, while the second has a prevalently adjectival function:

(26) This is a Creature so officious, that 'twill be known to every one at one time or other, so busie, and so impudent, that it *will* be intruding it self in every ones company, (HOOKE: 13, 5. 211)

(27) But if we will in good earnest apply our selves to the practice of Religion, and the obedience of God's Holy Laws, his Grace *will* never be wanting to us to so good a purpose. (TILLOTS: II, ii. 452)

Other patterns have been found in E3, such as WILL + perfect infinitive, WILL HAVE + noun phrase + past participle and WILL HAVE + noun phrase + bare infinitive. Here are examples of these three constructions:

(28) My Horse is at Mr. Marlo's at the dark house in Gravesend: I wish I had sent for him home within 3 or 4 days after I left him there: he *will* have been 5 weekes there next Wedensday or Thursday noone. (HOXINDEN: 281)

(29) weaker Electricks require to be as well wip'd as chaf'd; and even good ones *will* have their Operation promoted by the same means. (BOYLE: 10)

(30) If you *will* have him have the obedience of a son hereafter doe you be sure to keep and shew the authority (LOCKE: 54)

The two parts of the corpus do not contain any instances of modal verb combinations. E3 does, however, present cases in which two modals are followed by the same main verb, as can be seen in this quotation:[11]

(31) and I am sure I both *can* and *will* tell you more than any common Angler yet knows. (WALTON: 217)

In E3, WILL also coordinates with non-modal auxiliaries, e.g. *do*; this phenomenon is typical of a very formal style, as the following quotation from an official Letter shows:

(32) And therefore Wee doe not onely well approve yo[r] refusall of the desire he made as to Ballymartin, But further Wee *will*, and accordingly Wee *doe* hereby sufficiently authorise and require you to give order for the recalling and revokeing in such way (CHARLES: I, 25)

4. Time reference

In both parts of the corpus the most common time reference is towards the future (318 occurrences, i.e. 87%, in M3 and 510 occurrences, i.e 90%, in E3; cf. Table 3); indeed, WILL-forms usually appear in speech acts referring to an action to be performed, such as requests, commands, promises, prohibitions, predictions and hypotheses.

11 More examples of this construction are reported in 5.1.1.

	M3		*E3*	
	No.	*%*	*No.*	*%*
future	318	87	510	90
timeless	46	12	49	9
present	3	1	7	1
Total	367	100	566	100

Table 3. WILL time reference.

This type of time orientation is followed by that of timeless reference (46 cases, i.e. 12%, in M3 and 49, i.e. 9%, in E3) usually denoting habitual actions, constituent properties or dynamic possibility, as can be seen in the following examples (the first drawn from M3, the second from E3):

(33) This bawme groweth in no place but only þere And þough þat men bryngen of þe plauntes for to planten in oþer contrees þei growen wel & fayre but þei bryngen forth no fructuous thing. & the leves of bawme ne falle nought. And men kutten the braunches with a scharp flyntston or a scharp bon whanne men *wil* go to kutte hem, For who so kutte hem with jren it wolde destroye his vertue & his nature. (MAND: 32)

(34) And this is partly proved by tame and wild Rabbets, as also by some Ducks, which *will* lay eggs nine of the twelve months, and yet there be other Ducks that lay no longer than about one month. (WALTON: 293)

A small number of cases refer to the present and express reassurance or inference; for example, the following instance found in M3 expresses reassurance:

(35) And he seide to hem, Y am; *nyle* ȝe drede. (WYCNEW VI: 20)

The following cases of present reference found in E3 report the immediate reactions of the reader to the text or the reader's thought process:

(36) nothing else was talk'd of, no other sound was heard in every corner where there were whisperers, but Imoinda! Imoinda!. *'Twill* be imagin'd Oroonoko stay'd not long before he made his second visit; nor, considering his quality, not much longer before he told her, he ador'd her. (BEHN: 156)

(37) You *will* probably be the less dispos'd to believe, that Electrical Attractions must proceed from the Substantial Forms of the Attrahents, (BOYLE: 30)

No occurrences with past time reference have been identified.[12]

5. Types of modality

In both periods taken into consideration, WILL-forms express all kinds of modal meanings: deontic, epistemic and dynamic, covering most of the usages found in PDE.[13] The analysis of the corpus has revealed a wide range of semantic values; the results concerning these data are summarized in Tables 4 and 5.

In M3 there is virtually an equal distribution between deontic (52%) and dynamic (48%) aspects of modality. Only one case has been found of epistemic modality, expressing inference. Some modal meanings – such as prediction and volition – are distributed all over the various categories of texts, while others seem to correlate strongly with certain specific genres. This is the case of habit and dynamic possibility, which are particularly common in Handbooks and Travelogues, as these text types frequently deal with the specific characteristics of substances or the typical behaviour of human beings. Deontic necessity, instead, seems to be prevalent in Biblical texts, which often include statements expressing orders or prohibitions deriving from God's law.

In E3 dynamic meanings are prevalent (386 occurrences) and constitute over two thirds of the whole corpus (68%). The second largest group is that of deontic meanings (171 occurrences, i.e. 30%), while epistemic values only appear in a very limited number (9 cases corresponding to 2% of all occurrences). As can be seen from Table 5, certain types of modality are more widespread than others; this is the

12 Similarly in Kytö (1991) all the instances of WILL bear present or future reference.

13 For an analysis of the main semantic values of WILL cf., among others, Hermerén (1978), Coates (1983), Haegeman (1983), Perkins (1983) and Palmer (1990).

case of prediction (which is to be found in all text types except History books) and volition (which is only absent in Scientific treatises and Travelogues). Habit and deontic necessity are also quite common, while the other kinds of modal uses appear in a more limited number of text types. WILL expresses a variety of semantic values in some genres (such as Sermons, Educational books, Handbooks, Fictional works and Drama) while in others it has a narrower range of meanings. This is not only true for all those text types whose normalised figures are low (such as Statutes, History books, Travelogues and (auto)Biographies), but also for some other genres such as Philosophical works, Diaries, Letters, Scientific treatises and Trial proceedings.

	deontic			*epist.*	*dynamic*				*Tot.*
Text types	*volit.*	*nec.*	*Tot.*	*inf.*	*poss.*	*pred.*	*habit*	*Tot.*	
HOMILIES	11		11			19	4	23	34
FICTION	17		17			7	6	13	30
HANDBOOKS	6		6	1	2	10	9	21	28
RELIGIOUS TR	11	1	12		1	14	1	16	28
RULES	9	2	11			13	2	15	26
TRAVELOGUES	13		13			6	7	13	26
PHILOSOPHY	10		10			7	1	8	18
DOCUMENTS	12		12		1	2		3	15
LETTERS	6	6	12			1		1	13
BIBLE	6	6	12			1		1	13
HISTORY	9	1	10			1		1	11
SCIENCE	3		3						3
SERMONS	1		1		1	1		2	3
All texts	9	1	10	0.1	1	7	2	10	20
Abs. Numbers	171	19	190	1	8	128	40	176	367
ambig. cases	20	1	21	0	1	18	5	24	45
% ambig. cases	12%	5%	11%	0%	13%	14%	13%	14%	12%

Table 4. Occurrences of WILL by modality type in M3 (normalised frequencies; in order of overall text type frequency).

	deontic			epist.	dynamic				Tot.
Text types	*volit.*	*nec.*	*Tot.*	*inf.*	*poss.*	*pred.*	*habit*	*Tot.*	
HANDBOOKS	12	2	14		8	54	7	69	83
FICTION	16	10	26	1		41	2	43	70
LETTERS	14	4	18		1	43		44	62
EDUC TR	3	5	8	4		33	4	37	49
DRAMA	11	3	14	1	2	22		24	39
SERMONS	6	2	8	1	3	23	1	27	36
SCIENCE				1	1	22	3	26	27
TRIALS	17	4	21			1	1	2	23
PHILOSOPHY	7		7			15		15	22
DIARIES	5		5	1		10		10	16
BIOGRAPHIES	5	1	6			3		3	9
LAW	1		1			4		4	5
HISTORY	2		2						2
TRAVELOGUES						1	1	2	2
All texts	8	2	10	1	1	20	1	22	33
Abs. Numbers	131	40	171	9	19	337	20	386	566
ambig. cases	15	6	21	0	4	37	3	44	65
% ambig. cases	11%	15%	12%	0%	21%	11%	15%	11%	11%

Table 5 Occurrences of WILL by modality type in E3
(normalised frequencies; in order of overall text type frequency).

5.1. Deontic meanings

5.1.1. Volition

The semantic value of volition gives rise to the pragmatic values listed in Tables 6 and 7. None of the sentences containing WILL acts as an offer, as is the case in the following PDE example:

(38) I *will* get you a drink.[14]
(I offer to get you a drink)

14 The confirmation of the pragmatic value of offer of this question comes from the possibility of paraphrasing it as follows: *Shall I get you a drink?*

Text types	*intention*	*refusal*	*promise*	*Total*	*o/ooo*
FICTION	20	3	2	25	17
TRAVELOGUES	6	1		7	13
DOCUMENTS	14	1	3	18	12
RELIGIOUS TR	35	4	3	42	11
HOMILIES	2	6		8	11
PHILOSOPHY	12		1	13	10
HISTORY	14	3	6	23	9
RULES	5			5	9
BIBLE	10	2		12	6
HANDBOOKS	11	1		12	6
LETTERS	3			3	6
SCIENCE		1		1	3
SERMONS		2		2	1
All texts	132	24	15	171	9
ambig. cases	17	1	1	19	
% ambig. cases	13%	4%	7%	11%	

Table 6. Pragmatic uses expressing volition in M3 (absolute numbers; in order of normalized frequency, indicated in the last column).

Text types	*intention*	*refusal*	*promise*	*threat*	*Total*	*o/ooo*
TRIALS	15	1	5	3	24	17
FICTION	13	1	6		20	16
LETTERS	24	1	2		27	14
HANDBOOKS	9		5		14	12
DRAMA	7	3	4		14	11
PHILOSOPHY	6				6	7
SERMONS	6	1	1		8	6
BIOGRAPHIES	5		1		6	5
DIARIES	5	1			6	5
EDUC TR	3				3	3
HISTORY	1	1			2	2
LAW			1		1	1
SCIENCE					0	0
TRAVELOGUES					0	0
All texts	94	9	25	3	131	8
ambig. cases	13	0	2	0	15	
% ambig. cases	14%	0%	8%	0%	11%	

Table 7. Pragmatic uses expressing volition in E3 (absolute numbers; in order of normalized frequency, indicated in the last column).

5.1.1.1. Intention

The most frequent deontic value found in the corpus corresponds to that of intention; this meaning does not characterise any specific text type, but appears in the various genres analysed. Moreover, this kind of modality does not show any preference for a specific subject form, but combines with various nouns and pronouns. Here are a few quotations with a 1st person pronoun:

(39) Alle þis matere men may se þare, / þarfor here I *wil* spek þar-of na mare. (PRICK: 81)

(40) We *will* not direct you in any thing that's foul, but pray keep to those Questions that are pertinent. (OATES: IV, 75, C2)

This intentional function is very frequently found in Philosophical works, Handbooks and Sermons, especially in metatextual comments informing the reader of the argumentative structure and terminological conventions adopted by the writer; in these cases the subject is typically in the 1st person singular or plural:

(41) This tretis, divided in 5 parties, *wol* I shewe the under full light reules and naked wordes in Englissh, for Latyn ne canst thou yit but small, my litel sone. (ASTR: 662, C1)

(42) & þt the middel poynt of this plate wher as the fix fot of thy compas stondith / *wole* I calle centre .aryn. (EPLANETS: 18)

(43) And as before I have hinted somewhat touching the erecting of Petty-Schooles (whereof there is great need, especially) in *London*; so I *will* here presume (and I hope it will prove no offence) to publish what I have often seriously thought, (HOOLE: 220)

(44) But we *will* not at this time discourse of these. (BOETHPR: 181)

The following, instead, are intentional statements with a 2nd person pronoun:

(45) For understoond now, ye asken conseil to do wikkednesse; and if ye *wole* werken wikkednesse, and youre wif restreyneth thilke wikked purpos, and overcometh yow by reson and by good conseil, certes youre wyf oghte rather to be preised (CTMEL: 221, C1)

(46) I am proud of it, and so art thou I believe, but that thou *wilt* not confess it. (PENNY: 119)

The following quotations expressing intention contain WILL-forms which combine with a 3rd person pronoun:

(47) Of þe þridde maner o mekenes spekys sain benet to þa in his reul *wyl* be, (BENEDME: 12)

(48) L. C.J. *Will* the Prisoner ask this Person any Questions?
LISLE. No. (LISLE: IV, 115, C2)

Several instances expressing intention underline the volitional aspect, which is closely linked to the original semantic value of WILL and thus represents a clear case of 'persistence' (cf. Hopper 1991). Here are a few instances:

(49) Somtyme oure Lorde wil delaye it by a cauteel, for he *wol* bi soche a delaiing make it growe & be had more in deintee, when it is newe founden & felt aȝein, þat longe had be lost. (CLOUD: 132)

(50) Lo, what profit a man mai finde, / Which hindre *wole* an other wiht. / Forthi with al thin hole miht, / Mi Sone, eschuie thilke vice. (GOWER: I, 180)

At times this volitional aspect is made more manifest by the use of an adverb or an adverbial phrase expressing determination:

(51) For I *wol* be, certeyn, a wedded man, / And that anoon in al the haste I kan. (CTMERCH: 156, C1)

(52) But o thyng warne I yow, my freendes deere, / I *wol* noon oold wyf han in no manere. (CTMERCH: 156, C1)

In the following quotations the intentionality of the statements including WILL is highlighted by the contrast with other modal auxiliaries, such as *must* (expressing obligation) or *can* (conveying the meaning of ability):

(53) therefore Mary, I say I must, nay I *will*, and if thou deniest the refreshing of a Brother, thou are not worthy to be called a Sister. (PENNY: 151)

(54) Since then each of these things hath its unhappiness, it must of necessity be, that a threefold Misfortune must urge those Men who both *will*, can, and do commit Wickedness. (BOETHPR: 178)

WILL-forms expressing intention are often found in formulaic constructions of the following kind:[15]

(55) Sey what men seye *will* (CLOUD: 81)

(56) þink what he þink *will* (CLOUD: 123)

WILL is found in object clauses after a verb of requesting (typically *beseech*); a significantly high number of occurrences has been found in the genre of Documents, and in particular in petitions. Here are a few instances:

(57) Also worchepeful sires: we beseche ȝow at the reuerence of god: that ȝe *wole* praye to oure liege lord the kyng: that he *wole* fouche saf of his special grace and his Royal prerogatyf in this heye Court: (PET3: 199)

(58) Besechinge also (to) oure liege lord that he *wole* haue compassion and pyte vp on vs (PET3: 204)

As can be seen, the pragmatic function of the WILL-forms is made explicit by the use of the verb *to beseech* in the superordinate clause; this verb is superordinate to most of the text in petitions and is often left understood in a whole series of subclauses, presented graphically as separate sentences all containing WILL, as in (59) and (60):

(59) And also that ȝe *wole* praye the kyng to ȝeue in charge to myne aduersaries whanne thay comen to his worchopful presence (PET3: 200)

(60) That is to seyn that he *wole* at ȝoure instance and prayer in sauynge of his owne right and in fortherynge of (his) trewe lieges: ordeyne (PET3: 203)

A similar use of WILL in subclauses after a verb of requesting (like *beseech* or *pray*) is also found in other text types:

---

15 Cf. Ch. 4 § 3 (examples 4 and 5) for similar constructions with MAY.

(61) And þan I beseche þee þat þou *wilt* haue me excusid; for trewly I wolde haue profitid vnto þee in þis writyng at my simple kunnyng, (CLOUD: 129)

(62) And if any man þat es clerk, / Can fynde any errour in þis werk, / I pray hym he do me þat favour, / þat he *wille* amende þat errour; (PRICK: 258)

The following can be seen pragmatically as a request for confidence in the writer:

(63) And therfore, sire, if ye *wol* triste to my conseil, I shal restoore yow youre doghter hool and sound. (CTMEL: 221, C2)

The corpus analysed also includes requests for response from the interlocutor; these are often a formulaic set of words (*What wiltow seyn of this*), used to attract the reader's attention to the new point which the author intends to present or discuss. Here is an example:

(64) What *wiltow* seyn of this, that thei drawen alle here norysschynges by here rootes, ryght as thei hadden here mouthes yplunged wythinne (BOETHCH: 435, C2)

The following sentence – uttered to issue a challenge – may also be included in this section, as it may be interpreted as a request to take part in a fight:

(65) "*Wil* þou," coth goli, "fight wit me?" (CURSOR: 438)

5.1.1.2. Refusal

Refusals have been found with no particular preference for any specific genre; they are also expressed by different WILL-forms, associated with practically all subjects:

(66) For wel I wot sche wol noght take, / An yive *wol* sche noght also, / Sche is eschu of bothe tuo. (GOWER: II, 76)

(67) Yf Y do not the werkis of my fadir, *nyle* ȝe bileue to me; but if Y do, thouȝ ȝe *wolen* not bileue to me, bileue ȝe to the werkis; that ȝe knowe and bileue, that the fadir is in me, and Y in the fadir. (WYCNEW: X, 20)

(68) KA. Who shall be my Father to give me.
JO. Thou mayest ask Jack Wheeler, but I know he had rather had thee himself.
KA. Oh fie no, I *will* not ask him, he will take it for an affront, I will rather ask old father Bandol for he us'd to call me Daughter, and he will take it kindly.
(PENNY: 119)

In the next quotation the pragmatic function of refusal is made explicit by means of the negative form of WILL followed by the verb *to consent*:

(69) Sir Andrew," he saide, "*wil* ȝe *nouȝt consent* to destroye þe venyme of þe reaume, as we bene consented? (BRUT: 218)

In the quotation below, instead, refusal is underlined by the parallel structure, which presents "ye will not" as equivalent to "ye refuse":

(70) since ye refuse to accept of peace with your brethren, ye shall have War from your enemies; and since ye *will* not with us preach the word of life, to whom ye ought, from their hands ye shall receive death. (MILTON: X, 149)

The quotations below represent instances of strong refusal, usually implying insistence or persistence.

(71) And þan if he *will* noght tak hede / To ȝowre counsail, þan es it nede / þat þou tell vnto haly kirk / þe sins þat þou sese him wirk. / And þan if he *will* noght be boun / To haly kirk and to resoun, (NHOM: II, 70)

(72) þe leste mercy of men ys among clerkys, þat *wolen* not ȝyue goodus of grace but ȝif þei sullen hem. And þerfore þis sinne is heresye byfor God, þe moste and þe fyrste þat partiþ men fro God, (WSERM: I, 237)

In the following quotation the sentence expressing insistence reinforces the refusal expressed in the previous line:

(73) Mar mightes has vr lauerd wroght, / þan ani man mai thing in thoght, / Bot mani o trouth es sua vn-slei, / þai tru noght bot þat þai se wit ei; / And þat vnnethes *will* þai tru, / Wit-vten signe o gret vertu; (CURSOR: 1238)

In the next quotation, instead, the persistence of the negative action is made explicit by the use of the adverb *long* in the line before:

(74) ȝyf þou lygge long yn synne, / And *wylt* nat ryse, ne þerof blynne, / Certeynly, for eueri oure / þou shalt ȝelde a-counte ful soure; (HS: 159)

The category of refusals usually also includes those cases in which the subject is non-human and the verb phrase expresses the lack of accomplishment of a desired action,[16] as in the following instance:

(75) And when an hors is I-let blod & *wol* not staunche. Or ellus he strobuleþ his veyne with rubbynge of hym in self. þen schalt þou take felt & brenne it sumdel. (HORSES: 89)

5.1.1.3. Threat

In the corpus only three threats appear to be expressed by a WILL-form; all of them occur in a Trial transcript in the E3 subsection:

(76) I must know the Truth of that; remember that I gave you fair Warning, do not tell me a Lye, for I *will* be sure to treasure up every Lye that thou tellest me, and thou may'st be certain it *will* not be for thy Advantage: (LISLE: IV, 114.C1)

(77) L.C.J. and therefore look to it, that thou dost not prevaricate with me, for to be sure thou *wilt* come to the worst of it in the end?
DUNNE. My Lord, I will tell the Truth as near as I can. (LISLE: IV, 114.C1)

5.1.1.4. Promise

Many of the examples of WILL in the corpus have a 1st person subject and convey an undertaking to perform a certain action which is beneficial to the interlocutor, as can be seen in (78) and (79):

(78) wherfore y praye ȝow þat ȝe wil come wiþ vs, wiþ al þe power þat ȝe haue ordeynede, and helpe to destroie þe venyme of Engeland, and þe traitoures þat bene þerin, and we *wil* ȝif vnto ȝow þe best part of v Erldomes þar We haueþ & holdeþ; (BRUT: 218)

16 A PDE example of this usage is the following, in which the angry speaker anthropomorphizes the object and accuses it of deliberately refusing to do the action he wishes it to perform: e.g. 'The car *won't* start' (= The car refuses to start).

(79) PISC. but you must do me one courtesie, it must be done instantly.
HOST. I *will* do it, Mr Piscator, and with all the speed I can. (WALTON: 216)

Promises having a 3rd person subject have also been found, but mainly in reported speech; in three cases the pragmatic value of the WILL-form is emphasized by the harmonic superordinate verb *promise*:

(80) to perswade men, to put out their eyes, upon promise that they *will* help them to a much better and more faithful Guide? (TILLOTS: II, ii, 450)

(81) Christ hath promised y[t] where two or three are mett in his name hee *will* bee in ye midst of y[m] (FOX: 158)

(82) trust god in his promisses, for hee have saide, I *will* never lave thee nor for sake thee, (JPINNEY: 18)

Apart from *promise*, we find the verb *to swear* and the superordinate noun *oath* which also make explicit the pragmatic value of WILL:

(83) and We wil mak vnto ȝow an oth þat we *wil* neuer do þing wiþout ȝour consel, and so ȝe shul bene as wele at ese wiþ vs as euer was Robert Holande. (BRUT: 218)

(84) the said Justices are hereby impowered to impannel a Jury before them and to administer an Oath to the said Jury that they *will* assesse such Damages to be given and Recompense to be made to the Owners and others interested in the said Ground Rent or Charge respectively for their respective Interest' (STAT7: VII, 210)

(85) TOM. First, you shall kiss my hand and swear that you will acknowledge me to be your Lord and Master.
IONE. I *will* Sir. (PENNY: 268)

We still class as promises multiply-hedged undertakings such as the following to carry out an action:

(86) as the knowynge of thise thinges is a maner porcioun of the medycyne to the, al be it so that I have litil tyme to doon it, yit natheles y *wol* enforcen me to schewe somwhat of it. (BOETHCH: 451, C1)

5.1.2. Necessity

The semantic value of deontic necessity is expressed in various pragmatic forms, as can be seen in Tables 8 and 9.

Text types	*order*	*prohibition*	*advice*	*Total*
BIBLE		9	3	12
LETTERS	2	1		3
RELIGIOUS TR		2		2
HISTORY	1			1
RULES		1		1
DOCUMENTS				
FICTION				
HANDBOOKS				
HOMILIES				
PHILOSOPHY				
SCIENCE				
SERMONS				
TRAVELOGUES				
All texts	3	13	3	19
ambig. cases	0	1 (8%)	0	1 (5%)

Table 8. Pragmatic uses expressing deontic necessity in M3 (absolute numbers).

Text types	*order*	*prohibition*	*advice*	*proposal*	*Total*
FICTION	1			11	12
LETTERS	7				7
EDUC TR			6		6
DRAMA	2	1		2	5
TRIALS	5				5
HANDBOOKS	1		1		2
SERMONS			2		2
BIOGRAPHIES	1				1
DIARIES					
HISTORY					
LAW					
PHILOSOPHY					
SCIENCE					
TRAVELOGUES					
All texts	17	1	9	13	40
ambig. cases	3 (18%)	0	1 (11%)	2 (15%)	6 (15%)

Table 9. Pragmatic uses expressing deontic necessity in E3 (absolute numbers).

5.1.2.1. Order

This category includes statements demanding the interlocutor to perform an action. Orders appear in various text types, but are most frequent in official Letters, Trial proceedings and Drama. WILL-forms expressing orders usually have a 2nd person subject, as the recipient is addressed directly (e.g. in Fictional dialogues and Letters). Here are a few examples:

(87) The next Monday or Tuesday come seven-night, I expect to be Bachelor of Arts, so that you *will* but supply me with some money. (STRYPE: 183)

(88) The Letter goes enclosed which you *will* take care to deliver. (SPENCER: IV, 313)

To make orders more polite, they are often realized as questions, as can be seen in these examples:

(89) Come Hostess, how do you do? *Will* you first give us a cup of your best drink, and then dress this Chub, as you drest my last, when I and my friend were here about eight or ten days ago? (WALTON: 216)

(90) *Will* you do me the Favour to conduct me to a Chamber? (FARQUHAR: 62)

On the surface these questions resemble inquiries about someone's (good) intentions, but pragmatically they function as orders. They seem to be more frequent in the EModE period and can be made additionally indirect by the use of polite expressions such as *pray* and *be pleas'd*:

(91) Mr ffox: you are an eminent man amongst those of your profession: pray *will* you bee Instrumental to disswade ym from meetinge in such great numbers: (FOX: 158)

(92) Pray, sir Thomas, *will* you be pleas'd to give the Court an account, whether you saw Mr. Ireland in Staffordshire 1678, and what time it was? (OATES: IV, 85, C1)

In formal contexts, the order may be addressed using a 3rd person pronoun, as in these instances:

(93) Pray *will* your Lordship give my Lord and the Jury an account, when Mr. *Ireland* came to your House, and how far he travelled with you afterwards? (OATES: IV, 75.C1)

(94) OATES My Lord, is this any thing of Evidence?
L. C. J. The Jury hears it, and they *will* consider of it. (OATES: IV, 83.C1)

In addition to these, the M3 part of the Helsinki Corpus also includes one case of prescription, in which obligation is determined by the law rather than by the volition of a clearly identified individual:

(95) "Vr lagh," he said, "þat we in liue / *Wil* first our elder doghter giue. (CURSOR: 228)

5.1.2.2. Prohibition

Prohibitions are found in different genres, with the highest frequency in Biblical texts. In particular, in Wycliffe's rendering of the *Vulgata* the negative imperative *nile/nyle* forms are the English rendering of the Latin formulas *noli/nolite* used in the original work to perform the same function of prohibition. Here are a few examples of their usage:

(96) *Nyle* ȝe be rebel aȝens the Lord, nether drede ȝe the puple of this lond, for we moun deuoure hem so as breed; (WYCOLD: XIV, 1N)

(97) Go ȝe awey fro the tabernaclis of wickid men, and *nyle* ȝe touche tho thingis that parteynen to hem, lest ȝe ben wlappid in the synnes of hem. (WYCOLD: XVI, 20N)

Imperative *nile* and *nyle* are only found in Wycliffe's translations; in other texts, instead, prohibitions are expressed by means of a postponed negative particle:

(98) For þou *wilt* not late him fede him on soche swete meditacions touchid before. (CLOUD: 29)

In E3 there is only one example expressing prohibition, an instance recorded in Drama. In this unique case, it is reinforced by the co-occurence of *cannot*:

(99) ARCH. Your Lips must seal the Promise [...] They must, they must (Kisses her) [...] And the now conscious Stars have preordain'd this Moment for my Happiness. (Takes her in his Arms)
MRS. SULL. You *will* not, cannot sure. (FARQUHAR: 60)

5.1.2.3. Proposal

Proposals have been found only in E3 Fictional works and Drama, and always in the context of a dialogue. In general, the suggestion concerns the behaviour of the two interlocutors and is therefore accompanied by a 1st person plural pronoun; here are a few examples:

(100) KA. What Musick shall we have?
JO. We *will* have old Rowly and his company. (PENNY: 118)

(101) Come Mary, we *will* depart unto the Congregation of those Saints that be our Notions. (PENNY: 152)

In some instances the suggestion concerns the speaker and another person different from the interlocutor, as in the following example:

(102) if thou wilt begin, I and thy Maid *will* bear our parts, (PENNY: 151)

Proposals may also concern things or people different from the interlocutors; in this case the WILL-form is preceded by a 3rd person subject, as in the following quotation:

(103) KA. Who shall make the Sack Posset.
JO. The Bride-maids *will* take care of that. (PENNY: 119)

5.1.2.4. Advice

The cases of advice found in M3 usually contain the form *nyle*, as can be seen from the following examples:

(104) nether drede ȝe the puple of this lond, for we moun deuore hem so as breed; al her help passide awei fro hem, the Lord is with vs, *nyle* ȝe drede.
(WYCOLD: XIV, 1N)

(105) *Nyle* ȝe wondre this, for the our cometh, in which alle men that ben in birielis, schulen here the voice of Goddis sone. (WYCNEW: V, 20)

In E3, instances of advice have been found in Handbooks, Educational treatises and Sermons; whenever advice is meant to be general, a 3rd person subject is used; at times the subject is non-human, as can be seen in the following cases:

(106) But it *will* concern the Prudence of the Husbands love to make the Cares and Evils as simple and easie as he can, (JETAYLOR: 28)

(107) I think there are better ways of prevailing with them, and a gentle perswasion and reasoning [...] *will* most times doe much better. (LOCKE: 58)

No examples of requests for advice have been found, such as in the following PDE example:

(108) How *will* I get there?
(What must I do to get there? / How do you suggest that I should get there?)

5.2. Epistemic meanings

5.2.1. Inference

The only case of epistemic modality found in the M3 subsection of the corpus expresses a deduction made by the locutor:

(109) Scabbe wol brede in þe necke. [...] & þat *wol* come of superfluyte of blod. or of oþer wicked humourr. (HORSES: 103)

In the E3 part of the corpus, nine cases of epistemic usage expressing inference have been recorded.[17] Four of them appear in Educational books and single instances have also been found in five other text types. Besides the quotations reported in Section 4 above, here are some more examples:

---

17 This increase is in line with the wider use of WILL to express prediction. Indeed, "situating something in the future unavoidably involves an element of uncertainty" (Nuyts 2001: 173).

(110) But still it *will* be said, Who shall judge what things are plain and what doubtful? (TILLOTS: II, ii. 447)

(111) Igad, Sir, this *will* prove some Inchanted Castle; we shall have the Gyant come out by and by with his Club, and beat our Brains out. (VANBR: I, 57)

Epistemic WILL often combines with a harmonic verbal complement of opinion (such as *expect* or *think*), or is in a subclause following such a verb:

(112) Perhaps it *will* be expected from me that I should give him some directions of physick to prevent diseases. (LOCKE: 48)

(113) I imagine every one *will* judg it reasonable that their children when litle should looke upon their parents as their Lords, (LOCKE: 54)

(114) Mr. Busbie hath of late made at Westminster Schoole, where the Easterne Languages are now become familiar to the highest sort of Scholars, *will* undoubtedly think (as I do) that our children may be brought on to far more knowledge of Language and things, then hitherto they have been, (HOOLE: 220)

5.3. Dynamic meanings

5.3.1. Possibility

WILL-forms are sometimes used also to express dynamic possibility.[18] These forms are more frequent in Handbooks, as the following quotations show:

(115) Another cause is this, that sothly in any tretis of the Astrelabie that I have seyn, there be somme conclusions that *wol* not in alle thinges parformen her bihestes; and somme of hem ben to harde to thy tendir age of ten yeer to conceyve. (ASTR: 662, C1)

(116) Pigeons *will* fly forty miles for a breakfast, (WALTON: 211)

Here below are some quotations taken from other text types:

---

18 Apart from this term, others such as 'capacity', 'potential' or 'power' have been used to refer to this category (cf. Palmer 1979b, Haegeman 1983, Aijmer 1985).

(117) And þis fullyng ys not voydid but sadly replenyched and at þe laste hit is hepid as myche as hit *wole* take. (WSERM: I, 238)

(118) after the Laws of the lond made me able for to Zeue myne answeres in Lawe as my symple wittes *wole* seruen me (PET3: 199)

(119) My Chamber fellow & I differ someth in our apprehensions of things past, which *wil* not bee helpt, but for the unseen th. that are to come that are Eternal, wee are all one. (PHENRY: 340)

(120) This paper *will* not hold all the inconveniences I lay under before I came up to London, which now are in a great Measure abated. (HOXINDEN: 292)

(121) the Female Palms (which only Bear) *will* not Bring forth before they are Impregnated at the Roots with the Seed of the Male, first pounded into meal and sprinkled about them; (FRYER: II, 183)

5.3.2. Prediction

As shown above, the highest number of dynamic occurrences concerns prediction; its presence is particularly widespread in E3, where it corresponds to almost 60% of all WILL-forms (against 35% in M3) and covers nearly all the text types included in the corpus. The semantic value of prediction is expressed in different pragmatic meanings, as can be seen in Tables 10 and 11.

Text types	*prophecy*	*assurance*	*neutr. pred.*	*Total*	*o/ooo*
HOMILIES		1	13	14	19
RELIGIOUS TR	1	3	50	54	14
RULES			7	7	13
HANDBOOKS			19	19	10
FICTION			10	10	7
PHILOSOPHY			9	9	7
TRAVELOGUES			3	3	6
DOCUMENTS			4	4	2
HISTORY			3	3	1
BIBLE			2	2	1
SERMONS			2	2	1
LETTERS			1	1	1
SCIENCE					0
All texts	1	4	123	128	7

Table 10. Pragmatic uses expressing prediction in M3.

Text types	assurance	neutr. pred.	Total	o/ooo
HANDBOOKS	3	59	62	54
LETTERS	5	77	82	43
FICTION	6	43	49	41
EDUC TR		38	38	33
SERMONS		29	29	23
DRAMA	1	27	28	22
SCIENCE	1	24	25	22
PHILOSOPHY	1	12	13	15
DIARIES		11	11	10
LAW		5	5	4
BIOGRAPHIES		3	3	3
TRAVELOGUES		1	1	1
TRIALS		1	1	1
HISTORY				0
All texts	17	330	347	20

Table 11. Pragmatic uses expressing prediction in E3.

5.3.2.1. Neutral prediction

Neutral prediction (or 'pure future', as this category is often referred to in the literature) is very widespread in the corpus analysed; indeed, there are examples of usage with all persons, and in all kinds of sentences: affirmative, negative and interrogative. When the prediction is the result of some kind of hope, fear or confidence, it is commonly preceded by an explicit harmonic superordinate expression, as can be seen in the following quotations:

(122) It is <u>hoped</u> shee *will* recover. (HOXINDEN: 280)

(123) And now that those judgements have done no good upon us we may justly <u>fear</u> that he *will* appear once for all. (TILLOTS: II, ii, 430)

(124) I assure you I do of you wth as great kindness as any mother can doe for a childe, and <u>trust</u> God *will* hear the prayers y^{t} are made day and night for you by Y^{r} most truly affectionate mother, (EHATTON: II, 50)

Sentences predicting consequence and containing WILL-forms appear in various text types; they are commonly introduced by *(and) then, so, (so) that.* Here are a few examples taken from writings on Science:

(125) Put the ryng of thyn Astrolabie upon the thombe of thi right hond, and than *wol* his right side be toward thi lift side, and his left side *wol* be toward thy right side. (ASTR: 664, C2)

(126) innere or owtre til it stonde precise vp on the closere of the signes in the lymbe of thin equatorie / so *wole* thanne the centre of thin epicicle precise stonde vp on centre aryn the sixte (EPLANETS: 26)

Here are some more examples drawn from other text types:

(127) but þat hors be holpe in tyme þat mangew *wol* turne in-to a foule schabbe (HORSES: 101)

(128) For ȝyf þou dost, þan *wyl* she do / þyng þat she neuer þoghte to do. (HS: 68)

5.3.2.2. Prophecy

The only example of prophecy found in the corpus occurs in M3; it is the following:

(129) And therfore seith Salomon, "The wratthe of God ne *wol* nat spare no wight, for preyere ne for yifte"; and therfore, at the day of doom ther nys noon hope to escape. (CTPARS: 291, C1)

5.3.2.3. Assurance

Various cases of WILL-forms expressing assurance have been found both in the M3 and in the E3 parts of the Helsinki Corpus; they are not concentrated in any specific text type. In some cases propositions are made stronger by means of locutor-oriented boosters, intended to highlight the encoder's truthfulness and reliability. Here are a few examples:

(130) And trewly, who-so wil loke Denis bookes, he schal fynde þat his wordes *wilen* cleerly aferme al þat I haue seyde or schal sey, fro þe biginnyng of þis tretis to þe ende. (CLOUD: 125)

(131) Woman, trow what I þe tell: / Al men drinkes of þis well, / It *will* noght slokken ay þaire thrist, / Bot eftsones to drink sal þam list. (NHOM: II, 79)

(132) and not far from it you *will* find all her young ones, I dare warrant you, (WALTON: 212)

(133) He that shall diligently examine the *Phaenomena* of this Experiment, *will*, I doubt not, find cause to believe, that the reason I have heretofore given of it, is the true and genuine cause of it, (HOOKE: 13, 5, 45)

(134) I'll warrant thee all *will* go well: (VANBR: I, 58)

In other cases, the instances of assurance rely on content-oriented boosters, which are meant to increase the illocutionary force of the speech act by underlining the certainty of the proposition asserted and thus emphasize its validity. The following are examples of this usage:

(135) This *will* be brave indeed John, (PENNY: 117)

(136) she *will* verily conceive that we have gone astray, and Erred from the Light. (PENNY: 149)

Several expressions containing *sure(ly)* are used for this purpose, as may be seen in the following quotations:

(137) but sure enough hee *will* do mee no good. (HOXINDEN: 280)

(138) You may chance to have Suckers of an old Vine which *will* be sure to grow. (LANGF: 129)

(139) In the same manner, if we run through all other Beings, it *will* surely appear, that every thing, as long as it preserveth Unity doth subsist, (BOETHPR: 143)

5.3.3. Habit

WILL-forms expressing habit are quite widespread in both sub-sections of the corpus; the evolution of this habitual value may be a development from that of prediction, in the sense that it could be hypothesized that when one expects something to take place in a certain context basing one's own expectation on personal or general experience, one then infers that such regular behaviour is to be considered a habit or custom. Habitual statements appear in several text types and in particular in Handbooks, Educational works and

Scientific treatises. In most instances the subject is animate and possessed of a will:

(140) Or ellus take hors-cayme & grynd it wel & bynde it fast to þe veyne. Or ellus sum *wol* tak a feþer & twyne it in þe heere þer þe blod renneþ out & feþeres bynde þere-to. (HORSES: 91)

(141) for no wyght *nil* haten gode men, but yif he were overmochel a fool, and for to haten schrewes it nis no resoun. (BOETHCH: 449. C1)

(142) [This creature] *will* never be quiet till it has drawn blood (HOOKE: 13, 5, 211)

In other cases the subject denotes some other living thing and the speech act describes some aspects of its typical behaviour:

(143) Scabbe *wol* brede in þe necke. & on þe dok of þe taile riȝt as þe mangew. & it peliþ awei þe heere up bi þe rotes so þat þe hors *wille* rubbe him-self þat þe necke & þe dok of his taile schal be al bare (HORSES: 103)

(144) But þei *will* roten within .viij. dayes And for þat cause men may not carye of þo apples to no fer contrees. (MAND: 31)

(145) Apricocks *will* have buds sooner ready than other fruit; so that you may begin with them, and follow with other kinds. (LANGF: 34)

6. Concluding remarks

As has been seen above, in both periods taken into consideration WILL-forms express all three basic types of modal meaning: deontic, epistemic and dynamic. The distribution of tokens in these categories, however, varies considerably, as Table 12 shows. Between the two periods there is a considerable decrease in deontic meanings and a great increase in dynamic meanings; the percentages for epistemic use also increase, although to a more limited extent.[19] In particular, great

19 This confirms the evolution outlined by Traugott (1989: 37): the modal acquired at first deontic meanings, and then developed dynamic and epistemic meanings.

changes are involved in the expression of volition (-24%) and prediction (+26%).

Modality type		*M3*		*E3*
deontic	52		30	
volition		47		23
necessity		5		7
epistemic	0.3		2	
inference		0.3		2
dynamic	48		68	
possibility		2		3
prediction		35		61
habit		11		4
Total		100		100

Table 12. Percentages of WILL-forms according to modality type.

Smaller changes concern habit (-7%) and (probably insignificant) increases of less than 2% for deontic necessity, epistemic inference and dynamic possibility. Tables 13, 14 and 15 summarize the distribution of these changes in the various text types.

	deontic			*epist.*	*dynamic*				*Tot.*
Text types	*volit.*	*necess.*	*Tot.*	*inf*	*poss.*	*pred.*	*habit*	*Tot.*	
SCIENCE	100		100						100
BIBLE	46	46	92			7		7	100
HISTORY	85	4	89			11		11	100
LETTERS	43	43	86			14		14	100
DOCUMENTS	78		78		4	18		22	100
PHILOSOPHY	57		57			39	4	43	100
FICTION	57		57			23	20	43	100
TRAVELOGUES	50		50			21	29	50	100
RULES	36	7	43			50	7	57	100
RELIGIOUS T.	40	2	42		2	52	4	58	100
SERMONS	40		40		20	40		60	100
HOMILIES	32		32			56	12	68	100
HANDBOOKS	22		22	2	8	35	33	76	100

Table 13. Percentage distribution of WILL-forms by modality types in M3 (in descending order of total deontic modality).

	deontic			*epist.*	*dynamic*				*Tot.*
Text types	*volit.*	*necess.*	*Tot.*	*inf*	*poss.*	*pred.*	*habit*	*Tot.*	
HISTORY	100		100						100
TRIALS	78	16	94			3	3	6	100
BIOGRAPHIES	60	10	70	10		30		30	100
FICTION	24	14	38	1		58	3	61	100
DRAMA	28	10	38	2	4	56		60	100
PHILOSOPHY	32		32			68		68	100
LETTERS	23	6	29		2	69		71	100
SERMONS	18	4	22	2	9	65	2	76	100
LAW	17		17			83		83	100
HANDBOOKS	15	2	17		10	65	8	83	100
EDUC. TR.	6	11	17	7		69	7	76	100
SCIENCE				3	3	84	10	97	100
DIARIES						50	50	100	100

Table 14. Distribution of WILL-forms by modality types in E3
(in descending order of total deontic modality)

	deontic		*epistemic*		*dynamic*	
Text types	*M3*	*E3*	*M3*	*E3*	*M3*	*E3*
SCIENCE	100			3		97
HISTORY	89	100			11	
LETTERS	86	29			14	71
FICTION	57	38		1	43	61
PHILOSOPHY	57	32			43	68
SERMONS	40	22		2	60	76
HANDBOOKS	22	17	2		76	83

Table 15. Distribution of WILL-forms by modality types in M3 and E3 (comparable text types only, in descending order of total deontic modality in M3).

As the data in Tables 13, 14 and 15 show, the upward or downward trend is not uniform in all the text types included in the corpus. Total agreement can be found only as regards the expression of prediction (which increases in all the text types that appear in both periods) and of habit (which decreases in both Handbooks and Fiction). In contrast, the general decrease in the use of WILL to express volition (found in Handbooks, Philosophy, Sermons, Fiction and Letters) is not found in History, where there is a small increase.

The comparison between the two subcorpora has thus confirmed the trend in the grammaticalization process commonly pointed out in the literature on the evolution of central modals, and in particular the development of the prediction function according to the following sequence:

DESIRE > WILLINGNESS > INTENTION > PREDICTION
(Bybee / Perkins / Pagliuca 1994: 256)

The high number of intentional uses already found in the M3 subsection favoured the progress in the grammaticalization of WILL, as it is a very easy step for a statement expressing intention to be taken as expressing prediction, particularly when the value of intention is not very strong. The advanced stage of grammaticalization of WILL is confirmed by other data found in our analysis, such as the more complex verbal complements in which WILL-forms occur in the E3 part of the corpus and its use in tag questions, a feature which underlines its function as an auxiliary verb.

X. Would

The M3 part of the Helsinki Corpus contains 302 WOULD-forms, including 35 instances of non-modal usage, as in (1) and (2); when these are excluded, the M3 sub-corpus includes 267 forms (14 per 10,000 words).

(1) alle þynges þat ȝe *woolde* þat men dede to ȝouȝ, do ȝe to hem aȝenward: (AELR3: 36)

(2) But I nolde nat of schrewes, [...] that it were leveful to hem to don that. (BOETHCH: 4410.6.C2)

In the E3 part 404 WOULD-forms were recorded, including ten abbreviated forms.[1] Seven instances reflect non-modal usage of WOULD expressing wish or volition, as in (3). After these instances are excluded, the E3 subcorpus consists of 397 occurrences (23 per 10,000 words).

(3) KA. I *would* it were once over.
Jo. So *would* I, *i'd* as live as a groat. (PENNY: 119)

In the time span between M3 and E3 there is thus an increase of 65% in the use of WOULD and this, in turn, appears to be related to a decrease by about 33% in the use of SHOULD (cf. Ch. 8); it will be interesting to observe whether the respective patterns of increase and decrease can be outlined in specific text types or syntactic contexts.

1 These have been included in the calculations on the basis of their occurrence in the neighbourhood of WOULD-forms in contexts in which SHOULD was a less plausible choice in view of its more marked meaning in the diachronic period under discussion (cf. Ch. 8). In addition, the fact that the OED attributes *'d* to this modal and not to others was also deemed to be significant. As regards distribution, these abbreviated forms (*I'd, you'd, she'd* and *they'd*) still appear to be rather marginal and only occur in unstressed positions in Fictional dialogues, Drama and (in one case) in a Travelogue.

1. Spelling variants

In the M3 sub-corpus no single spelling variant appears to correlate with all subjects. Forms ending with *-st* (*woldest, woldist* and *wuldyst)* correlate only with 2nd person singular subjects, whereas *wolden* and *nolden* only occur with plural subjects. The vowel-less form *wlde* only occurs once, which may be accidental, since elsewhere in the same text other variants are used:

(4) And how þey *wulde* haue dampned hym þere, ȝyf mercy of Ihesu Cryst ne were [...] Moche *wlde* hyt helpe at nede, with gode wyl do almes dede [...] Of alle men he *wuld* haue doute, And to here byddyng mekly loute (HS: 185, 189)

Agglutinated negative forms *nolde* and *nolden* occur in a range of texts, albeit rather infrequently:

(5) Ther was no dore that he *nolde* heve of harre, (CTPROL: 32.C1)

(6) For ȝe *nolden* assente to the Lord, nether the Lord schal be with ȝou. (WYCOLD: XIV, 40N)

In M3 geographical variation is still clearly marked, with *wald*-forms only occurring in Northern texts (where no other forms are found) and *wuld*-forms only occurring in Southern ones (where, however, a clear majority of tokens are *-o*-forms). *Wold*-forms characterize the texts from both the East and the West-Midlands.

In E3 the 397 occurrences of WOULD-forms conveying modal values are expressed in three basic spelling variants correlating with all subjects. Of these, *would* accounts for 80% of all occurrences; *wou'd* signals a phonological rendition of the auxiliary; and *woulde* maintains a disappearing form with final *-e*. Morphologically marked forms occurring with 2nd person singular subjects are restricted to 7 instances of *wouldst.*[2] The following quotations provide instances of the various forms employed in the different text types; as shown in example (7), different variants could still occur in the same text:

2 These were all recorded in dialogues, both Fictional and Philosophical.

(7) Wee *woulde* have ye parlament men to put ye certificate Into ye Gazette [...] frendes askt mee to what meetinge I *would* goe; (FOX: 155-156)

(8) It's well I have a Husband a coming, or Icod, *I'd* marry the Baker, I *wou'd* so. (VANBR: I, 59)

2. Distribution according to text type

Table 1 shows the distribution of the various forms in the different text types included in the corpus. As we can see, the average frequency of WOULD-forms increases by over 60% between M3 and E3; Historical texts and Travelogues are the only text types in which there is a significant decrease, possibly due to a change in the stylistic and epistemological approach to historical chronicle and journal writing, less based on reported dialogues between protagonists, and more on the narration of events. Considerable increases are recorded in Philosophical texts, Handbooks, Sermons, Fiction and Letters; however, the most remarkable change is possibly witnessed in Scientific texts, where the rise in the use of tentative forms appears to be inextricably related to the change in thought-styles to which reference has already been made elsewhere in this volume (cf. Ch. 8, n. 13). Another interesting result is the complete absence of WOULD-forms in E3 Legal documents. This is understandable, as rules, by definition, leave no margin for the tentativeness associated with hypothetical forms. On the other hand, in M3 above-average frequencies were recorded in genres in which hypotheses are made and volition is reported: for instance, in narrative texts, whether Historical or Fictional.

If we now compare normalized frequencies for SHOULD and WOULD, some interesting patterns begin to emerge. Overall data are summarized in Table 2 for the text types included in both sub-corpora: while both decrease in Historical texts and appear to be fairly stable in Travelogues, they increase in Philosophical texts, Letters and Handbooks. However, in Sermons and Scientific texts a decrease in the frequency of SHOULD corresponds to an increase in the frequency of WOULD, a pattern also reflected in the figures expressing average values. Whether this can be related to a change in modal values and syntactic patterns of usage will be discussed in the next paragraphs.

Text type	*M3*	*E3*
FICTION	31	49
HISTORY	27	19
PHILOSOPHY	13	28
TRAVELOGUES	9	6
SERMONS	8	22
LETTERS	6	26
HANDBOOKS	3	11
SCIENCE	0	28
DOCUMENTS	21	-
HOMILIES	19	-
RELIGIOUS TREATISES	16	-
RULES	7	-
BIBLE	4	-
EDUC. TREATISES	-	30
DRAMA	-	27
TRIALS	-	25
BIOGRAPHIES	-	19
DIARIES	-	19
LAW	-	0
All texts	14	23

Table 1. Normalized occurrences of WOULD-forms according to text type.

	M3		*E3*	
Text type	*SHOULD*	*WOULD*	*SHOULD*	*WOULD*
SERMONS	75	8	22	22
HISTORY	36	27	9	19
FICTION	29	31	29	49
PHILOSOPHY	29	13	43	28
SCIENCE	22	0	13	28
LETTERS	9	6	21	26
TRAVELOGUES	3	9	4	6
HANDBOOKS	2	3	10	11
All texts	27	14	18	23

Table 2. Normalized frequencies of SHOULD and WOULD
(text types included in both subcorpora).

3. Sentence structure

Table 3 summarizes the number of occurrences of WOULD-forms in different sentence structures; as we can see, the majority of these are in subordinate clauses. Among these, noun clauses (including indirect questions) were found to account for nearly 30% in E3 – quite a dramatic increase in relation to the values of M3.

Clause type		*M3* %	*E3* %
Main		37	42
Subordinate clauses		63	58
	Noun	16	23
	Relative	19	11
	Conditional	8	6
	Cause	6	5
	Final	6	4
	Indirect questions	1	4
	Comparative	2	3
	Time	2	1
	Concessive	1	1

Table 3. Percentage of WOULD-forms occurring in different clause types.

The high number of tokens in this type of subclause may of course be related to usage of WOULD in the context of reported predictions and expectations:

(9) He told me when I saw him, That he hoped I *would* come to him upon that general Insinuation of the desire he had of my Company (BURNETROC: 136)

(10) He began to suspect them of falshood, and that they *would* delay him till the time of his wife's delivery (BEHN: 191)

As regards WOULD-forms in conditional clauses,[3] the type-token ratio was found to be similar in both periods. The following quotations provide a few examples:

3 On this point see, among others, Bybee (1995).

(11) yf that a wyght *wolde* ryden for cause of hele, he ne desireth not so mochel the moevyng to ryden, as the effect of his hele. (BOETHCH: 434.C1)

(12) She would have com to you[u] longe or this tim if I *would* have let her com (JPINNEY: 40)

If may be omitted after a main clause, as in example (13), so that the hypotheticality of the clause derives from its syntactic environment:

(13) My deare Lord, I should be very glad you *would* bring some chocolate along with you (FHATTON: I, 148)

Occasionally, the conditional clause can be marked by an introductory verb-subject inversion, as in (14); an alternative subordinator is *provided*, which dictates the necessary conditions for the predication to become factual:

(14) *wulde* þey bydde hym sytte or stande, Euer he wulde be bowande. (HS: 189)

(15) he had brought her a Ring, provided she *would* give him another kiss (PENNY: 159)

4. Verb phrase structure

Both in M3 and E3 the most widespread construction has the modal followed by an active infinitive, which may be expressed or ellipted; the two possibilities together account for 84% of the total in M3 and for 85% of the total in E3. The following quotations provide examples of both cases recorded in the two subcorpora:

(16) And on the morewe he *wolde* go out in to Galilee, (WYCNEW: I, 40)

(17) I am so ravisht of the syhte, That speke unto hire I ne myhte [...], thogh I *wolde*: (GOWER: I, 319-320)

(18) Some *would* have the princesse made Queene without any more dispute (EVELYN: 896)

(19) odoriferous Gums and Perfumes, which, being heated, send forth their fragrant steams, both further and more copiously than otherwise they *would*
(BOYLE: 8)

On occasion, two or more infinitives may follow the same modal – either for symmetry and balance, as in poetry, or for the sake of narrative density:

(20) Sownynge in moral vertu was his speche, And gladly *wolde* he lerne and gladly teche. (CTPROL: 28.C1)

(21) If they *woulde* lett mee see it & give mee time to consider of it: I might aunswer: (FOX: 83)

In both M3 and E3 the modal verb and infinitive could be separated by an adverbial phrase – as in (22) – or indeed a subordinate clause – as in (23) – so that discourse development could be delayed and therefore made more interesting:

(22) wiþ a special beholding to hem, as þou *woldest* bi þat beholding fede and encrees þi purpos (CLOUD: 25)

(23) He had found an Experiment to do it, provided she *would* when her Husband and she was a walking in the Garden, pretend to Long for some Fruit
(PENNY: 160)

In one case in M3 the modal precedes a progressive form which signals the persistence of the predication, also reinforced by the adverbial *ever*; however, no occurrences of this structure were recorded in the E3 section:

(24) wulde þey bydde hym sytte or stande, Euer he *wulde* be bowande; (HS: 189)

Perfect infinitives are the second most frequent verb complement in both subperiods and have been generally found to follow the modal in those instances in which counterfactuality is expressed (cf. also Boyland 1998 and Molencki 1999):

(25) &, truly, had noght the aldermen kome to trete, [...] they *wolde* haue go to a Newe eleccion, & in that hete haue slayn hym that *wolde* haue letted it, yf they had myght. (USK: 28-29)

(26) I am glad that I have setled my busines so well as I have, so that what ever come of mee, things will be better for Thee and Thine then they *would* have been in case I had not made any agreement. (HOXINDEN: 293)

In two cases in M3, however, the sequence 'HAVE + past participle' expresses the causative meaning conveyed by PDE 'to want sth done' with the object anticipated in the pronominal form:

(27) and what-so-euer the Spensers *wolde* haue done, it was don. (BRUT: 224)
[Whatever the Spensers wanted done]

(28) All þat his fader *wald* ha wroght Thoru him til end it suld be broght.
[wanted done] (CURSOR: 548)

If we now consider the passive voice, we see that in M3 passive infinitives generally occur in narrative texts, whether Fictional or Historical, and in Religious instruction:

(29) Aboute þat tyme Ricoldus duke of Frisons was i-tornede by the prechynge of Seynt Wilfranus þe bisshop, and *wolde* i-cristned be. (TREVISA: VI, 227)

(30) ȝe wymmen also, comunly, *wulde* be kallede 'madame' or 'lady;' Al þys comþ of grete pryde; [...] ȝyf þou delyte þe yn grete meyne, [...] And for þy meyne *wuldyst* preysed be, þou for þy meyne shalt dampned be ȝyf þou to euyl vowe þy meyne. (HS: 118)

In E3 the range of text types in which passives occur is broader, encompassing Drama, private Letters and Scientific texts, in addition to Fiction, Philosophy and Sermons:

(31) I see not the silver buckles I was promised; yet they *would* be received very thankfully, if they came (STRYPE: 182)

(32) the Town *wou'd* be robb'd of one of its chief Diversions, if it shou'd become a Crime to laugh at a Fool. (VANBR: I, 35)

No perfect passive forms have been found in the M3 section of our subcorpus; however, they do occur in the E3 section, typically in formal contexts; for instance, in Scientific texts and in a Diary at a point in which political issues are discussed:

(33) so great a multitude of Hair *would* not have been easily attracted by an ordinary Electrical Body [...] all she could tell me of the Circumstances, which I *would* have been inform'd about, was, that (BOYLE: 28)

(34) [Jesuites] hindred the Emperor to make a most advantagious peace, by which France *would* have ben forc'd to abate of his so insolent progresse (EVELYN: 932)

No examples of modal verb combinations occur in either M3 or E3.

5. Time reference

As in the case of SHOULD, occurrences of WOULD-forms have been found to express time reference that may be either simultaneous or subsequent to the main predication; in addition to these, there is a relatively large number of occurrences in which the modal relates to predications the validity of which encompasses both the situation at the time of encoding and its future consequences; for instance, this is the case of Religious instruction, which intends to provide principles of universal validity. Although WOULD-forms are related to a past form of WILL, no instances have been found to express past time reference; as previously mentioned (cf. Ch. 8, § 4 – see also Declerck / Reed 2001, Ch. 5), in those instances in which the modal is followed by a perfect infinitive, reference is made to the counterfactuality of the predication, rather than its collocation in the past; in fact, it generally refers to an event that was predicted or expected to take place in the future, but was unfulfilled (cf. Fischer *et al.* 2000: 100-101), as in (35). When a subject's typical behaviour is described, the time reference of WOULD-forms is simultaneous with that of the other predications in the narrative context, as in (36):

(35) summe of hem *wolden* haue take hym, but no man sette hondis on hym (WYCNEW: VII, 40)

(36) And so wel the Kyng louede ham, þat þai might do wiþ him al þat þai *wolde* (BRUT: 224)

6. Type of modality

WOULD-forms have been found to express a very similar range of semantic values and pragmatic meanings to that conveyed by WILL; however, these values and uses are normally recorded in contexts in which they also convey an additional meaning of hypotheticality, counterfactuality or tentativeness.

In some instances at least two semantic values may combine and it is difficult to attribute them to either category (cf. Coates 1983: 68); for instance, in the following quotation both a deontic meaning of volition and a dynamic meaning conveying typicality co-occur:

(37) Thou farst as he betwen tuo stoles That *wolde* sitte and goth to grounde (GOWER: I, 318)

The deontic meaning could be deemed to be more relevant in the light of the greater emphasis placed on the proverbial contrast between the subject's volition and the actual outcome of the predication – however, the predictability of the situation is also stressed.

Table 4 shows a summary of all occurrences (in absolute numbers and in percentage) with their different values in M3 and E3. In addition to the three main modal categories used in this study a separate category lists occurrences in which co-existing or underdetermined meanings – as in (37) – are found. Most occurrences, however, were disambiguated in relation to their prevalent function in the context of the text analysed.

As shown in Table 4, in M3 deontic meanings account for 68% of all tokens, whereas dynamic values correspond to 29%; in E3 there is a slight decrease in the percentage of deontic values (51%), while dynamic meanings rise to 41%. As regards epistemic values, their percentage more than doubles between the two diachronic sections; similarly, cases of coexisting meanings appear to increase slightly.

Within the three main categories we see that deontic meanings normally convey volition and, to a much lesser extent, obligation; no instances of permission expressed by WOULD-forms have been recorded in the subcorpus. As for dynamic meanings, these mostly convey prediction (whether reported or hypothetical) and habit, though instances expressing ability and possibility were also recorded; cases signalling necessity were extremely rare. Finally, in the case of epistemic meanings we see that all these convey inference in E3, while in M3 one case of epistemic possibility was also observed.

		M3		*E3*	
Modal cat.	*Meaning*	*No.*	*%*	*No.*	*%*
deontic	volition	178	67	186	47
	necessity	1	1	17	4
	possibility	0	0	0	0
	deontic total	179	68	203	51
dynamic	ability	2	1	19	5
	possibility	3	1	16	4
	prediction	49	18	106	27
	necessity	1	1	1	0.2
	habit	22	8	22	5
	dynamic total	77	29	164	41
epistemic	possibility	1	1	0	0
	inference	4	1	19	5
	necessity	0	0	0	0
	epistemic total	5	2	19	5
bleached and underdet. meanings		6	1	11	3
TOTAL		267	100	397	100

Table 4. Distribution of WOULD-forms in relation to modal meaning in both subcorpora.

In the next sections these semantic and pragmatic values will be discussed in greater detail, especially as far as distribution within different text types is concerned. At this stage a general overview is provided in Table 5, which summarizes the distribution of WOULD-forms in their different values in each text type included in our subcorpus.

	M3				*E3*			
	de	*dy*	*ep*	*mix*	*de*	*dy*	*ep*	*mix*
FICTION	14	14	1	0	28	18	0	2
HISTORY	23	3	0	0	9	6	0	3
PHILOSOPHY	6	6	0	0	10	12	6	0
TRAVELOGUES	1	7	0	0	0	5	0	1
SERMONS	3	3	0	0	9	9	3	1
LETTERS	5	0	0	0	16	11	0	0
HANDBOOKS	2	0	0	0	4	6	1	0
SCIENCE	0	0	0	0	2	24	1	1
DOCUMENTS	12	5	0	1	-	-	-	-
HOMILIES	12	5	0	1	-	-	-	-
REL. TREATISES	11	3	0	0	-	-	-	-
RULES	3	5	0	0	-	-	-	-
BIBLE	2	0	0	0	-	-	-	-
BIOGRAPHIES	-	-	-	-	16	11	0	0
ED. TREATISES	-	-	-	-	22	7	1	0
DRAMA	-	-	-	-	16	9	1	1
TRIALS	-	-	-	-	23	1	1	0
DIARIES	-	-	-	-	11	4	4	0
LAW	-	-	-	-	0	0	0	0
All texts	9	4	0	0	12	10	1	1

Table 5. Distribution of WOULD-forms by modal meaning and text type (normalized figures per 10,000 words).

From this outline we can see that the significant increase in the type/token ratio of WOULD-forms already mentioned in relation to Scientific texts is mainly attributable to a more widespread use of WOULD for the expression of prediction (for instance, when the scientist reports his speculations about the expected results of a certain experiment). In the case of Philosophical texts the rise is partly due to an increase of WOULD-forms expressing epistemic values, in addition to deontic and dynamic ones; as we shall see in the latter part of this study, it will be interesting to investigate to what extent this occurs at the expense of SHOULD. Epistemic meanings also increase in Historical texts and Travelogues, but this time there is a certain decrease in dynamic or deontic uses. On the other hand, in Fiction and (to an even greater extent) in Letters there is a remarkable increase in deontic and dynamic values – the latter, on average, more than double;[4] again, the interplay of SHOULD and WOULD as competing forms will be discussed in the final section.

6.1. Deontic meanings

6.1.1. Volition

Intention is the deontic value that appears to occur most frequently in our subcorpus; it does not appear to correlate specifically with any text type and it may combine with an equally wide range of subjects and syntactic constructions:

(38) I trowe thou *woldest* loke me in thy chiste! (CTBATH: 109.C1)

(39) the Year after, when it hath put forth Branches, cut off the top sloap-wise, where it is alive, at the uppermost Branch you *would* preserve, and then clay it (LANGF: 122)

In some cases the expression of intention serves argumentative purposes, as the WOULD-form is used to introduce the encoder's pragmatic aim; this may be made explicit through the use of the harmonic noun *entent*:

(40) I *wolde* by soche a hid schewyng bryng þee oute of þe boistouste of bodely felyng into þe purete and depnes of goostly felyng [...] And þan I beseche þee þat þou wilt haue me excusid; for trewly I *wolde* haue profitid vnto þee in þis writyng at my simple kunnyng, & þat was myn entent. (CLOUD: 88, 129)

In other cases, typically in Handbooks, the argumentative structure develops from the encoder's stated wish to find out about a certain phenomenon:

4 It should be remembered that the typology of Letters included in the two subcorpora is quite different: non-private, administrative documents in M3 and both official and private letters in E3. This may account for different types of modal usage.

(41) The yeer of oure lord 1391, the 12 day of March, I *wolde* knowe the tyde of the day [...] Anothir day I *wolde* knowen the degre of my sonne.
(ASTR: 670.C1; 669.C1)

In several instances individual volition is shown to correspond or contrast with actual possibility or ability. The expression of this interdependence of desire and (lack of) impediment may be employed for argumentative purposes, as in (42) and (43):[5]

(42) I had leuer be so nowhere bodely, [...] þan to be so grete a lorde þat I miȝt when I *wolde* be euerywhere bodely (CLOUD: 122)

(43) if they *woulde* lett mee see it & give mee time to consider of it: I might aunswer (FOX: 83)

From the pragmatic point of view, volitional WOULD can have the illocutionary force of an indirect request; in these cases the co-occurrence of adverbial intensifiers like *fayn, gladly* or *willingly* is observed:

(44) Oold fissh and yong flessh *wolde* I have fayn (CTMERCH: 1510.6.C1)

(45) If þou me dere flesse ani gete, Gladli *wald* .i. þar-of ete; (CURSOR: 214)

(46) I *would* willingly hear those Reasons. (BOETHPR: 183)

In the following instance the modal is followed by two co-ordinated verbal complements, one expressing an intention and the other a refusal, i.e. an intention not to do something:

(47) & than the comunes [...] seiden truly they *wolde* go to a-nother eleccion, & noght soeffre thys wrong, (USK: 28)

In other cases the negative element immediately follows the modal or (in M3) an agglutinated form may occur:

(48) And, for as moche þat þei *nolde* nat assente to hym, he amercied hem excessiflich fro court to the somme of xl s. (PET3: 226)

5 Volitional WOULD in conditional clauses is also discussed by Molencki (1998 and 1999).

(49) ye Judge *woulde* not lett mee plead to these later errors (FOX: 85)

In the following instance the expression of refusal is emphasized by means of the phrase *for all the world*:

(50) being asked if he knew anything against him, he answered he did not, adding, God forbid he should say any thing more than he knew, he *would* not do that for all the world (BURNETCHA: 1, ii, 160)

6.1.1.1. Promise

Volitional meanings acquire additional illocutionary force when harmonic lexical choices and the context stress the encoder's commitment to make the predication become factual; this is typically the case of reported promises, in which explicit reference is made to the agreement between the two parties:

(51) and prayede him of helpe and of socoure [...] oppon þat couenaunt, þat he *wolde* haue his douȝter to wyf; (BRUT: 24)

(52) Innocently trustyng to her wordes and behest, behot hym for to do all þat he desired, with that condicion that he *wolde* perfourme and do as he hadde hight and promised (JUDG: 95)

(53) he assur'd me, that whatsoever resolutions he should take, he *would* act nothing upon the white people; (BEHN: 193)

(54) I have now sent for Dick, but had it not been to fullfill my promise that I *would* send for him this mounth, I had trespased one your patience a while longer (EOXINDEN: 321)

6.1.1.2. Threat

From the syntactic and pragmatic point of view, threats function like promises, except that their connotation is negative; as the text types in which tokens of reported promises and threats appear in our subcorpus are typically narrative, these occurrences have 3rd-person subjects. As with promises, the condition(s) depending upon which the threat will become factual are often made explicit: in (55) the injunction of one party is followed by a clause introduced by the typical threatening phrase *or else*; in (56), instead, the threat is made stronger by the oath and the iconic gesture of drawing the sword:

(55) and sent to his broþer Belyn, þat he shulde ȝelde aȝeyne his lande to his wif and to his folc, & his castelles also, or elles he *wolde* destroye his lande (BRUT: 25)

(56) and drow his suorde, & swore by Almygty God and by his holy names, but if þat he wolde go wiþ ham, he shulde be dede, and þat he *wolde* slee him þere (BRUT: 217)

No instances of reported threats conveyed by means of WOULD-forms were recorded in the E3 section of our subcorpus.

6.1.2. Necessity

6.1.2.1. Order and request

A clear semantic value of obligation has been detected only in instances in which a polite request is made:

(57) þan al þa men of Samary […] Praied him if it war his will With þam þat he *wald* dwell still (NHOM: II, 85)

In the following cases WOULD-forms are employed to express reported orders (as in 58) or occur after forms like 'I wish', or 'I'd rather', that pragmatically introduce polite requests, as in (59) and (60):

(58) The King commands me to send you the enclosed Letter […], which he *would* have you deliver as soon as you can. (SPENCER: IV, 312)

(59) I wish you *wou'd* dispense with the Canonical Hour, and let it be this very Night. (VANBR: I, 60)

(60) If Thou canst not send him thether, yet I pray send him to Ospring to our Brother Cater's; but I had rather Thou *would* send him to the Dark House. (HOXINDEN: 292)

6.1.2.2. Instruction and advice

The vast majority of WOULD-forms expressing advice were recorded in Educational treatises; given the pragmatic aim of the text type, it may be difficult to decide the extent to which the encoder is simply advising as to a recommended course of action, or wishes to instruct on what is taken to be ideal practice, in which case tentative forms function as politeness markers.[6] The following quotations provide a few instances of this ambiguity between what, on the surface, is an apparent expression of the encoder's volition and the expression of guidance:

(61) I *would* have children very seldome beaten. […] Two faults and only two there be that I *would* have them whipd for to give them the greater abhorrence of them, and that is Lyeing and obstinacy or rebellion (LOCKE: 56)

(62) Other Characters I *would* have forborn, till one be well acquainted with these, because so much variety at the first doth but amaze young wits, (HOOLE: 10)

(63) But till that Reformation can be made, I *wou'd* not leave the whol'some Corn, for some intruding Tares that grow amongst it. (VANBR: I, 33)

This type of usage was not recorded in M3 samples.

6.2. Dynamic meanings

6.2.1. Ability

The use of WOULD-forms for the expression of ability (described by Visser 1963-73: § 1597)increases in E3; these instances occur in a range of text types, especially in narrative contexts, even when the description of scientific experiments is under discussion:

(64) ȝif a lond *wolde* bere good corn wiþowte tylyng and donghyng þerof, it were but ydel to traueyle þerfore, whonne it encresuþ not þe fruyt (WSERM: I, 588)

6 On distal forms as hedges and politeness markers cf. Ch. 8 § 6.1.2.4.

(65) but she would not yield to his Desire, unless he *would* contrive some way to cornute her Husband in his presence and he not to believe it (PENNY: 160)

(66) To examine this, I say, I thought the fittest way, if 'twere practicable, would be, to try, whether Amber *would* draw a light Body in a Glass whence the air was pumpt out (BOYLE: 29)

As we can see, in all these cases the modal form could be replaced with COULD (cf. Ch. 3) or MIGHT (cf. Ch. 5).

6.2.2. Possibility

WOULD-forms expressing dynamic possibility also seem to become more frequent in E3 and to concentrate in narrative contexts:

(67) we *wolde* neuer han leved it, had wee not a seen it. (MAND: 144)

(68) I hearde they had sent ye Indictment to London to see if it *woulde* stande & they was Informed y[t] It *woulde* not stande & soe they woulde not lett mee pleade to it. (FOX: 85)

(69) what love *wou'd* not oblige Imoinda to do, duty wou'd compel her to.
[what it would not be possible for love to oblige her to do...] (BEHN: 158)

Other instances occur in Letters, both official and private, and in a Philosophical text:

(70) I wish my mony *would* have extended itself into a larger maner, for if it may be beleft I have but three shillinges to keep me untill our Lady day.
(EOXINDEN: 322)

(71) For such is the Matter of it, that one Doubt being removed, innumerable others, like the Heads of Hydra, grow up. Nor *would* there indeed be any End of them, unless they were restrained by the Quickness and lively Fire of the Mind (BOETHPR: 190)

6.2.3. Prediction

As far as dynamic modality is concerned, the largest number of occurrences expresses reported or hypothetical prediction. These are distributed across a range of text types, but appear to be most frequent in Letters (both private and official), in Philosophical texts and Religious treatises, in Documents, Fiction and Drama.

From the semantic point of view a distinction ought to be made between reported predictions and hypotheses; both are expressed by WOULD-forms and both convey future time reference, but the former generally occur in the context of narratives set in the past, as shown in the following quotations:

(72) me trowed þat þe kyng *wolde* nevere come aȝen hom. (TREVISA: VIII, 89)

(73) I writ to him, and desired him to give her a Visit, for I knew she *would* be glad to see him. (OATES: IV, 82.C1)

In the case of hypotheses the possibility of the predication ever becoming factual depends on an action or factor expressed by means of a conditional clause, the typical structure of which has been discussed in section 3 above. The following quotations exemplify both M3 and E3 cases:

(74) And þerfore and I miȝt gete a wakyng and a besi beholdyng to þis goostly werk wiþ-inne in my soule, I *wolde* þan haue a rechelesnes in [...] alle myn outward doynges. (CLOUD: 81)

(75) If they were never sufferd to obteine any thing by the impatience they expresse for it, they *would* noe more crye for other things then they doe for the moon. (LOCKE: 52)

In official Letters relatively long phrases may be employed to express the encoder's agreement to the predication being theorized:

(76) I acknowledge ye great honour and favour of yr Excellency's letter by Mr Godolphin, and concurre with you yt itt *would* be of great use to have yr Excellency here to conferr with his Ma[tie] upon those important matters mentioned therein. (OSBORNE: 21-22)

In contrast, private Letters can be much more direct:

(77) It *would* be good if the remainder of the money due to this Bill could be sent by the next. The next Quarter, which is approaching, *would* be the more tolerable. (STRYPE: 180)

6.2.4. Necessity

In each section of the sub-corpus one occurrence has been found to express dynamic necessity, i.e. the inevitability of the predication being hypothesized; this may be supported by the co-occurrence of the harmonic adverbial form *needs*:

(78) Every wight *wolde* holde me thanne a fool (CTMEL: 220.C1)

(79) At last, he *wou'd* <u>needs</u> go view his land, his house, and the business assign'd him (BEHN: 186)

6.2.5. Habit

The expression of habit by means of WOULD-forms has been found to be most frequent in Fictional texts; indeed, numerous occurrences were recorded in the Prologue to *The Canterbury Tales*, in which the main traits and typical behaviour of each pilgrim are described. However, Biographical accounts also include several instances of this usage:

(80) She *wolde* wepe, if that she saugh a mous Kaught in a trappe, if it were deed or bledde. (CTPROL: 25.C2)

(81) At other times, meerly for diversion, he *would* go about in odd shapes (BURNETROC: 28)

These forms are typically observed in narrative contexts in which the behaviour of a certain character is described – at times hyperbolically, as in (82) – or in connection with harmonic adverbs like *always* and parallel clauses containing *used to*:

(82) Of his metscip was mesur nan, He *wald* ete seuen scep him an. (CURSOR: 430)

(83) A VVoman sitting with Fish in Canterbury Market, *would* <u>always</u> have a saying to Men when they came to buy any thing (PENNY: 159)

(84) Eh, God's Blessing on the sweet Face on't; how it us'd to hang at this poor Tett, and suck and squeeze, and kick and sprawl it *wou'd*, till the Belly on't was so full, it *wou'd* drop off like a Leech. (VANBR: I, 63)

In Scientific texts the properties of a certain material or the typical development of certain phenomena can be described in similar ways:

(85) I afterwards repeated the Trial, and found, that in warm Weather it *would* retain a manifest power of attracting for several minutes (BOYLE: 30)

6.3. Epistemic meanings

6.3.1. Possibility

The following M3 occurrence was found to express the encoder's subjective perception of a possible event:

(86) wher anoþer man *wolde* bid þee gader þi miȝtes & þi wittes holiche wiþ-inne þi-self, [...] ȝit for feerde of disseite & bodely conceyuyng of his wordes, me list not byd þee do so (CLOUD: 121)
[while it is possible that another man could bid thee gather thy strength and thy wits within thyself [...] yet, fearing deceipt and an earthly understanding of his words, I wouldn't bid thee do so.]

6.3.2. Inference

Instances in which WOULD-forms have been found to express the encoder's deductions concerning a counterfactual predication are more numerous in the E3 section of the subcorpus. In M3 texts the subjectivity of the point of view is frequently strengthened by the co-occurrence of an epistemic adverb like *certes*:

(87) For certes, sire, oure Lord Jhesu Crist *wolde* nevere have descended to be born of a womman, if alle wommen hadden been wikke. [And] if that wommen were nat goode, and hir conseils goode and profitable, oure Lord God of hevene *wolde* nevere han wroght hem, ne called hem help of man, but rather confusioun of man. (CTMEL: 221.C2)

(88) For certes, if ther ne hadde be no synne in clothyng, Crist *wolde* nat so soone have noted and spoken of the clothyng of thilke riche man in the gospel. (CTPARS: 300.C2)

In E3 cases of epistemic deduction are often also recorded in association with harmonic superordinate verbs like *believe*, *know, fear* and *think* and same-clause adverbs like *doubtless(ly)*, both of which emphasize the fact that the predication is perceived subjectively. The following quotations provide a few examples of this:

(89) It was believed that they both, especialy the Princesse, *would* have shewed some (seeming) reluctancy at least, of assuming her Fathers Crowne & made some Apologie (EVELYN: 902)

(90) now she fear'd the storm *wou'd* fall on the prince (BEHN: 159)

(91) these scoffers twitted the Christians withall; and because Christ did not come when some looked for him they concluded he *would* not come at all. (TILLOTS: II.ii.418)

In the following example the idea of subjective conjecture is stressed by a parenthetical clause functioning as epistemic adverbial:

(92) [Those] Histories, if well consider'd, and the tree, substance, and manner of growing, if well examin'd, *would*, I am very apt to believe, much confirm this my conjecture about the origination of Cork. (HOOKE: 13.5, 115)

7. A comparison between SHOULD and WOULD

Although the distinctive usage of SHOULD and WOULD with different subjects has been the object of fierce debate for many centuries, especially on the part of grammarians and prescriptivists, the aim of this paragraph is not to investigate this issue.[7] Instead, we

7 This will be taken up in a subsequent study, which will encompass a broader set of data, in an attempt to compare English and Scots usage, as different patterns have often been described for the two varieties under discussion (cf. Visser 1963-73: 1724-1725; 1733).

shall try and comment on the different modal values conveyed by SHOULD and WOULD in the text types that make up the two diachronic sections of our subcorpus and to discuss their patterns of increase or decrease. Table 6 shows the occurrence of both modals in each text type (with their different modal values) in terms of normalized figures per 10,000 words.

It is immediately clear that (in both sections) SHOULD is the prevalent form in those genres in which prescription – i.e., a deontic value – is typical: Educational and Religious treatises, Rules and Legal documents, Homilies and Sermons. It is true that the average frequency of deontic meanings in E3 is actually higher in the case of WOULD, but this is due to the expression of volition, rather than obligation, such as we see in Biographies, Trial proceedings, Diaries and Drama – that is, in those genres in which WOULD occurs more frequently than SHOULD. Dynamic meanings which, on average, were more normally conveyed by SHOULD in the M3 period, become more frequently associated with WOULD in E3. E3 also sees a very small increase in the number of epistemic uses expressed by means of WOULD.

If we now focus on the eight text types that appear in both sections, the increase of WOULD as a form to express dynamic meanings appears to be very clear in the case of Handbooks; Fiction, which displayed similar values for the two modals in M3, shows an increase in the type/token ratio of WOULD-forms in E3 – with volitional (deontic) meanings of WOULD also showing a notable increase. An equally important increase in dynamic WOULD is to be observed in Letters (which in E3 contain speech-influenced private correspondence). In Historical texts, instead, both modals decrease. A similar pattern is outlined in Sermons: in M3 SHOULD was the dominant form, especially for deontic meanings; in E3 both modals display similar values, due to an increased use of WOULD to convey all types of modal meaning, including epistemic ones. Travelogues, instead, seem to follow a different trend, as WOULD appears to decrease. Finally, the case of Scientific and Philosophical texts shows interesting change: as regards the former, we see that in E3 dynamic meanings, previously conveyed by SHOULD, are more frequently expressed by WOULD. In addition, deontic and epistemic values are also conveyed by the same modal. In Philosophical texts, on the other hand, we observe that in the later period both modals occur more frequently with dynamic and epistemic meanings, while SHOULD decreases as a medium for the expression of deonticity, in favour of WOULD.

	M3						*E3*					
	deontic		*dynamic*		*epistemic*		*deontic*		*dynamic*		*epistemic*	
	SH	*W*	*SH*	*W*	*SH*	*W*	*SH*	*W*	*SH*	*W*	*SH*	*W*
SERMONS	53	3	17	3	0	0	12	9	5	9	0	3
HISTORY	20	23	14	3	0	0	6	9	2	6	0	0
PHILOSOPHY	16	6	6	6	1	0	7	10	23	12	2	6
FICTION	14	14	13	14	0	1	14	28	12	18	0	0
SCIENCE	0	0	22	0	0	0	1	2	10	24	0	1
LETTERS	5	5	3	0	0	0	8	16	8	11	0	4
TRAVELOGUES	0	1	3	7	0	0	0	0	1	5	0	0
HANDBOOKS	2	2	0	0	0	0	4	4	5	6	0	1
HOMILIES	16	12	9	5	0	0	-	-	-	-	-	-
DOCUMENTS	20	12	7	5	0	0	-	-	-	-	-	-
REL. TREATISES	8	11	13	3	0	0	-	-	-	-	-	-
RULES	16	3	3	5	0	0	-	-	-	-	-	-
BIBLE	10	2	7	0	0	0	-	-	-	-	-	-
ED. TREATISES	-	-	-	-	-	-	47	22	3	7	0	1
BIOGRAPHIES	-	-	-	-	-	-	8	16	9	11	0	1
DRAMA	-	-	-	-	-	-	5	16	9	9	0	1
TRIALS	-	-	-	-	-	-	7	23	3	1	0	1
DIARIES	-	-	-	-	-	-	2	11	5	4	0	4
LAW	-	-	-	-	-	-	2	0	0	0	0	0
All texts	14	9	10	4	0	0	9	12	7	10	0	1

Table 6. Modal values of SHOULD and WOULD in the M3-E3 subcorpora.

XI. Conclusion

This final chapter summarizes the main results of the investigation carried out on occurrences of the nine central modal verbs in the corpus analysed, in order to present a picture of the syntactic and semantic variation of verbal modality in the time span under discussion. The data will be compared with those of previous studies and comments will be made in order to provide a contribution to the theoretical debate on the development of English modal auxiliaries. In particular, in §3 attention will be paid to the varying distribution of modal forms in different text types, in an attempt to relate modal meaning and pragmatic function in a broader perspective pertaining to the evolution of genre characteristics.

1. Quantitative data

The number of occurrences examined in this study is shown in terms of normalized figures per 10,000 words in Table 1.

	M3	*E3*	*Variation*	*% variation*
CAN	5	24	+ 19	+380
COULD	2	11	+ 9	+450
MAY	37	28	- 9	- 24
MIGHT	12	8	- 4	- 33
MUST	6	13	+7	+117
SHALL	72	32	- 40	- 56
SHOULD	27	18	- 9	- 33
WILL	20	33	+13	+65
WOULD	14	23	+ 9	+65

Table 1. Occurrences of the central modal verbs in the corpus.

As can be seen, the most common modal in the M3 subsection is SHALL, followed by MAY and SHOULD. In contrast, COULD, CAN, and MUST occur much less frequently. Comparing M3 and E3 frequencies we note significant changes: in particular, there is a remarkable increase in the occurrences of COULD, CAN, and MUST, a relative increase in the occurrences of WILL and WOULD, and a considerable decrease in the occurrences of MAY, MIGHT, SHALL and SHOULD.

The dramatic increase in CAN and COULD is largely at the expense of dynamic MAY and MIGHT, combined with the acquisition of new semantic values: epistemic use in negative and interrogative clauses (expressing disbelief or request for opinion) and (to a limited extent and only for COULD) deontic use (conveying prohibition). We also recorded a higher incidence of 'merger' in E3, particularly with reference to COULD, whereby both epistemic and dynamic interpretation appeared to be possible.

As regards SHALL, its considerable decrease is only partially due to the more frequent use of WILL-forms to convey the pragmatic value of prediction in the second period; indeed, normalized figures for predictive SHALL-forms fall by 24, while the general decrease corresponds to 40; SHALL is also less commonly used to express volition (-5) and deontic necessity (-12); the loss in the latter is compensated by an increase in the use of MUST to express the same pragmatic function. The increase in the use of WILL (+13) corresponds to the change in normalized figures of WILL-forms used to express prediction in the two periods taken into consideration (7 vs 20).

MAY is about three times more frequent than MIGHT in both periods and both modals decline in frequency in a similar way, partly due to less frequent dynamic uses of both modals in E3. SHOULD, instead, is almost twice as frequent as WOULD in M3, but slightly less frequent in E3, on account of the increase of WOULD in the context of hypothetical predictions and in the expression of epistemic inference.

Many of the forms occurring in the corpus show non-modal usage. However, the evolution towards the auxiliary function is not uniform, as can be seen from Table 2. This shows that the process of grammaticalization was completed earlier in the case of MAY,

MIGHT, SHALL, and MUST, which present no main verb usage in either of the two periods taken into consideration. On the other hand, some of them – such as WILL and WOULD – still had a main verbal function, although in very few cases, in the Early Modern period. Compared to all other modals, CAN and COULD appear to lag behind in the pace of grammaticalization, since in M3 up to 27% of CAN-occurrences and 28% of COULD still feature main verb values.

	M3	*E3*
CAN	32	0
COULD	13	0
MAY	1	0
MIGHT	0	0
MUST	0	0
SHALL	0	0
SHOULD	2	0
WILL	40	5
WOULD	35	7

Table 2. Occurrences of modals as main verbal forms in the corpus.

2. Spelling variants

For all the modals taken into consideration, spelling variability declines drastically between the two periods.

Negative forms deriving from the combination of negation + verb – e.g. *nil, nolde(n)* – appear only in the earlier period, as do enclitic forms such as *shaltou* and *wyltow*. Contracted forms (both affirmative and negative) only occur in the later subsection; their numbers, however, are still low – indeed, no instances were recorded for MUST or COULD – and their occurrence is generally limited to dialogues.

3. Distribution according to text type

The results of the analysis point to a correlation in the use of a few modal auxiliaries within specific text types. This is the case, for example, of SHALL, which shows a frequency clearly above average in Rules, Religious treatises, Biblical texts and Statutes; in the case of Rules, frequency is almost double and can be explained by the relevant number of occurrences expressing obligation which characterises this kind of text. As regards Religious treatises and Biblical texts, the particular preference for SHALL-forms can be explained by the frequent reference to future events (as in prophecies) and the expression of deontic meanings, mainly occurring in sentences in which God's will is reported. The frequent adoption of SHALL in Statutes may be explained by its double possibility of expressing both obligation and futurity, implicit in the very nature of regulative acts.

We find MAY and MIGHT with above-average frequencies in the formal variety of non-private Letters in both periods. Philosophy texts have above-average frequencies of MAY in both periods but (being non-narrative) below-average frequencies of MIGHT, while narrative History texts show the reverse configuration. Perhaps most interesting is the relative abandonment of MAY and MIGHT in Fictional texts between the two periods and their adoption by Scientific texts. All this, together with low-frequency of use in Diaries and Trial transcripts in E3, suggests a clear polarization in uses with speech-based text types using MAY and MIGHT less frequently.

The reverse is true for CAN and COULD. Both of them show a very limited frequency in both subperiods with reference to History and Scientific data and a corresponding high frequency in speech-based texts. Indeed, CAN frequently occurs in the dialogical sections of Chaucer's *Canterbury Tales*, in Religious samples, Sermons, and Letters in M3, but also in Trials, Drama, and also notably in the translation of Boethius' *De Consolatione Philosophiae*, which is fully dialogical. COULD is found frequently in speech-based texts to express tentativeness, like Letters, and also in narrative sequences of text types like Science, Fiction and History. Unsurprisingly, E3 Legal texts exhibit no occurrence of COULD. This can be explained both with their lack of tentativeness and with their time reference, as Rules are laid down to guide future action.

As for MUST, a general increase in E3 texts has been found, except for Sermons. Handbooks have an average frequency of MUST in M3 but clearly above-average frequency in E3. The same applies to E3 Educational Treatises, which are very similar to Handbooks. Since the most frequent use in E3 is found in Drama, Philosophy (in dialogue form), Fiction (which contains dialogue), and Handbooks (in fictionalised form with dialogues), we can draw the conclusion that evolving MUST is mainly observed within speech-related texts.

Distal forms SHOULD and WOULD also show interesting patterns of increase and decrease in the text types, samples of which are included in both sections of the subcorpus. Uses of both decrease in Historical texts and increase in Handbooks, Letters and Philosophy, while Fiction and Travelogues see only an increase in WOULD. Remarkable increases in frequency of WOULD are also found in Sermons and (even greater) in Scientific texts, where this possibly signals the greater attention (on the part of encoders) to epistemic meanings and to hedged statements that was to become typical of modern Scientific discourse. Indeed, a similar phenomenon is observed in the case of MAY and MIGHT.

4. Verb phrase structure

The most frequent structure in both periods is MODAL + bare infinitive, followed by MODAL + passive infinitive, the latter structure showing a general increase in the second period. The perfect infinitive is associated with the historical past tense forms of the modals: it only occurs in E3 with COULD (8%, mostly in the active voice), is very rare in both periods with MAY, but found more frequently with MIGHT (4% in M3, 11% in E3). SHOULD, instead, appears to be followed by perfect infinitives less frequently in E3 than in M3. On the other hand, perfect infinitives are the second most frequent verbal complement for WOULD, normally in contexts in which counterfactuality is expressed. The same is true for the few E3 examples of MUST followed by a perfect infinitive which are associated with epistemic use.

As regards the construction MODAL + no verb, the data collected are not uniform; most cases refer to elliptical forms, commonly avoiding the repetition of a verb already mentioned in the same or previous sentence. There is a general decrease in the cases of omission of verbs of motion and of *be*, which we still find – although in small numbers – in M3, but which becomes rare in E3. A few cases in E3 (but only with WILL) are found in tag questions; this is another confirmation of the ongoing but irregular process of grammaticalization of these verbs and their increasing use as auxiliaries. The same is true for modal combinations, occurrences of which have been found (only for CAN, MAY, SHALL, and SHOULD) in M3, while none have been found in E3.

Both parts of the corpus contain cases in which the modal is followed by BE + *ing*-form, a structure which was still rare in ME (cf. Visser 1963-73: 2413 and Strang 1970: 208). In the instances found in M3, indeed, the *ing*-form seems to have prevalently an adjectival function. In contrast, most examples of this construction are more clearly verbal in E3.

5. Type of modality

The analysis of the occurrences found in the corpus has shown an extensive use of the central modals to express a wide range of pragmatic functions, as shown in Table 3 (data are expressed in terms of normalized figures per 10,000 words).

To make the data more easily comparable and to find the prevalent pragmatic uses of the various modal verbs we could adopt a table similar to the one suggested by Coates (1983: 26, fig. 3.2) to distinguish the primary, secondary and the infrequent uses for each modal. To achieve this purpose, we could assign frequency values to the data found, e.g. 3 to indicate very high frequency (over 15 tokens per 10,000 words), 2 for lower frequency (5-14.9 tokens per 10,000 words), 1 for limited frequency (more than nought but less than 5 tokens per 10,000 words). Applying these conversions to the numbers inserted above, we obtain Table 4 (for each modal the figure on the left refers to M3, the one on the right to E3).

			CAN		*COULD*		*MAY*		*MIGHT*		*MUST*		*SHALL*		*SHD*		*WILL*		*WD*	
modal meaning			*M3*	*E3*	*M3*	*E3*	*M3*	*E3*	*M3*	*E3*	*M3*	*E3*	*M3*	*E3*	*M3*	*E3*	*M3*	*E3*	*M3*	*E3*
Deontic	volition	intention									0.4		6	4		1	7	5	8	8
		refusal															1	1	1	1
		threat									0.1		2	0.4				0.2		
		promise											3	2			1	2		
	necess.	order					0.3	2	0.1	0.1	3	6	10	7	4	2	0.2	1		
		prohib.				0.2						1	1	2	1		1	0.1		
		instruc.									1	1	7	0.1	6	3				
		proposal												1				1		
		advice											4	0.3			0.2	1		
	possib.						1	2	0.2	0.4	0.4			1						
Dynamic	ability		4	15	2	7	7	2	5	0.1										
	possib.		0.1	5	0.2	3	19	10	5	4			0.2		1	1	1	1		
	predict.	neutr.pred.					3	1	0.3	0.2	1		32	15	6	5	7	19	2	6
		prophecy											4	0.2			0.1			
		assurance											3	1			0.2	10		
	necessity							0.1				1	0.1	0.2	1					
	habit							0.1	0.1	0.1			0.3	0.3			2	1	1	1
Epistemic	possib.			1		0.2	1	5	1	2	0.4									
	infer.						0.1										0.1	1		1
	necess.						0.1				1	4								

Table 3. Pragmatic functions expressed by the central modals occurring in the corpus.

modal meaning			*CAN* *M3*	*E3*	*COULD* *M3*	*E3*	*MAY* *M3*	*E3*	*MIGHT* *M3*	*E3*	*MUST* *M3*	*E3*	*SHALL* *M3*	*E3*	*SHD* *M3*	*E3*	*WILL* *M3*	*E3*	*WD* *M3*	*E3*
Deontic	volition	intention									1		2	1		1	2	2	2	2
		refusal															1	1	1	1
		threat									1		1	1				1		
		promise											1	1			1	1		
	necess.	order					1	1	1	1	1	2	2	2	1	1	1	1		
		prohib.				1						1	1	1	1		1	1		
		instruc.									1	1	2	1	2	1				
		proposal												1				1		
		advice											1	1			1	1		
	possib.						1	1	1	1	1			1						
Dynamic	ability		1	3	1	2	2	1	2	1										
	possib.		1	2	1	1	3	2	2	1			1		1	1	1	1		
	predict.	neutr.pred.					1	1	1	1	1		3	3	2	2	2	3	1	2
		prophecy											1	1			1			
		assurance											1	1			1	2		
	necessity							1				1	1	1	1					
	habit							1	1	1			1	1			1	1	1	1
Epistemic	possib.			1		1	1	2	1	1	1									
	infer.						1										1	1		1
	necess.						1				1	1								

Table 4. Frequency of pragmatic functions expressed by the central modals in the corpus (Data shown in relation to normalized figures).

The data in Tables 3 and 4 allow for the following considerations.

Deontic meanings:

- *Intention / Refusal:* in both periods intention can be expressed by different modals; however, the most frequently used are SHALL (in M3) and WILL (in both M3 and E3). WOULD was also observed to occur with higher-than-average frequency in both subperiods on account of its use in narrative contexts, in which the intentions of third parties are reported. As regards refusal, the only modals used to express the non-intention to carry out an action in both periods are WILL and WOULD.

- *Promise / Threat:* in both subsections promises are expressed both by SHALL and WILL; however, the former decreases in the period taken into consideration, while the latter shows an increase. As regards threats, in M3 these are typically conveyed by means of SHALL (there are only two examples with MUST). In E3, instead, WILL-forms expressing threats have also been found. In both subperiods both SHOULD and WOULD may be employed to report threats and promises, though the number of their occurrences is small.
- *Order / Prohibition:* Different modals are used to express commands; however, in both periods SHALL is the most frequent. Most examples of MUST in both periods also convey the pragmatic function of imposing or proposing some course of action or pattern of behaviour and indicating that it should be carried out. In E3 SHALL appears to decrease slightly in favour of MUST. We also see a decrease in SHOULD associated with orders, typically in reported speech. We also find SHALL and WILL for reported orders, with SHALL increasing in this function in E3 and WILL decreasing. Both MUST and COULD are overtly used to indicate prohibition only in E3, and for COULD the deontic source is a regulation or an official authority rather than one single subject.
- *Instruction / Advice:* In both subsections only SHALL and MUST are used for explicit instructions, while both SHALL and WILL are used in both periods to express advice, with a prevalence of SHALL-forms in M3. In the 2nd person the meaning of MUST may easily develop into that of a counsel or advice. However, such examples are always tinged with some instructional purposes on the part of the encoder. A similar case can be made for SHOULD, which – as a distal form – may express hedged instruction or subjective advice.
- *Proposal:* in E3 this is expressed by SHALL and WILL.
- *Possibility:* The modal form mainly used to express permission is MAY, which appears to become more frequent in E3; also SHALL is used for this purpose, although in very limited cases

and only in E3. A few examples of MUST, where the OE sense 'be allowed', 'be permitted' can still be attached to it, have been found in the M3 sub-corpus.

Dynamic meanings:

- *Ability:* This meaning is typically expressed by MAY, MIGHT, CAN, and COULD; while MAY and MIGHT become less frequent in E3, CAN and COULD become much more frequent.
- *Possibility:* The modal WILL has been found in both periods to express dynamic possibility; SHALL is also found with this meaning, but only in a very limited number of cases and only in M3. In fact, as above, this meaning is typically expressed by MAY and MIGHT, CAN and COULD, with frequencies decreasing in E3 for MAY and MIGHT, increasing for CAN and COULD.
- *Neutral prediction:* The two main modals used to express futurity are SHALL and WILL; however, the former is prevalent in M3, while the latter is more frequent in E3. Modally coloured predictive meanings ('X is fated / certain to …', 'X shall / will certainly / inevitably …') are conveyed by MUST in M3 Sermons and Religious texts. As regards the use of distal forms SHOULD and WOULD in the expression of hypothetical or reported predictions (including reported prophecies), in E3 the frequency of WOULD increases as SHOULD becomes less widespread.
- *Prophecy:* Prophecies are mainly expressed by SHALL-forms; the use of WILL is very limited and occurs only in M3.
- *Assurance:* Both SHALL and WILL are used to strengthen a prediction; however, the former is more frequent in M3, while the latter becomes prevalent in E3 and covers almost all the cases found.
- *Necessity:* In both subsections SHALL and SHOULD have been found to refer to those cases of obligation deriving from external factors. The latter, however, becomes less frequent in E3. Instances of MUST posed as objectively grounded are present only in E3.

Habit: Both SHALL and WILL occur in both subsections to express habitual actions and typical behaviour; of the two, however, WILL is more frequently used. As regards distal forms MIGHT and WOULD, their frequency appears to remain stable in the two diachronic sections under discussion.

Epistemic meanings:

- *Possibility:* There is only one example of MUST in Chaucer's Fiction which may allow for an interpretation in terms of epistemic possibility. On the other hand, MAY appears to be the modal form which expresses this meaning most frequently in E3. CAN and COULD also appear to occur with epistemic possibility values, mostly in interrogative and negative contexts.
- *Inference:* In both periods deductions are expressed by WILL and its corresponding distal form WOULD. Occurrences appear to increase in the E3 subsection.
- *Necessity:* Unambiguous examples of MUST conveying this type of meaning are quite frequent in M3 (20%) and increase in E3 (30%).

6. Final remarks

Although our study has mainly focussed on semantic and pragmatic values, the analysis of the two subcorpora has enabled us to verify the process of grammaticalization commonly discussed in recent literature on the evolution of verbal modality. In the periods taken into consideration all central modals have completed the change from full predicates to auxiliary predicates, many of them becoming predicate operators for tenses such as the future and the conditional, or for moods such as the subjunctive. The progress followed thus confirms the one pointed out in Functional Grammar terms by Goossens (1987: 118) in this scale:

Full predicates > predicate formation > predicate operators

However, modal forms do not seem to have developed in strict synchronicity. Owing to competition inside the modal system, some of the central modals – such as SHALL – have gone beyond the last stage of the scale, reducing their function as predicate operators, and privileging instead their deontic and/or epistemic values.

The picture that thus emerges from our analysis is the one summarized in Table 5 below, giving the main functions of each modal (the unbracketed positions indicate the predominant use). As can be seen, although the grammaticalization trend is similar for all, the evolutionary process of each central modal takes place in different stages and in different periods; however, the process may be a global one, in the sense that the changes of each central modal verb probably depend on – and give rise to – the changes of the others.

		Full predicate / Main verb	*Predicate formation / Modal verb*	*Predicate operator*
CAN	M3	(X)	X	
	E3		X	
COULD	M3	(X)	X	
	E3		X	
MAY	M3	(X)	X	
	E3		X	(X)
MIGHT	M3		X	
	E3		X	(X)
MUST	M3		X	
	E3		X	
SHALL	M3		(X)	X
	E3		X	(X)
SHOULD	M3	(X)	(X)	X
	E3		X	(X)
WILL	M3	(X)	X	(X)
	E3	(X)	(X)	X
WOULD	M3	(X)	X	(X)
	E3	(X)	X	(X)

Table 5. Main functions of central modal verbs.

In general, this study has taken into consideration morpho-syntactic and semantic and pragmatic variation in the use of central modal auxiliaries over time. In addition, geographical variation has been discussed in individual chapters in relation to the M3 samples and (as pointed out in the Introduction) further investigation is in progress as far as uses in Northern English and Older Scots texts are concerned.

However, diachronic and diatopic variation has not been the only focus of our study: indeed, diastratic and diatypic variation has also been taken into consideration as an equally important approach to the phenomena under discussion. Indeed, occurrences in different text types and the varying level of formality of these may be seen to have influenced the encoders' use of the modal forms which we had chosen to follow on their path to grammaticalization. In addition, their varying proximity to spoken language was also perceived to have played a significant role in their encoders' syntactic choices. In this respect, then, through this study some light may have been shed not only on modality as an important grammatical phenomenon, but also on language use as it is and as it was.

References

Adamson, Sylvia *et al.* (eds.) 1990. *Papers from the 5th International Conference on English Historical Linguistics.* Amsterdam: Benjamins.

Aijmer, Karin 1985. The Semantic Development of *Will.* In Fisiak, Jacek (ed.) *Historical Semantics – Historical Word-Formation.* Berlin: Mouton, 11-21.

Anderson, John 1971. Some Proposals Concerning the Modal Verbs in English. In Aitken, Adam J. / McIntosh, Angus / Pálsson, Hermann (eds.) *Edinburgh Studies in English and Scots.* London: Longman, 19-120.

Anderson, John 1991. Should. In Kastovsky, Dieter (ed.) *Historical English Syntax*, Berlin / New York: Mouton de Gruyter, 11-30.

Anderson, John 2001. Modals, Subjunctives and (Non-)Finiteness. *English Language and Linguistics*, 5/1, 159-166.

Arnovick, Leslie K. 1985. The Semantic Development of *Will.* In Fisiak, Jacek (ed.) *Historical Semantics – Historical Word-Formation.* Berlin: Mouton, 11-21.

Arnovick, Leslie K. 1990. *The Development of Future Constructions in English: The Pragmatics of Modal and Temporal* Will *and* Shall *in Middlle English.* Frankfurt am Main: Peter Lang.

Auwera, Johan van der / Plungian, Vladimir A. 1998. Modality's Semantic Map. *Linguistic Typology,* 2, 79-124.

Bailey, Charles-James N. 1981. English Verb Modalities. *Zeitschrift für Dialektologie und Linguistik,* 2, 161-188.

Barber, Charles L. 1962. Some Measurable Characteristics of Modern Scientific Prose. *Gothenburg Studies in English*, 14, 21-43.

Battistella, Edwin L. 1995. The Syntax of the Double Modal Construction. *Linguistica Atlantica*, 17, 19-44.

Behre, Frank 1955. *Meditative-Polemic* Should *in Modern English* That-*Clauses.* Stockholm: Almqvist & Wiksell.

Biber, Douglas / Johansson, Stig / Leech, Geoffrey / Conrad, Susan / Finegan, Edward 1999. *Longman Grammar of Spoken and Written English*. London: Longman.

Blake, Norman (ed.) 1992. *The Cambridge History of the English Language*, vol. 2: *1066-1476*. Cambridge: Cambridge University Press.

Boyd, Julian / Boyd, Zelda. 1980. *Shall* and *Will*. In Michaels, Leonard / Ricks, Christopher (eds.) *The State of the Language*. Berkeley: Univ. of California Press, 43-53.

Boyd, Julian / Thorne, James P. 1969. The Semantics of Modal Verbs. *Journal of Linguistics,* 5, 57-74.

Boyland, Joyce T. 1998. A Corpus Study of *would+have*+past-participle. In Hogg, Richard M. / van Bergen, Linda (eds.) *Historical Linguistics 1995*. Amsterdam: Benjamins, 2, 1-17.

Burrow, J. A. / Turville-Petre, Thorlac 1992. *A Book of Middle English*, Oxford: Blackwell.

Butters Ronald R. 1991. Multiple Modals in United States Black English: Synchronic and Diachronic Aspects. In Edwards, F. / Winford, D. (eds.) *Verb Phrase Patterns in Black English and Creole*. Detroit: Wayne State University Press, 165-176.

Bybee, Joan L. 1995. The Semantic Development of Past Tense Modals in English. In Bybee / Fleischman (eds.), 503-517.

Bybee, Joan / Perkins, Revere / Pagliuca, William 1994. *The Evolution of Grammar.* Chicago: University of Chicago Press.

Bybee, Joan / Fleischman, Suzanne (eds.) 1995. *Modality in Grammar and Discourse*. Amsterdam / Philadelphia: John Benjamins.

Coates, Jennifer 1983. *The Semantics of the Modal Auxiliaries*. London: Croom Helm.

Coates, Jennifer 1995. The Expression of Root and Epistemic Possibility in English. In Aarts, Bas / Meyer, Charles F. (eds.) *The Verb in Contemporary English*. Cambridge: Cambridge University Press, 145-156.

Danet, Brenda 1980. Language in the Legal Process. *Law & Society Review*, XIV/3, 445-564.

de Beaugrande, Robert 1996. The 'Pragmatics' of Doing Language Science: The 'Warrant' for Large-Corpus Linguistics. *Journal of Pragmatics*, 25, 503-535.

De la Cruz, Juan M. 1994. The Modals Again in the Light of Historical and Cross-linguistic Evidence. In Fernandez / Fuster / Calvo (eds.), 145-156.

De la Cruz, Juan M. 1995. The Geography and History of Double Modals in English: A New Proposal. *Folia Linguistica Historica*, XVI/1-2, 75-96.

Declerck, Renaat / Reed, Susan 2001. *Conditionals. A Comprehensive Empirical Analysis*. Berlin / New York: Mouton de Gruyter.

Denison, David 1993. *English Historical Syntax: Verbal Constructions*. London: Longman.

Dossena, Marina 2001a. *The cruel slauchtyr that vas cruelly exsecutit*: Intensification and Adverbial Modality in the Helsinki Corpus of Older Scots – A Preliminary Overview, *Neuphilologische Mitteilungen*, 102/3, 287-302.

Dossena, Marina 2001b. *For the aduancement of the commoun weilth*: Hypotheses in Scots Scientific Discourse of the 16th-17th Centuries. A Preliminary Investigation. *Scottish Language*, 20, 47-65.

Ehrman, Madeline E. 1966. *The Meanings of the Modals in Present-Day American English*. The Hague: Mouton.

Facchinetti, Roberta 1997. Modal Combinations in Modern English: A Socio-historical Interpretation. In Barisone, Ermanno / Hughes, Geoffrey (eds.) *Linguistic Change in English: A Socio-Cultural Overview*, monographic issue of *Textus*, X/2, 377-393.

Facchinetti, Roberta 2000. *Be Able to* vs. *Can* / *Could* in Present-day British English. In Mair, Christian / Hundt, Marianne (eds.) *Corpus Linguistics and Linguistic Theory*. Amsterdam: Rodopi, 117-130.

Fennell, Barbara / Butters, Ronald 1996. Historical and Contemporary Distribution of Modals in English. In Schneider, Edgar W. (ed.) *Focus on the U.S.A.* Amsterdam: Benjamins, 265-288.

Fernandez, Francisco / Fuster, Miguel / Calvo, Juan José (eds.) 1994. *English Historical Linguistics 1992*. Amsterdam: Benjamins.

Fischer, Olga 1992. Syntax. In Blake (ed.), 207-408.

Fischer, Olga / van Kemenade, Ans / Koopman, Willem / van der Wurff, Wim 2000. *The Syntax of Early English*. Cambridge: Cambridge University Press.

Fleischman, Suzanne 1982. *The Future in Thought and Language*. Cambridge: Cambridge University Press.
Goossens, Louis 1984. The Interplay of Syntax and Sematics in the Development of the English Modals. In Blake, Norman / Jones, Charles (eds.) *English Historical Linguistics: Studies in Development*. Sheffield: The Centre for English Cultural Tradition and Language, University of Sheffield, 149-159.
Goossens, Louis 1987. The Auxiliarization of the English Modals: A Functional Grammar View. In Harris / Ramat (eds.), 111-143.
Goossens, Louis 1999. Metonymic Bridges in Modal Shifts. In Panther, K.U. / Radden, G. (eds.) *Metonymy in Language and Cognition*. Amsterdam: Benjamins, 193-210.
Görlach, Manfred 1991. *Introduction to Early Modern English*. Cambridge: Cambridge University Press.
Gotti, Maurizio 1996. *Robert Boyle and the Language of Science*. Milano: Guerini.
Gotti, Maurizio 2001. Semantic and Pragmatic Values of *Shall* and *Will* in Early Modern English Statutes. In Gotti / Dossena (eds.), 89-111.
Gotti, Maurizio (ed.) 1993. *English Diachronic Syntax*. Milano: Guerini.
Gotti, Maurizio / Dossena, Marina (eds.) 2001. *Modality in Specialized Texts*. Bern: Peter Lang.
Haegeman, Liliane M.V. 1981. Modal *Shall* and Speaker's Control. *Journal of English Linguistics*, 15, 4-9.
Haegeman, Liliane M.V. 1983. *The Semantics of* Will *in Present-Day British English: A Unified Account*. Brussels: AWLSK.
Halliday, Michael A.K. 1976. Modality and Modulation in English. In Kress, Günther. (ed.) *Halliday: System and Function in Language*. Oxford: Oxford University Press, 189-213.
Halliday, Michael A.K. / Hasan, Ruqaia (^{2}1987). *Cohesion in English*. London: Longman.
Harris, Martin 1987. Syntactic and Semantic Change within the Modal Systems of English and Afrikaans. In Harris / Ramat (eds.), 181-189.
Harris, Martin / Ramat, Paolo (eds.) 1987. *Historical Development of Auxiliaries*. Berlin: Mouton de Gruyter.

Hermerén, Lars 1978. *On Modality in English: A Study of the Semantics of the Modals*. Lund: CWK Gleerup.

Hickey, Raymond / Kytö, Merja / Lancashire, Ian / Rissanen, Matti (eds.) 1997. *Tracing the Trail of Time*. Amsterdam: Rodopi.

Hoffman, Thomas R. 1966. *Past Tense Replacement and the Modal System*. The Computational Laboratory of Harvard University Linguistics and Automatic Translation Report No. NSF-17. Harvard: Harvard University.

Hogg, Richard 1992. Phonology and Morphology. In Hogg (ed.), 67-167.

Hogg, Richard (ed.) 1992. *The Cambridge History of the English Language*, vol. 1: *The Beginnings to 1066*, Cambridge: Cambridge University Press.

Holmes, John 1984. Modifying Illocutionary Force. *Journal of Pragmatics*, 8, 345-365.

Hopper, Paul J. 1991. On Some Principles of Grammaticalization. In Traugott, Elizabeth Closs / Heine, Bernd (eds.) *Approaches to Grammaticalization*. Amsterdam: Benjamins, vol. 1, 17-35.

Hoye, Leo 1997. *Adverbs and Modality in English*. London: Longman.

Huddleston, Rodney D. 1971. *The Sentence in Written English*. Cambridge: Cambridge University Press.

Huddleston, Rodney D. 1976. *An Introduction to English Transformational Syntax*. London: Longman.

Huddleston, Rodney D. 1995. The Case Against a Future Tense in English. *Studies in Language,* 19, 2, 339-446.

Hyland, Ken 1998. *Hedging in Scientific Research Articles*. Amsterdam / Philadelphia: Benjamins.

Jacobsson, Bengt 1979. Modality and the Modals of Necessity *Must* and *Have to*. *English Studies,* 60, 239-312.

Jacobsson, Bengt 1994. Recessive and Emergent Uses of Modal Auxiliaries in English. *English Studies,* 72, 2, 166-182.

James, Francis 1986. *Semantics of the English Subjunctive,* Vancouver: University of British Columbia Press.

Jespersen, Otto 1949. *A Modern English Grammar on Historical Principles*. Copenhagen: Ejnar Munksgaard; repr. London: George Allen and Unwin (1961).

Johannesson, Niels-Lennart 1976. *The English Modal Auxiliaries: A Stratificational Account. Stockholm Studies in English*, 36, Stockholm: Almqvist & Wiksell.

Kakietek, Piotr 1972. *Modal Verbs in Shakespeare's English.* Poznan: Adam Mickiewicz University.

Kemenade, Ans van 1992. Structural Factors in the History of English Modals. In Rissanen, Matti / Ihalainen, Ossi / Nevalainen, Terttu / Taavistsainen, Irma (eds.) *History of Englishes: New Methods and Interpretations in Historical Linguistics*. Berlin / New York: Mouton de Gruyter: 287-309.

Kiefer, Ferenc 1997. Modality and Pragmatics. *Folia Linguistica,* 31/3-4, 241-253.

Krogvig, Inger / Johansson, Stig 1984. *Shall* and *Will* in British and American English: A Frequency Study. *Studia Linguistica*, 38, 70-87.

Kurzon, Dennis 1986. *It is Hereby Performed ...: Explorations in Legal Speech Acts.* Amsterdam / Philadelphia: Benjamins.

Krug, Manfred G. 2000. *Emerging English Modals.* Berlin: Mouton de Gruyter.

Kytö, Merja 1987. On the Use of Modal Auxiliaries Indicating 'Possibility' in Early American English. In Harris / Ramat (eds.), 145-170.

Kytö, Merja 1991. *Variation and Diachrony, with Early American English in Focus: Studies on CAN/MAY and SHALL/WILL.* Frankfurt am Main: Peter Lang.

Kytö, Merja 1996. *Manual to the Diachronic Part of the Helsinki Corpus of English Texts.* Helsinki: Department of English, University of Helsinki.

Kytö, Merja / Rissanen, Matti / Wright, Susan (eds.) 1994. *Corpora across the Centuries.* Amsterdam: Rodopi.

Lass, Roger 1992. Phonology and Morphology. In Blake (ed.), 23-155.

Lass, Roger 1999. Phonology and Morphology. In Lass (ed.), 56-186.

Lass, Roger (ed.) 1999. *The Cambridge History of the English Language*, vol. 3: *1476-1776.* Cambridge: Cambridge University Press.

Leech, Geoffrey N. [1]1971, [2]1987. *Meaning and the English Verb.* London: Longman.

Leirbukt, Oddleif 1997. Dimensions of Epistemicity in English, German and Norwegian Conditionals. In Swan, Toril / Westvik, Olaf Jansen (eds.) *Modality in Germanic Languages – Historical and Comparative Perspectives*. Berlin / New York: Mouton de Gruyter, 49-73.

Lew, Robert 1997. Towards a Taxonomy of Linguistic Jokes. *Studia Anglica Posnaniensia,* 31, 123-152.

Lightfoot, David W. 1979. *Principles of Diachronic Syntax*. Cambridge: Cambridge University Press.

Lima, Maria 1993a. Notes on the History of the English Modals of Necessity. In Gotti (ed.), 77-87.

Lima, Maria 1993b. *Must* in Shakespeare's Sonnets. In Caliumi, Grazia (ed.) *Shakespeare e la sua eredità*. Parma: Zara, 323-336.

Lyons, John 1977. *Semantics*. Cambridge: Cambridge University Press.

Meurman-Solin, Anneli 1995. A New Tool: The Helsinki Corpus of Older Scots (1450-1700). *ICAME Journal*, 19, 49-62.

Meurman-Solin, Anneli 1997. Differentiation and Standardization in Early Scots. In Jones, Charles (ed.) *The Edinburgh History of the Scots Language*. Edinburgh: Edinburgh Univ. Press, 3-23.

Meurman-Solin, Anneli 1999. Point of View in Scottish and English Genre Styles. In McMillan, Neil / Stirling, Kirsten (eds.) *Odd Alliances. Scottish Studies in European Contexts*. Glasgow: Cruithne Press, 25-51.

Meurman-Solin, Anneli 2001. Women as Informants in the Reconstruction of Geographically and Socioculturally Conditioned Language Variation and Change in 16th and 17th Century Scots. *Scottish Language*, 20, 20-46.

Mindt, Dieter 1995. *An Empirical Grammar of the English Verb: Modal Verbs*. Berlin: Cornelsen Verlag.

Mitchell, Bruce 1985. *Old English Syntax*, 2 vols, Oxford: Clarendon Press.

Mitchell, Bruce / Robinson, Fred C. 1964/1986. *A Guide to Old English*, Oxford: Blackwell.

Molencki, Rafał 1998. Modals in Past Counterfactual Conditional Protases, in Fisiak, Jacek / Krygier, Marcin (eds.) *Advances in*

English Historical Linguistics (1996). Berlin / New York: Mouton de Gruyter, 241-251.

Molencki, Rafał 1999. *A History of English Counterfactuals*. Katowice: Wydawnictwo Uniwersytetu Śląskiego.

Molencki, Rafał 2001. Counterfactuals in the Different Manuscripts of the *Cursor Mundi*. *Neuphilologische Mitteilungen*, 102/1, 11-22.

Mossé, Fernand 1952/1968. *A Handbook of Middle English*. (Transl. by J. A. Walker), Baltimore: The Johns Hopkins Press.

Mustanoja, Tauno F. 1960. *A Middle English Syntax*. Helsinki: Société Néophilologique.

Nagle, Stephen J. 1986. *Inferential Change and Syntactic Modality in English*. PhD Thesis, University of South Carolina.

Nagle, Stephen J. 1993. Double Modals in Early English. In Aertsen, Henk / Jeffers, Robert J. (eds.) *Historical Linguistics 1989*. Amsterdam / Philadelphia: Benjamins, 363-370.

Nagle, Stephen J. 1994. The English Double Modal Conspiracy. *Diachronica*, 11/2, 199-212.

Nagle, Stephen J. 1995. The English Double Modals: Internal or External Change?. In Fisiak, Jacek (ed.) *Linguistic Change under Contact Conditions*. Berlin: Mouton de Gruyter, 207-215.

Nagle, Stephen J. 1997. What is Double about Double Modals? In Hickey, Raymond / Puppel, Stanislaw (eds.) *Language History and Linguistic Modelling*. Berlin: Mouton de Gruyter, 1513-1526.

Nordlinger, Rachel / Traugott, Elizabeth Closs 1997. Scope and the Development of Epistemic Modality: Evidence from *Ought to*. *English Language and Linguistics*, 1, 295-317.

Nuyts, Jan 2001. *Epistemic Modality, Language, and Conceptualization. A Cognitive-Pragmatic Perspective*. Amsterdam / Philadelphia: Benjamins.

OED = *The Oxford English Dictionary* 2002. On-line edition. Oxford: Oxford University Press.

Palmer, Frank R. [1]1979a, [2]1990. *Modality and the English Modals*. London: Longman.

Palmer, Frank R. 1979b. *Can*, *Will* and Actuality. In Greenbaum, Sydney / Leech, Geoffrey / Svartvik, Jan (eds.) *Studies in*

English Linguistics for Randolph Quirk. London: Longman, 91-99.

Palmer, Frank R. [1]1986, [2]2001. *Mood and Modality*. Cambridge: Cambridge University Press.

Palmer, Frank R. [2]1987. *The English Verb*. London: Longman.

Papafragou, Anna 2000. On Speech-Act Modality. *Journal of Pragmatics*, 32, 519-538.

Pérez-Guerra, Javier 1999. *Historical English Syntax: A Statistical Corpus-based Study of the Organisation of Early Modern English Sentences*. München / Newcastle: LINCOM Europa.

Perkins, Michael R. 1983. *Modal Expressions in English*. London: Frances Pinter.

Plank, Frans 1984. The Modals Story Retold. *Studies in Language*, 8/3, 305-364.

Quirk, Randolph / Greenbaum, Sidney / Leech, Geoffrey / Svartvik, Jan 1985. *A Comprehensive Grammar of the English Language*. London / New York: Longman.

Rescher, Nicholas 1968. *Topics in Philosophical Logic*, Dordrecht: Reidel.

Rissanen, Matti 1999. Syntax. In Lass (ed.), 187-331.

Rissanen, Matti 2000a. The World of English Historical Corpora: From Cædmon to the Computer Age. *Journal of English Linguistics*, 28/1, 7-20.

Rissanen, Matti 2000b. Standardisation and the Language of Early Statutes. In Wright, Laura (ed.) *The Development of Standard English: Theories, Descriptions, Conflicts*. Cambridge: Cambridge University Press, 117-130.

Rissanen, Matti / Kytö, Merja / Palander-Collin, Minna (eds.) 1993. *Early History in the Computer Age: Explorations through the Helsinki Corpus*. Berlin: Mouton de Gruyter.

Rissanen, Matti / Kytö, Merja / Heikkonen, Kirsi (eds.) 1997a. *Grammaticalization at Work: Studies of Long-term Developments in English*. Berlin: Mouton de Gruyter.

Rissanen, Matti / Kytö, Merja / Heikkonen, Kirsi (eds.) 1997b. *English in Transition: Corpus-based Studies in Linguistic Variation and Genre Styles*. Berlin: Mouton de Gruyter.

Rivière, Claude 1981. Is *Should* a Weaker *Must?*. *Journal of Linguistics*, 17, 179-195.

Romaine, Suzanne 1982. *Socio-Historical Linguistics, Its Status and Methodology*. Cambridge: Cambridge University Press.

Ross, John R. 1969. Auxiliaries as Main Verbs. In Todd, W. (ed.) *Studies in Philosophical Linguistics*. Evanston (Ill.): Great Expectations, 77-102.

Searle, John 1975. Indirect Speech Acts. In Cole, Peter / Morgan, Jerry (eds.) *Syntax and Semantics 3: Speech Acts*. New York: Academic Press, 59-82.

Skeat, Walter W. ^{2}1884. *Etymological Dictionary*. Oxford: Clarendon Press.

Skeat, Walter W. (ed.) 1906. *The Complete Works of Geoffrey Chaucer*. Oxford: Clarendon Press.

Standop, Ewald 1957. *Syntax und Semantik der Modalen Hilfsverben im Altenglischen: Magan, Motan, Sculan, Willan.* Bochum-Langendreer: Poppinghaus.

Strang, Barbara 1970. *A History of the English Language.* London: Methuen.

Sweet, Henry 1891. *A New English Grammar*. Vol. 1. Oxford: Oxford University Press.

Sweetser, Eve 1990. *From Etymology to Pragmatics: Metaphorical and Cultural Aspects of Semantic Structure.* Cambridge: Cambridge University Press.

Taavitsainen, Irma 1994. On the Evolution of Scientific Writings from 1375 to 1675: Repertoire of Emotive Features. In Fernandez / Fuster / Calvo (eds.), 329-342.

Taavitsainen, Irma 2000. Metadiscursive Practices and the Evolution of Early English Medical Writing 1375-1550. In Kirk, John M. (ed.) *Corpora Galore: Analyses and Techniques in Describing English*. Amsterdam / Atlanta: Rodopi, 191-207.

Taavitsainen, Irma 2001. Evidentiality and Scientific Thought-Styles: English Medical Writing in Late Middle English and Early Modern English. In Gotti / Dossena (eds.), 21-52.

Traugott, Elizabeth Closs 1972. *A History of English Syntax A Transformational Approach to the History of English Sentence Structure*. New York: Holt, Rinehart & Winston.

Traugott, Elizabeth Closs 1989. On the Rise of Epistemic Meanings in English: An Example of Subjectification in Semantic Change. *Language*, 65/1, 31-55.

Traugott, Elizabeth Closs 1990. From Less to More Situated in Language: The Unidirectionality of Semantic Change. In Adamson *et al.* (eds.), 497-516.

Traugott, Elizabeth Closs 1992. Syntax. In Hogg, Richard (ed.), 168-289.

Traugott, Elizabeth Closs / Dasher, Richard B. 2002. *Regularity in Semantic Change*. Cambridge: Cambridge University Press.

Vanparys, Johan 1987. Towards a Pragmatic Approach to Modality: The Case of Permissive *Can* and *May*. In Verschueren, Jef / Bertuccelli-Papi, Marcella (eds.) *The Pragmatic Perspective.* Amsterdam: Benjamins, 229-238.

Visser, Frederick Th. 1963-1973. *An Historical Syntax of the English Language*. 3 parts; 4 vols. Leiden: Brill.

Warner, Anthony R. 1990. Reworking the History of the English Auxiliaries. In Adamson, Sylvia / Law, Vivien / Vincent, Nigel / Wright, Susan (eds.) *Papers from the 5th International Conference on English Historical Linguistics.* Amsterdam: Benjamins, 537-558.

Warner, Anthony R. 1993. *English Auxiliaries: Structure and History*, Cambridge: Cambridge University Press.

Watts, Victor.E. 1969. *Boethius. The Consolation of Philosophy*, Harmondsworth: Penguin.

Werlich, Egon 1983. *A Text Grammar of English*. Heidelberg: Quelle & Meyer.

Westney, Paul 1995. *Modals and Periphrastics in English*. Tübingen: Niemeyer.

Wierzbicka, Anna 1991. *Cross-Cutural Pragmatics. The Semantics of Human Interaction.* Berlin: Mouton de Gruyter.

Wright, Georg Henrik von 1951. *An Essay in Modal Logic.* Amsterdam: North Holland.

Zadeh, Lofti 1965. Fuzzy Sets. *Information and Control,* 8, 338-353.

Zadeh, Lofti 1970. Fuzzy Languages and their Relation to Human and Machine Intelligence. In *Proceedings of the International Conference on Man and Computer*. Bordeaux, 130-165.

Zadeh, Lofti 1971. Quantitative Fuzzy Semantics. *Information Sciences,* 3, 159-176.

Zadeh, Lofti 1972. A Fuzzy-set Theoretic Interpretation of Linguistic Hedges. *Journal of Cybernetics,* 2/3, 4-34.

General Index

Authors

MAURIZIO GOTTI is Professor of English and Director of the Language Centre at the University of Bergamo. He is currently President of CERCLES (the European Confederation of University Language Centres) and member of ESSE (the European Society for the Study of English). He is the Director of CERLIS, the research centre on specialized languages based at the University of Bergamo. His main research areas are the features and origins of specialized languages, both in a diachronic (*Robert Boyle and the Language of Science*, Milan: Guerini, 1996) and in a synchronic perspective (*I linguaggi specialistici*, Florence: La Nuova Italia, 1991). He is also interested in the development of the English language (*English Diachronic Syntax*, Milan: Guerini, 1992) and in English lexicology and lexicography, with particular regard to specialized languages (The 'Hard Words' of Levins' Dictionary, Berlin: Mouton de Gruyter, 1997; John Bullokar's 'Terms of Art', Berlin: Mouton de Gruyter, 1998) and to 'canting' (*The Language of Thieves and Vagabonds*, Tübingen: Niemeyer, 1999).

MARINA DOSSENA is Associate Professor of English at the University of Bergamo (Faculty of Foreign Languages and Literatures). Her published and current research focuses on the features and origins of British varieties of English, particularly Scots and Scottish Standard English (*"Like runes upon a standin' stane": The Perception of Scotticisms in Grammar and Vocabulary*, East Linton (Scotland): Tuckwell Press, forthcoming). As far as domain-specific discourse is concerned, her main interests relate to argumentation and political language. She also devotes considerable attention to the role of technology in research and pedagogical issues.

RICHARD DURY, Associate Professor of English at the University of Bergamo (Faculty of Literature and Philosophy), teaches and researches in both literature (Stevenson, children's literature) and history of the English language. His published work on historical linguistics has covered the pronouns of address, alliterative formulas and the question of parallel drift in the history of the European languages.

ROBERTA FACCHINETTI is Associate Professor of English at the University of Verona. Her research field and publications are mainly concerned with language description, textual analysis and pragmatics, with specific reference to modality (*Modality in Contemporary English*, Berlin: Mouton de Gruyter, forthcoming). This is done mostly by means of computerized corpora of both synchronic and diachronic English (Drawbacks and Pitfalls of Machine-Readable Texts for Linguistic Research, Amsterdam: Benjamins, 1998). She has also dealt with Early Modern English grammatical theory and lexicography (Anthony Huish: A 17th-Century English Grammarian, Berlin: Mouton de Gruyter, 1998), and has lectured on specialized languages in a number of Italian universities.

MARIA LIMA is Associate Professor of English at the University of Salerno, Faculty of Political Science, and lecturer of the PhD course in English for Specific Purposes at the University of Naples. She has published in the field of historical linguistics, modality, word-formation processes and pragmatics. Recent books of which she is the author or co-editor include *Appartenenza e Alterità nei Familiar Dialogues (1586) di Jacques Bellot: Uso linguistico e verbi modali* (Naples: Bibliopolis, 1999) and *English Diachronic Pragmatics* (Naples: CUEN, 2000). She has also written essays and a book on Allen Ginsberg (*One of them. Allen Ginsberg e la sua America*, Naples: CUEN, 1998) and translated his poetry into Italian.

Linguistic Insights

Studies in Language and Communication

This series publishes mainly the work of scholars linked to the Centro di Ricerca sui Linguaggi Specialistici (CERLIS) and aims to promote specialist language studies, both in the fields of linguistic theory and applied linguistics. The volumes focus on specific aspects of language use in one or several languages and provide valuable insights into language and communication research. A cross-disciplinary approach is favoured and most European languages are accepted.

The series includes two types of books:

- **Monographs** – featuring in-depth studies on special aspects of language theory, language analysis or language teaching.
- **Collected papers** – assembling papers from workshops, conferences or symposia.

Vol. 1 Maurizio Gotti & Marina Dossena (eds.)
Modality in Specialized Texts. Selected Papers of the 1st CERLIS Conference. 421 pp. 2001.
ISBN 3-906767-10-8. US-ISBN 0-8204-5340-4

Vol. 2 Giuseppina Cortese & Philip Riley (eds.)
Domain-specific English. Textual Practices across Communities and Classrooms.
420 pp. 2002.
ISBN 3-906768-98-8. US-ISBN 0-8204-5884-8

Vol. 3 Maurizio Gotti, Dorothee Heller & Marina Dossena (eds.)
Conflict and Negotiation in Specialized Texts. Selected Papers of the 2nd CERLIS Conference. 470 pp. 2002.
ISBN 3-906769-12-7. US-ISBN 0-8204-5887-2

Vol. 4 Maurizio Gotti, Marina Dossena, Richard Dury, Roberta Facchinetti & Maria Lima
Variation in Central Modals. A Repertoire of Forms and Types of Usage in Middle English and Early Modern English.
364 pp. 2002.
ISBN 3-906769-84-4. US-ISBN 0-8204-5898-8

Vol. 5 Stefania Nuccorini (ed.)
Phrases and Phraseology. Data and Descriptions.
187 pp. 2002.
ISBN 3-906770-08-7. US-ISBN 0-8204-5933-X

Editorial address:

Prof. Maurizio Gotti Università di Bergamo, Facoltà di Lingue e Letterature Straniere,
Via Salvecchio 19, 24129 Bergamo, Italy
Fax: 0039 035 235136, E-Mail: m.gotti@unibg.it

Stefania Nuccorini (ed.)

Phrases and Phraseology – Data and Descriptions

Bern, Berlin, Bruxelles, Frankfurt/M., New York, Oxford, Wien, 2002. 187 pp.
Linguistic Insights. Studies in Language and Communication. Vol. 5
General Editor: Maurizio Gotti

ISBN 3-906770-08-7 / US-ISBN 0-8204-5933-X pb.
sFr. 52.– / €1 35.80 / €2** 33.50 / £ 22.– / US-$ 31.95*

* The €1-price includes VAT and is only valid for Germany and Austria. ** The €2-price does not include VAT.

Phraseology has been acquiring increasing relevance in the fields of linguistics, lexicography and language teaching. This volume brings together data from a variety of sources to arrive at a better understanding and description of various types of 'phrases' and 'phraseological units' as used in 'real' language. The different approaches and objectives of the papers attest to the pervasiveness of phraseology in different languages, sub-languages and registers. The role of different types of corpora is highlighted and native speakers' expectations, culture-specific factors, context-dependent choices and genre specifications are explored.

Contents: Anna Rita Puglielli: Preface – Stefania Nuccorini: Introduction – John Sinclair: Phraseognomy – Rema Rossini Favretti: Corpus Linguistics and Italian Studies – Fabio Tamburini/Cristiana De Santis/Edoardo Zamuner: Identifying Phrasal Connectives in Italian. Using Quantitative Methods – Elena Tognini-Bonelli: Between Phraseology and Terminology in the Language of Economics – David Oakey: Lexical Phrases for Teaching Academic Writing in English: Corpus Evidence – Susan Kermas: The Translation of Katherine Mansfield's Botanical Terms: Some Phraseological Insights – Peter Howarth: The Conventional Language of Press Conferences: Scripted and Spontaneous English Speech – Judith Munat: In search of the Nominal Compound – Tita Kyriacopoulou/Vasso Sfetsiou: Les constructions nominales à verbe support en grec moderne.

The Editor: Stefania Nuccorini is Professor of English Linguistics at Roma Tre University and a member of the CLA (Centro Linguistico di Ateneo) scientific board. She has previously taught at the University of Perugia and at La Sapienza University, Roma.

PETER LANG
Bern · Berlin · Bruxelles · Frankfurt/M. · New York · Oxford · Wien

Lightning Source UK Ltd.
Milton Keynes UK
UKHW021441070722
405523UK00021B/325

9 783906 769844